DISCOVERING PORTLAND PARKS

DISCOVERING PORTLAND PARKS

A LOCAL'S GUIDE

OWEN WOZNIAK

MOUNTAINEERS
BOOKS

To Poppy—our companion on the trail, on the water, and in the snow. You are loved and missed.

MOUNTAINEERS BOOKS is dedicated to the exploration, preservation, and enjoyment of outdoor and wilderness areas.

1001 SW Klickitat Way, Suite 201, Seattle, WA 98134
800-553-4453, www.mountaineersbooks.org

Printed in China
Distributed in the United Kingdom by Cordee, www.cordee.co.uk
First edition, 2021

Copyeditor: Mary Rosewood
Design: Jen Grable
Layout: McKenzie Long
Cartographer: Lohnes+Wright
All photographs by the author unless credited otherwise
Cover illustration: McKenzie Long

Library of Congress Cataloging-in-Publication Data is on file for this title at https://lccn.loc.gov/2020039312. The ebook record is available at https://lccn.loc.gov/2020039313.

Printed on FSC®-certified materials

FSC www.fsc.org MIX Paper from responsible sources FSC® C001701

ISBN (paperback): 978-1-68051-294-6
ISBN (ebook): 978-1-68051-295-3

An independent nonprofit publisher since 1960

Contents

INNER SOUTHEAST PORTLAND

THE WEST SIDE: SOUTHWEST PORTLAND, BEAVERTON, TIGARD, AND HILLSBORO

UP THE WILLAMETTE: MILWAUKIE, OREGON CITY, WEST LINN, AND WILSONVILLE

EAST PORTLAND, GRESHAM, AND BEYOND

ACROSS THE COLUMBIA: VANCOUVER AND CLARK COUNTY

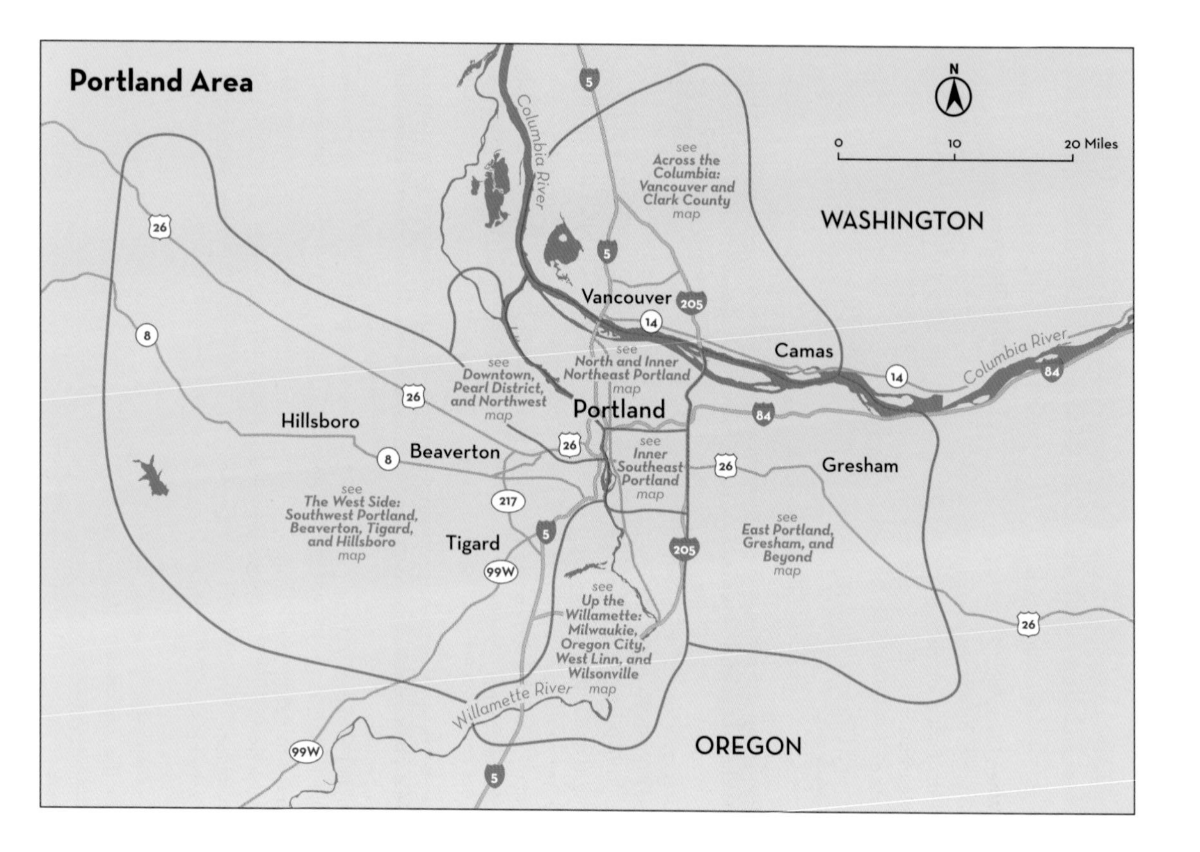

Portland Area
N
0
10
20 Miles
WASHINGTON
OREGON
see
Across the Columbia: Vancouver and Clark County
map
see
North and Inner Northeast Portland
map
see
Downtown, Pearl District, and Northwest
map
see
Inner Southeast Portland
map
see
East Portland, Gresham, and Beyond
map
see
The West Side: Southwest Portland, Beaverton, Tigard, and Hillsboro
map
see
Up the Willamette: Milwaukie, Oregon City, West Linn, and Wilsonville
map
Columbia River
Columbia River
Willamette River
Portland
Vancouver
Camas
Gresham
Hillsboro
Beaverton
Tigard
5
26
8
14
205
84
217
99W

Introduction

When I moved to Portland in 2001, I was an ardent cyclist and mountain climber looking for places to ride or get into the wild. Local parks were not on my radar. Then I got a job with an organization that protects natural places to benefit people in urban areas. I started working on projects that involved acquiring vacant lots and overgrown bits of forest in Portland suburbs I hardly knew existed. The projects intrigued me, and their capacity to focus the civic energy of their communities inspired me.

Then I had a kid. Hours spent carrying an infant strapped to my chest or on my bike through local parks made clear—to the extent anything was clear during those sleep-deprived years—how critical parks are to making city life bearable. I have now visited the majority of the region's five hundred–plus parks and dragged my wife and son to a significant number of them. I feel motivated and perhaps even qualified to share my passions and opinions with you.

I began this book during a summer of bike rides and canoe trips. I'm finishing it under a stay-at-home order due to the COVID-19 pandemic. I thus have a new and urgent reason to appreciate parks, this one tinged by tragedy rather than joy. If any good comes of this pandemic, I hope it includes a renewed wave of investments in parks. Do we need any *more* proof of how important they are?

PARKS FOR THE PEOPLE

Many of Portland's parks are beautiful in the same understated way that Portland is beautiful. They reflect what I believe to be a core value of Portlanders: a desire to live in some kind of balance with the natural world.

How well the parks—and Portlanders—actually succeed in this respect is open to debate. Here is the evidence in favor: Our parks are full of green, low on frills and bling. Rare is the blockbuster play area or elaborate pavilion with a billionaire benefactor's name plastered over it. Instead, parks highlight the amazing capacity of this climate to nourish plant growth. They invite people into nature for a few moments, a lunch hour, or a whole day.

They are truly parks for the people. That's what landscape architect John Charles Olmsted proposed after his pivotal visit in 1903. His vision of a connected, natural, and democratic park system has stayed relevant, even as our

Enjoying winter sun at Luuwit View Park

culture and demographics have changed and our city has mushroomed into a sprawling metropolitan region.

Region is a key word. The Portland region has over thirty different governments involved in the park business, from cities to park districts to the regional government, and even a handful of utilities. Yet the nature they all seek to sustain disregards jurisdictional boundaries.

So do many park users. Even folks living within a few blocks of the zigzagging border between Portland and Gresham would be hard-pressed to locate that line on a map, though the two cities take very different approaches to their parks. Likewise the western edge of Portland and its neighbor Beaverton, where a property tax–funded, directly elected parks district operates in a starkly different fiscal and political environment from Portland Parks and Recreation, which fights for resources alongside other city bureaus in a governance structure that virtually guarantees parks get short shrift.

This diversity of approaches has its upsides, but it complicates regional coordination. And coordination is imperative—to ensure equitable access to parks, to secure wildlife refuges and migration corridors, and to stay resilient in the face of climate change and other disruptions. In one sense, we are ahead of the curve, having long ago entrusted regional planning and open space conservation to a highly competent regional government called Metro. Yet the distance we still have to travel is obvious to anyone paying attention.

Portland is a case in point. Portlanders can be very parochial about their parks, in both good and bad ways. Many parks have a "Friends of" group, often run by a small core of super-volunteers. These groups are essential to keeping the wheels on our park system. Yet their highly place-specific passions can be a challenge for the chronically underfunded parks department in a city where consultation and egalitarian decision-making is prized. Portland Parks and Recreation must constantly navigate the challenge of distributing inadequate resources to seemingly infinite needs.

This challenge is most evident in Portland's glaring park inequities. When I first moved here, I noticed how much more numerous and well equipped the parks on the west side of the river were compared to those in my Inner Southeast neighborhood. Only later did I realize that much of Portland east of me, especially the areas beyond 82nd Avenue, made my neighborhood look park-rich.

Outer neighborhoods like Lents, Powellhurst-Gilbert, and Centennial have a disproportionate share of kids and lower-income people, precisely the folks who most need a park nearby for their physical and mental health. Yet these neighborhoods have fewer parks and have consistently received less investment. About a decade ago, elected officials woke up to this fact and started rebalancing. There is a long way to go, though, before we reach anything resembling park equity.

Nevertheless, when it comes to parks, we have many reasons to love Portland. As voters, we consistently tax ourselves to preserve open space, restore natural areas, protect water quality, and secure access to nature. We have a tradition of leaders and philanthropists supporting the park system, citizens working at the grassroots level to expand and sustain it, and public servants thinking creatively to maintain and enhance it. Our parks speak well of us, imperfections and all.

I firmly believe Portlanders want this to be an inclusive, just, and sustainable region. These ideals aren't yet reality, to be sure. But if they are ever achieved, it will be in large measure thanks to our parks. Does that sound like a bold claim? Well, get out and see for yourself.

How to Use This Book

The park entries are divided into seven sections, working outward from the center. The first section, covering downtown and Northwest Portland, showcases parks ranging from lively, hardscaped urban plazas to the wildest recesses of giant Forest Park. The next sections cover North, Northeast, and Southeast Portland west of Interstate 205. These older neighborhoods are blessed with many stately parks dating from the early twentieth century.

From here, the book jumps over the Willamette River and the West Hills to the Tualatin Valley, sampling a few of the many excellent parks in Southwest Portland and the towns of Beaverton, Hillsboro, and Tigard. This section also includes some natural areas along the Tualatin River and farther-flung destinations tucked in the Coast Range foothills.

The book then loops back to the region's heart and soul, the Willamette River, visiting the best parks and natural areas upstream from Portland. If your view of the river is limited to the seawall downtown, you owe it to yourself to discover just how lush and natural the river can be.

Completing the circle, the book heads east to visit parks—many of them larger natural areas—east of I-205. This part of the region has fewer compelling neighborhood parks, but more than compensates with scenic buttes and access to the wild and beautiful Clackamas and Sandy Rivers. Finally, the journey ends across the biggest river of them all, the mighty Columbia, with a mix of urban plazas, neighborhood parks, and natural areas in and around Vancouver, Washington.

ABOUT THE PARK ENTRIES

The entries are designed to give you relevant facts at the top, then a flavor for the place within the text. Here's a quick rundown of the components.

Icons These highlight what I feel are the key features—the reasons you should visit each park.

OPPOSITE: *A quiet summer morning at High Rocks Park. (Photo by Monica Vogel)*

Location If a park has a main entrance, I use the street address; otherwise I provide a general description or a convenient intersection. Entries for parks that aren't in Portland include the city or county location as well.

Maps Due to space constraints, I include maps for only a handful of parks, typically those with many points of entry or an abundance of features. You can find maps from the park agencies; the Northwest Family Daycation app also provides a great one-stop shop for park maps and information.

Acreage For parks over ten acres, I round to the nearest acre.

Amenities The word "path" describes a paved and generally accessible route; "trail" indicates a soft surface that may or may not be accessible—I try to note which. Remember that some amenities, including restrooms and drinking fountains, close seasonally in some parks.

Jurisdiction This indicates who manages the park. A full list of websites is at the back of the book.

Getting There The Portland region is getting ever more congested, so ease of access factored into my park choices. Please take transit, walk, or bike whenever possible!

By Car: Driving directions commence from the nearest major freeway. Where the directions include a distance greater than three-quarters of a mile between turns, I specify the distance.

By Transit: Most entries refer to TriMet, the agency that operates the MAX Light Rail and buses throughout the region. In the central city, you can also ride the Portland Streetcar with a TriMet ticket. The C-TRAN bus system provides service for much of Vancouver and Clark County in Washington. It connects to TriMet at the Expo Center MAX station. (C-TRAN also operates express buses from downtown Portland, mostly on weekdays. These are oriented toward commuters and less useful for park visitors, so I largely omit them.)

MAP LEGEND

Road
Trail
Paved trail
Stairs
Other trail
Trailhead
Parking
Restroom
Picnic area
Playground
MAX stop
Bridge/Tunnel
Building or landmark
Gate
Wetland
River or stream
Lake
Park

Transit directions assume you start downtown. If a bus route runs in two directions from downtown, I specify which direction to take. I also include a rating for the "hassle" factor: three stars indicates a straightforward, if not necessarily quick, trip with no transfers and minimal walking; two stars suggests a transfer and/or some walking; one star could mean multiple transfers, limited service on certain days of the week, and/or a long walk.

By Bike: For biking, I use similar ratings. Three stars indicates a car-free path suitable for all riders. Two stars indicates a straightforward approach via bike lanes and/or quiet streets. One star indicates a route requiring competent bike skills due to hills, distance, or busy roads. For some entries, I provide a recommended route if it's especially scenic and/or bike-friendly. For other entries, consult the excellent *Bike There!* map and app created by Metro.

WHAT THE ICONS MEAN

The icons in each entry summarize each park's defining features.

Accessible

 Kid-friendly

 Dog-friendly

 Barbecue grills

 Gardens

 Historical or cultural significance

 Natural areas

 Paths or trails

 Public art

 Views

 Water access

Accessible The park—in particular restrooms, parking areas, and paths—is generally accessible to people with mobility issues.

Kid-Friendly There is a play structure and/or other kid-focused feature like a splash pad.

Dog-Friendly There is a dog off-leash area, fenced dog park, or adequate space for a dog to roam without breaking rules or hassling others. (Note: dogs are not allowed in parks operated by Metro.)

Barbecue Grills Some require reservations, so check with the relevant park agency.

Gardens This means formal gardens, not community garden plots.

Historical or Cultural Significance The park has historical significance or commemorates a past era.

Natural Areas The park has substantial areas of natural habitat.
Paths or Trails There are paved paths or soft-surface trails geared toward walking or running.
Public Art You'll find major artworks that merit a visit for their own sake.
Views You know, *views!*
Water Access There is a beach, boat launch, or swimming area; none have lifeguards except where noted.

A FINAL NOTE

I have visited every park in the book and have done my best to verify all details. I take sole responsibility for errors and welcome your corrections—and your differing opinions! You can reach me through Mountaineers Books.

The information in this book is based on the research and expertise of the author. It is incumbent upon readers to confirm park details, such as hours, fees, facilities, or transit access, and to be aware of any changes in public guidelines, jurisdiction, or other city, county, or state regulations. The publisher and author are not responsible for any adverse effects or consequences resulting from the use of any of the suggestions presented in this book.

OPPOSITE: *Strolling above the reservoirs at Mount Tabor Park.*

10 FUN FACTS
ABOUT PORTLAND PARKS

1. Pioneer Courthouse Square, "Portland's Living Room" since 1984, changed hands for the first time in 1849. The price: $24 and a pair of boots.

2. The rose gardens at Washington Park and Peninsula Park are venerable, but for *really* old roses, visit the Pioneer Rose Garden at the Lone Fir Cemetery. In the 1930s, members of the Pioneer Rose Association roamed the Northwest, collecting cuttings from rose bushes brought across the Oregon Trail by early settlers. The association established four gardens; only the one at Lone Fir remains.

3. Bogus superlative: Portland claims Forest Park is the "largest, forested natural area within city limits in the United States." According to the Trust for Public Land, the prize actually goes to Jefferson Memorial Forest in Louisville, Kentucky. A good reason to keep expanding Forest Park!

4. Actual superlative: Portland's claim to World's Smallest Park is legit, according to the *Guinness Book of World Records*. Mill Ends Park fills a two-foot-diameter traffic island in the middle of SW Front Avenue.

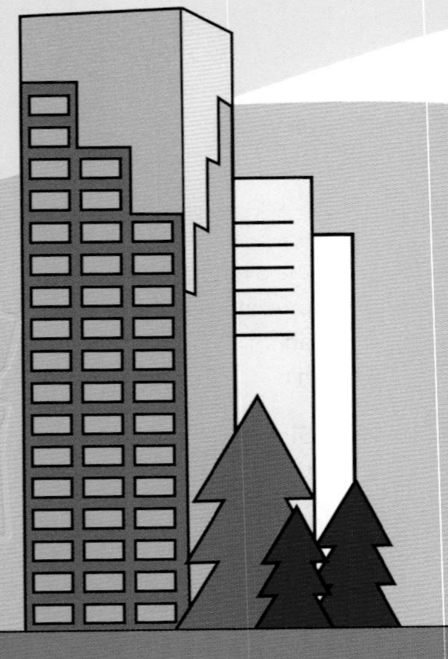

5 Portland's most remote city park? That would be Dodge Park, 11 miles east of the city limits. Visit for great fishing, boating, and picnicking.

6 In 2004, a runner in Forest Park discovered a man and his twelve-year-old daughter living under a tarp. They'd been there four years. The police officer in charge of evicting them noted they seemed happy and healthy, with a Bible, an encyclopedia, and a small vegetable garden. The officer helped them relocate to a friend's farm nearby, but within a month they vanished again. Their whereabouts remain unknown.

7 Un-fun fact: Heron Lakes Golf Course and the Portland International Raceway occupy the site of what was once the largest public housing project in American history—Vanport, home to nearly forty thousand shipyard workers during World War II. In 1948, a levee along the Columbia River failed, flooding Vanport and killing fifteen residents and leaving thousands homeless.

8 Forget about Woodstock. In 1970, the only state-sponsored rock festival in US history took place at Milo McIver State Park on the Clackamas River. Called Vortex I: A Biodegradable Festival of Life, it was devised by Governor Tom McCall as a way to head off potentially violent antiwar protests set to greet President Richard Nixon's planned Portland visit. The governor tacitly agreed to allow the cops to turn a blind eye to the nudity and weed smoking in exchange for a peaceful week. It worked.

9 Creepiest park? Kelly Butte Natural Area in Southeast Portland. Atop the overgrown hill is an abandoned bunker, built by the city in 1956 to shelter officials and documents from a nuclear attack. (CBS made a documentary about it titled *The Day Called 'X'*.) The bunker proved impractical and the city has since sealed and buried the entrance.

10 Sick of all the hipster bicyclists and dog lovers? Head to River View Natural Area, where neither is allowed.

A Brief History of Portland Parks

The little clearing on the Willamette River's left bank made a convenient spot to camp while paddling from Willamette Falls to the Columbia River. Native peoples, fur traders, and the earliest settlers all used it. In 1843, two Oregon City businessmen, William Overton and Asa Lovejoy, staked a claim to it. Overton promptly sold out to Francis Pettygrove. Both men—Lovejoy and Pettygrove—fancied naming a town after their home cities: Boston, Massachusetts, for Lovejoy; Portland, Maine, for Pettygrove. They tossed a coin on November 1, 1846. You can visit the room where it happened, at the Francis Ermatinger House across from the Oregon City Library.

Thus was Portland born. The little town spent its first few decades mired in mud as the small clearing grew into a landscape of stumps, shacks, and rutted roads. Early Portlanders were pragmatic, mostly merchants looking to grow trade up and down the rivers. They congregated at the Plaza Blocks, Portland's first public space, to do business and debate governance. Few saw a need for formal parks or open space, though. After all, just beyond the clearing's edge was trackless wilderness.

Soon, though, new ideas about the value of parks in cities reached Portland from the East. In 1852—a year before the New York Legislature established what would become Manhattan's Central Park—Portland landowner Daniel Lownsdale platted a series of city blocks at the edge of town as a public park. These would become the South Park Blocks.

From this promising beginning followed . . . not much. For decades, the South Park Blocks were little more than a muddy parkway. In 1871, after stiff debate, the city acquired forty acres of brushy second-growth timber up Burnside Street to create City Park (later renamed Washington Park), with no clear sense of what to put there. In 1877, someone finally planted trees along the South Park Blocks. In 1885, the city hired a "park keeper," Portland's first park employee.

By then, the new ideas from the East were coalescing into a movement that would become known as City Beautiful. Social reformers, appalled at living

OPPOSITE: *Visit Pittock Mansion for a glimpse of nineteenth-century upper crust life.*

conditions in the tenements filling America's ballooning cities, found common cause with urban elites anxious to blunt the growing power of immigrant underclasses. Both groups—elites and reformers—fixated on beautification projects and urban planning. These would, they believed, increase the quality of proletarian life while promoting respect for the social order. Their vision took shape in the famous "White City" at the World's Columbian Exposition of 1893 in Chicago.

Portland was paying attention. In 1899, city leaders established a board of park commissioners. Voters approved a levy to acquire park properties. With leadership and funding, Portland could at last create a park system. But what should the system look like?

The answer came thanks to another fair. Hoping to boost Portland's profile, as the Columbian Exposition had done for Chicago, civic leaders announced the Lewis and Clark Centennial and American Pacific Exposition and Oriental Fair, to be held in 1905. Eager to top the White City's grandeur, they brought in the nation's most prestigious name in landscape design: the Olmsted Brothers, sons of famed Central Park designer Frederick Law Olmsted.

The new parks board was anxious to benefit from the gilded Olmsted name and to repurpose exposition land as parks when the fair ended. Accordingly, they too hired the Olmsteds to make recommendations for a city park system although they lacked the funds for a full-blown plan. John Charles Olmsted journeyed to Portland in 1903. The park commission's tight budget afforded him precious little time to explore, yet he managed to produce a dazzlingly ambitious vision.

Olmsted proposed Portland create a comprehensive and interconnected system of parks, parkways, and natural areas; that it preserve hilltops and river islands; that it create a vast meadow park on the Columbia Slough; that it transform Guilds Lake, site of the exposition, into a park; that it create a forest reserve in the Tualatin Mountains north of town; and much more. Of equal importance, Olmsted urged Portland to create a plan for maintaining its parks and to hire park professionals. Perhaps most significantly, he recommended the parks board be funded independently of the city budget and be led by qualified, volunteer officials.

Olmsted's report landed with a thud. Funding and leadership were in short supply. His top recommendation—creation of Forest Park—was ignored for a generation. Guilds Lake and the Columbia Slough were sacrificed to industry.

And yet, Olmsted's work proved remarkably durable. His vision set the framework for much of the parks advocacy and conservation that has happened since.

Though many of Olmsted's proposals languished, his work did prompt the parks board to hire a former Olmsted employee named Emanuel Mische as the parks superintendent. The previous two occupants of the job had been, respectively, corrupt and incompetent. Mische was neither. He was instead the rare parks professional with a genius for both design *and* administration. To him we owe some of our best parks, including Laurelhurst, Mount Tabor, Kenilworth, and the rose gardens at Peninsula Park and Ladds Circle.

The Mische era was the first golden age of Portland parks. It ended around 1913, when Portland's switch to a commission form of government curtailed the parks board's independence by transforming it into the Portland Parks Bureau. Mische briefly led the bureau, but chafed against city politics and departed the following year.

More significant than these changes, however, was the arrival of the automobile in the city. Cars remade Portland, including its parks, in their image. Parks Superintendent Charles Paul Keyser bowed to the new reality and spent precious funds to repave Terwilliger Parkway at the behest of auto enthusiasts. In the 1920s, the Parks Bureau developed auto campgrounds and other car-centric attractions. As more people took to driving out of town to recreate, investment in inner-city parks slowed.

A second golden age began, somewhat paradoxically, in the depths of the Great Depression. Though the bureau was broke, lacking money for basic park maintenance and upkeep, federal stimulus from the New Deal poured in money and manpower to expand the park system.

In 1936, Keyser oversaw a "Plan for a System of Public Recreation Areas," which updated the Olmsted vision to include play areas, community centers, neighborhood parks, and "pleasureways"—scenic driving routes like Fairmount Boulevard in the West Hills below Council Crest. It also called for tripling the city's park acreage.

The Second World War brought this expansion to a halt. Instead, public concern about newly unsupervised kids, with their parents serving abroad or in the domestic war economy, prompted new investments in recreation programs. These programs reached many more Portlanders than before, even the Japanese American citizens held, in violation of their constitutional rights, at the Pacific International Livestock Exposition Pavilion awaiting removal to wartime internment camps.

Following the war, the park system resumed its expansion, notably with acquisition of much of Vanport, the wartime-era public housing development that catastrophically flooded in 1948. Portland also, at long last, created Forest Park from the tax delinquent parcels Multnomah County had acquired over decades. Investment in community centers and recreation programs again surged as the baby boom brought a new wave of kids into the system.

In the 1970s, the Parks Bureau returned yet again to Olmsted's proposal, with Superintendent Douglas Bridges working to revive the 40-Mile Loop, Olmsted's vision of parkways circling the city. In the 1980s, the bureau rediscovered

Polished basalt boulders celebrate neighborhood history at Dawson Park.

an interest in natural areas and launched its first naturalist programs. At the same time, though, a deep recession early in the decade gutted the bureau's budget and created a structural funding deficit that persists to this day.

The bureau formally changed its name to Portland Parks and Recreation (PP&R) in 1991 and renewed its push for resources—from the city council, donors, corporate sponsors, and voters. A successful 1994 bond measure gave the system a huge boost, supporting new and renovated facilities across the city. As the millennium drew to a close, PP&R engaged in a deep round of public engagement to create its *Parks 2020 Vision*, which prioritized park equity, natural areas, and solutions to the structural deficit.

Now the page is set to turn again as PP&R works to renew its vision amid another funding crisis, a public health crisis, renewed attention to racial injustice, and anxieties around public order. Never has the park system been so vital to our health, our sanity, and even our survival.

This pocket history does not do justice to the many other park stories across the region, like Gresham's legacy of acquiring parkland on its volcanic buttes, or the Tualatin Hills Park and Recreation District's dramatic postwar growth and exemplary professionalism. It fails to tell the twisted tale of how Clark County in

Washington and its main city, Vancouver, each with strong park systems, joined in an innovative partnership and then landed in a messy divorce.

There's a larger story, as well, about the role of regional collaboration in the development of the parks we enjoy today. Following limited but crucial efforts in the 1960s and early 1970s, in 1978 regional leaders referred a measure to voters to create a directly elected regional government, called Metro. It's the only such body in the United States.

Among its many duties, Metro owns the Oregon Zoo, oversees the solid waste system, establishes the urban growth boundary, and—since the 1990s—operates regional parks and natural areas. Working with greenspace advocates, in 1992 Metro created the Metropolitan Greenspaces Master Plan. This set the stage for further collaboration among Metro, local governments, and community partners to secure open space. Nearly thirty years and several major funding measures later, Metro owns over seventeen thousand acres of parks and natural areas and has supported acquisition and restoration of many more by other park agencies. Thanks to a successful measure in 2019, this essential work is set to continue.

These accomplishments depend on citizens voting to fund land acquisition as well as parks development, maintenance, and restoration. Much of the needed coordination has come thanks to tireless efforts among parks advocates working with committed professionals in the alphabet soup of local, regional, state, and federal agencies.

The legacy of success to date is impressive—but so are the challenges. Like society as a whole, our parks experience the impacts of gross economic and racial inequality, climate change, and public health and safety challenges. These issues don't respect jurisdictional boundaries, making it more important than ever for everyone to work together.

One of the most innovative venues for collaboration is the Intertwine Alliance, a network of governmental, nonprofit, and business partners working around the region to improve and expand access to nature. They do so in large part by facilitating coordination across organizations and sectors. As a longtime volunteer, I wholeheartedly urge you to visit www.theintertwine.org to learn more. While you're there, you might also get some good ideas for parks to visit!

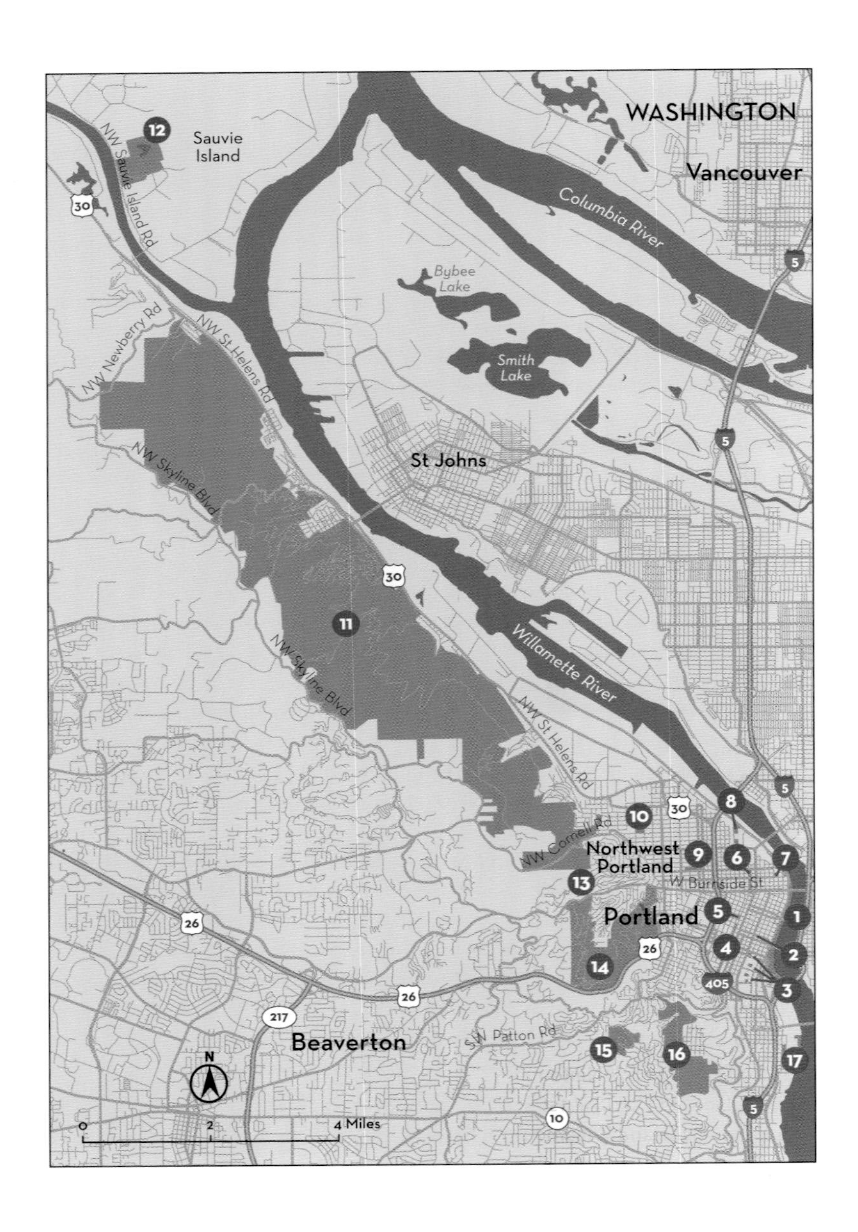

WASHINGTON
Vancouver
Sauvie Island
NW Sauvie Island Rd
Columbia River
Bybee Lake
Smith Lake
NW Newberry Rd
NW St Helens Rd
NW Skyline Blvd
St Johns
Willamette River
NW St Helens Rd
NW Cornell Rd
Northwest Portland
W Burnside St
Portland
Beaverton
SW Patton Rd
N
0
2
4 Miles

DOWNTOWN, PEARL DISTRICT, AND NORTHWEST

1 TOM McCALL WATERFRONT PARK

Portland's waterfront is home to lively festivals, fountains, and the Saturday Market

Location: Naito Pkwy. between SW Harrison St. and NW Glisan St.
Acreage: 37
Amenities: Restrooms, splash pads and fountain, bike rental, beach, monuments, public art, promenade, food vendors (on market days)
Jurisdiction: Portland Parks and Recreation

GETTING THERE

BY CAR I-5 southbound to exit 300B (City Center); across the bridge, take right-hand off-ramp to SW Naito Pkwy. Street parking. **BY TRANSIT** ★★★ MAX (Red or Blue Line) to Oak/SW 1st Ave.; walk one block east. **BY BIKE** ★★★ Via Eastbank Esplanade and Willamette Greenway Trail.

Waterfront Park is Portland's front yard. The city got its start here in 1843 as a muddy collection of riverside shacks, huddled in a clearing hacked from ancient forest. It was a layover on the paddle between Oregon City at Willamette Falls and Fort Vancouver, home base of the Hudson's Bay Company, on the Columbia River. Portland soon found its footing as a river port and never looked back.

The nineteenth-century riverfront bustled with docks, warehouses, canneries, and saloons. The river, undammed and prone to spring floods, routinely inundated the fledgling city. In 1929, the city built a seawall, replacing the waterfront with a (mostly) flood-proof open space. City leaders briefly considered creating a park; but then Robert Moses, New York City's master road builder, arrived with grand freeway plans. This led to the construction of Harbor Drive, a modern four-lane highway, leaving only a narrow, noisy, exhaust-choked, and hard-to-reach sidewalk pinned between the seawall and highway.

By the late 1960s, with I-5 completed across the river, traffic on Harbor Drive dwindled. Governor Tom McCall, the visionary behind Oregon's pioneering bottle deposit bill, public beaches, and progressive land use planning, proposed removing Harbor Drive. Thus in 1975, when most American cities were building downtown freeways as emblems of progress, Portland tore up Harbor Drive and built Waterfront Park in its place.

Now the park is home to Portland's major summer festivals, notably the Rose Festival in early June, when navy ships line the seawall for Fleet Week and thousands trample the midway grass. Other big events include Cinco de Mayo, the Waterfront Blues Festival, and the Oregon Brewers Festival. The park may be at its best in late spring, though, when blossoming cherry trees explode with color. Seen from the Burnside and Morrison Bridges, the park nearly glows. There's no better sign that Portland's long, gray winter is nearly done.

Start at Salmon Springs Fountain, near the Hawthorne Bridge. The plaza bustles with office workers on lunch hour and kids squealing in the fountain. The adjacent building, from 1949, houses the Rose Festival offices and a shop where you can rent a surrey. Famed Oregon architect John Yeon, who pioneered a Northwestern spin on modernism and helped protect the Columbia River Gorge, designed it.

Head south under the Hawthorne Bridge to visit the Bowl, a grassy field sloping to the water. One of my favorite events takes place on the river here in July: the Big Float, when thousands gather to float on kayaks, inner tubes, pool toys, and other more outlandish vessels. It's organized by the Human Access Project, a group dedicated to reconnecting Portlanders to the river. For too long, raw sewage polluted the Willamette River, but thanks to expensive new pipes (for which we pay huge sewer bills), the water is now clean and safe for swimming.

Loop back from the Bowl and continue north. Beyond the Morrison Bridge, a plaque on the seawall marks the former landing of the Stark Street Ferry, the sole means of crossing the Willamette prior to construction of the Morrison Bridge in 1887. (That bridge burned. The current Morrison Bridge dates from 1958.) Nearby, a gangway leads down to the stern-wheeler *Portland*, the last steam-powered stern-wheel tugboat made in the United States. It's now home to the Oregon Maritime Museum. Across the lawn, along Naito Parkway, the Battleship Oregon Memorial commemorates the USS *Oregon* and its role in the Spanish-American War. Be sure to come back in 2076, when the memorial's time capsule (placed in 1976) is scheduled to be opened.

Farther along is a broad plaza, home to the Portland Saturday Market on weekends from March through Christmas. You'll find everything here, from exquisite fine arts and crafts to that velour Bob Marley–themed tapestry you've always wanted. Plus a lot of street food. When the market is closed, there's a splash-pad park here, with gentle jets suited to toddlers.

From the plaza, detour across Naito Parkway to visit the Skidmore Fountain, dedicated in 1888. If any place could be called the spiritual center of Portland, this is it. Here in the heart of Old Town, Portland's earliest streets thronged with people and horses, both species finding refreshment at the fountain.

Back in Waterfront Park, continue through the market area and under the Burnside Bridge to reach the Japanese American Historical Plaza. The city blocks west of here formed one of Portland's *Nihonmachi*, or Japantowns. It was emptied virtually overnight in May 1942, following President Franklin D. Roosevelt's infamous executive order designating military zones from which potential spies—including American citizens—could be removed. As in many western cities, this led to the forcible removal of Portland's Japanese Americans to concentration camps for the duration of the war.

The park ends nearby at the Friendship Circle, where today twinned steel sculptures celebrate Portland's sister city relationship with Sapporo, Japan.

EXTEND YOUR VISIT

South of the Bowl, a promenade continues a quarter mile past cafes, shops, and a marina to South Waterfront Park and Poet's Beach, under the Marquam Bridge. Here, volunteers from the Human Access Project transformed a derelict riverbank into a swimming beach. Look for the river-inspired poetry by local students inscribed on stones lining the path to the beach. The swimming area is shallow and muddy: great for kids, less so for adults. In the summer heat, the looming freeway bridge casts welcome shade. By the time you read this, the promenade will likely be linked up with the Tilikum Crossing Bridge and the South Waterfront Greenway.

2 PLAZA BLOCKS

Public squares in Portland's civic heart

Location: SW 3rd Ave. and Main St.
Acreage: 2.8
Amenities: Benches, monuments, restrooms
Jurisdiction: Portland Parks and Recreation

GETTING THERE

BY CAR I-5 southbound to exit 300B (City Center); cross bridge; left onto SW 3rd Ave.; five blocks to the park. **BY TRANSIT** ★★★ MAX (Blue or Red Line) to Yamhill District; walk two blocks west to SW 3rd Ave. and go left to reach the parks. **BY BIKE** ★★

Steeped in history and ringed by public buildings, the Plaza Blocks are Portland's original public space. Since 1869, they've been the place where citizens meet to mingle, debate, and rally. Today, tourists, office workers, jurors, politicians, protestors, and transients alike gather under a canopy of ancient elms and gingkos. Grab a coffee or a sandwich, find an empty bench, and spend a while people watching.

The northern block, Lownsdale Square, was for "gentleman" in an era when men and women were not to fraternize in public. It centers on a tall obelisk, sculpted in 1906 by Daniel Tilden as a monument to Oregon soldiers killed in the Spanish-American War. Cannons used in the epochal opening battle of the American Civil War at Fort Sumter flank it. From this martial core, bench-lined paths radiate to the four corners.

Chapman Square, originally reserved for the women and children, is next door. Its elegant rows of gingko trees (all female, of course) cast welcome shade in summer. Paths crisscross the park, lined with wrought-iron benches. Along the east edge, a 1993 sculpture by David Manuel depicts an idealized family of pioneers, commemorating in sentimental fashion the 150th anniversary of the Oregon Trail.

Between the two squares runs Main Street, which since 1900 has curved around a giant bronze elk. As of this writing, however, the elk has gone into hiding because city officials feared that during recent protests, it might get toppled and injure protesters. The elk sat, and presumably one day will again sit, atop a foundation donated in 1900 by a former mayor, David P. Thompson. As a sheepherder and later founder of the Oregon Humane Society, Thompson desired that Portland have a place for "bird, beast, and human" to all get a drink of water.

Politics and protests sometimes roil elegant Chapman Square.

South of Chapman is a third square, named for former mayor Terry Schrunk. In pleasing contrast to the straight lines of the Plaza Blocks, Schrunk Plaza features a sunken circular brick plaza and a lawn sloping up to a ghostly taihu stone. This rock, made of a highly porous limestone unique to China's Lake Tai region, is a gift from Portland's sister city of Suzhou.

Ringing the three blocks are City Hall, the Portland Building (home to most city bureaus), the former Multnomah County Courthouse, the federal courthouse, and a massive federal office building housing the US Forest Service and Bureau of Land Management. This constellation of officialdom makes the plazas potent sites for civic action. From anti-war protests to marches for a more equitable city and nation, the Plaza Blocks serve as a symbolic—and at times actual—battleground for the movements of our times.

3 PORTLAND OPEN SPACE SEQUENCE

Four linked, landmark urban spaces that bring nature and city together

Location: Multiple sites near and along SW 3rd Ave.
Acreage: 2.6
Amenities: Fountains, public art
Jurisdiction: Portland Parks and Recreation

The New York Times once called Keller Fountain Park "one of the most important urban spaces since the Renaissance."

GETTING THERE

BY CAR I-5 southbound to exit 300B (City Center); cross bridge and exit right for southbound Naito Pkwy.; from Naito, go right onto SW Lincoln St.; the Source Fountain is at right just beyond 1st Ave. **BY TRANSIT** ★★★ MAX (Orange Line) to Lincoln St./SW 3rd Ave.; walk east to the SW Pedestrian Trail and Source Fountain at left. **BY BIKE** ★★

The Portland Open Space Sequence is a series of fountains set in urban plazas, designed by Lawrence Halprin and constructed between 1966 and 1970. They are internationally famous among designers and widely hailed as a turning point in the history of American cities, sparking an urban renaissance after decades of soul-crushing, auto-oriented redevelopment.

Start your visit at the source—the Source Fountain, that is. Like a headwater stream, it is modest: a brick pile quietly spilling water within a tidy little square, half-hidden among offices and apartments. It portends more than it shows.

A pedestrian path leads north from the Source, downhill to the Lovejoy Fountain. Of the four plazas in Halprin's sequence, this is my favorite. The space is profound, using little more than concrete and water to evoke elemental forces. In the southwest corner, water emerges from the ground to cascade over ragged steps into a shallow pool. Marked by water stains and moss, this mass of concrete suggests an abandoned dam, or the basalt ledges carved by the Columbia River at now-drowned Celilo Falls.

The space is oddly gloomy, even foreboding, as it focuses your attention on the majesty of flowing water. The surrounding plaza is desolate. The lone cluster of trees sits on a slightly elevated island below the fountain, as if growing on a gravel bar midstream. Yet the line of trees ringing the plaza make the square somehow cozy, and the meandering lines of concrete steps invite exploration and movement. On each visit, I pick a different spot from which to admire the water's grace and complexity: from above, from below, even from within. Keep an eye on kids, who will (and should) climb all over the fountain. Like a real waterfall, it has some drop-offs with serious consequences.

Two more blocks along the path is Pettygrove Park, a green and hilly rejoinder to Lovejoy Fountain's rectilinear austerity. A brass sculpture (*The Dreamer* by Manuel Izquierdo) set in a circular reflecting pool greets you, beckoning toward the forest beyond. Izquierdo fled civil war in his native Spain to settle in Portland during World War II, going on to teach for nearly half a century at what is now the Pacific Northwest College of Art. Beyond the sculpture, a path leads up steps past perfectly rounded hillocks. So evocative of nature, while so consciously sculpted by human hands, these hills use grass to achieve the same imaginative tension as Lovejoy Fountain's concrete.

Two more blocks, across busy SW Market Street, is the finale: Keller Fountain Park. On the uphill side, a wooded lawn gives way to concrete expanses dotted with pines. These in turn step down to tiered basins shimmering with water that emerges from underground. It cascades down several short drops, then plunges over jagged concrete cliffs to a basin set below street level. It is truly exhilarating, a grandiose synthesis of urban forms with natural processes. (And yes, your kid could get hurt here. I doubt such a design would be approved today.)

Each of these plazas manages, in different vocabularies, to compress a sense of vast nature into an intimate urban space. It's as though Halprin somehow bottled the essence of that awe you feel among sheer, waterfall-shrouded mountain walls and smuggled it into some ancient town square—and then translated it all to a twentieth-century American city. Fifty years ago, *New York Times* architectural critic Ada Louise Huxtable described it as "one of the most important urban spaces since the Renaissance." The judgment stands.

4 SOUTH PARK BLOCKS

Museums, monuments, and historic sites along one of Portland's first parks

Location: SW Park Ave. from SW Salmon St. to SW Jackson St.
Acreage: 8.7
Amenities: Playground, paved paths, accessible restroom
Jurisdiction: Portland Parks and Recreation

GETTING THERE

BY CAR I-405 northbound to exit 1D (SW 12th Ave.); right on SW Market St.; three blocks to the park. **BY TRANSIT** ★★★ MAX (Green, Orange, or Yellow Line) to City Hall; walk three blocks west to the park. **BY BIKE** ★★

Eleven elegant, slender city blocks, a hundred by two hundred feet, march downhill from Portland State University to the heart of downtown lined with monuments, gardens, and cultural institutions. I love to stroll here, taking in the solidity and gravitas of nineteenth-century Portland.

At the southern end is Portland State University, where the park blocks function as a campus quadrangle. The blocks fit the role so well it's easy to forget they predate the university by almost a century. Portland State, Oregon's largest public university, started as the scrappy Vanport Extension Center in 1946, serving veterans returning from World War II. It survived the disastrous Vanport Flood and found a new home here in 1953.

The university blocks are fully pedestrianized and exude calm even when full of students. Only on Saturday mornings do they fill up; that's when the mother of all farmers markets sets up here, a glorious if overwhelming celebration of Portland's food scene. Tourists and locals alike should experience this market at least once.

North of Market Street, the park narrows and gets a touch more formal. The next block has my favorite of the park's many artworks: a 1984 piece by Paul Sutinen titled *In the Shadow of the Elm*. Granite laid flush with the ground forms the shape of an elm's trunk and branches, suggesting the ghost of a tree long gone. It feels like a memorial to something or someone left intentionally unnamed.

At Columbia Street, you'll find a restroom and a trio of imposing old churches: First Christian; Sixth Church of Christ, Scientist; and St. James Lutheran. The Portland Art Museum and Oregon Historical Society face off along the next block. Both are must-sees; the latter is free to all Multnomah County residents.

The park blocks' emotional and aesthetic peak comes, to my mind at least, in the next block, where a statue of Abraham Lincoln stands near the First Congregational United Church of Christ, which has championed social justice and inclusion for decades. The sight of the Great Liberator—lost in thought, freighted with concern for the fate of his nation, and dwarfed by this Venetian Gothic fortress of rectitude—never fails to move me. Great swaths of time separate Portland of the twenty-first century from Lincoln's world, yet the moral and political challenges with which he wrestled remain.

As of this writing, the city is reimagining the South Park Blocks to "activate" them with social seating arrangements, performance spaces, and integration with the Green Loop, a linear park-cum-bicycle/pedestrian path planned to encircle the central city.

5 DIRECTOR PARK

A genuine piazza in the heart of downtown, full of bustle and activity year-round

Location: SW Taylor St. and SW Park Ave.
Acreage: 0.5
Amenities: Food vendors, picnic tables, public art, restrooms, splash pad with wading pool
Jurisdiction: Portland Parks and Recreation

GETTING THERE

BY CAR I-5 southbound to exit 300B (City Center); across bridge, continue on SW Washington St.; left onto SW 9th Ave.; three blocks to the park. **BY TRANSIT** ★★★ MAX (Blue or Red Line) to Galleria/SW 10th Ave.; walk south along SW 9th one block. **BY BIKE** ★★

Director Park breaks the mold of Portland parks, with virtually no green space and a design intended to meld with, rather than separate from, the surrounding world of concrete and steel. The place is often lively, even in winter. In summer, it's a true piazza. If nearby Pioneer Square is Portland's modern living room, this is the den.

The park opened in 2009 after a long career as a surface parking lot. In the late 1990s, the landowner unveiled plans to build a twelve-story parking garage. A competing developer stepped in to buy the land, cheered on by city leaders hoping for a park here. Instead, the developer announced plans to build a tower on the adjacent block. This killed, probably once and for all, the 150-year-old dream of a continuous string of park blocks spanning downtown.

An unusually quiet moment in Director Park, which is a lively place year-round.

As a partial recompense, the developer tucked a parking garage under the block and donated the surface to the city. He also kicked in a million dollars to help build a park on top. Another developer added a few million more, enough to name the place after his grandparents, Simon and Helen Director.

Generous though these gifts were, they left taxpayers with much of the park's nearly $10 million tab. When recession struck in 2008, the optics of shoveling limited park funds into a lunchtime playground for downtown office workers started looking bad. Meanwhile, vacant park properties in East Portland that had been waiting decades for a swing set and bathroom kept waiting. Fanfare surrounding Director Park's opening was understandably muted.

Fortunately, its completion coincided with a new push for investment in those underserved areas. Places like Cully Park and Luuwit View are the hard-won results. With the costs to create Director Park now fading from public memory, we're in a better place to appreciate its achievement. I think it succeeds as a beautiful and inviting twenty-first-century urban space.

The main feature is a wooden bench arcing around a plaza that becomes a wading pool and splash fountain in summer. It brings together office workers on lunch hour with food-cart-sampling tourists and sharp-eyed parents overseeing their toddlers giggling in the water. In the southeast corner, a bench-lined grove of trees called "The Bosque" provides a hint of green and summer shade. Bollards along Park Avenue help extend the park into the street, supplying some all-too-rare shared space between cars and pedestrians. It suggests what a whole city could look like with enough care, planning, and—yes—money.

EXTEND YOUR VISIT

Pioneer Courthouse Square is just a block away. A century ago, it was home to Portland's most elite hotel and the true center of town. In the 1950s, the hotel was demolished and replaced with (what else?) a parking lot. Luckily, Portland was not long in rediscovering urbanism. By the mid-1980s, the superfluous parking lot found a new life as one of America's first revived town squares.

6 NORTH PARK BLOCKS

Leafy, linear park at the intersection of an urban arts zone and underbelly

Location: Along NW Park Ave. between SW Ankeny St. and NW Hoyt St.
Acreage: 3.1
Amenities: Basketball courts, picnic tables, play structure, public art, accessible restrooms
Jurisdiction: Portland Parks and Recreation

GETTING THERE

BY CAR I-5 southbound to exit 300B (City Center); across bridge, continue on SW Washington St.; right onto SW 4th Ave.; left onto NW Davis St.; four blocks to the park. **BY TRANSIT** ★★★ MAX (Yellow or Green Line) to NW 6th and Davis; walk two blocks west. **BY BIKE** ★★

The North Park Blocks run between the Pearl District and Chinatown. Thirty years ago, the former was a warehouse district and the latter a diverse inner-city neighborhood. Now, the Pearl is a playland of the wealthy, full of high-end condos and shops. Chinatown is in transition, as the forces of gentrification deadlock with Portland's persistent challenge of homelessness.

The North Park Blocks are a frontier of sorts. Frankly, they can be rough, especially at night. Even during the day, you'll encounter people living outdoors—not surprising, as the city's social service agencies and shelters are concentrated nearby. You'll also see tourists, young families enjoying the playground, art lovers gallery hopping, and a diverse crowd at work on the basketball courts. It's a conflicted and disharmonious—but often vibrant—urban tableau.

Portland received the blocks in 1865 as a gift from Captain John Couch. Couch was a canny speculator whose land claim ran from the Willamette River up Burnside and north, encompassing today's Pearl District, Chinatown, and Nob Hill. At the time of the donation, the park blocks were essentially a greenbelt at the edge of town. Unlike the South Park Blocks, which became a prestigious address, the North Park Blocks developed into a humble neighborhood with light industrial uses, warehouses, and flophouses.

In 1904, the city council passed an ordinance setting aside one of the blocks for women and children, presumably to keep them safe from the dockworkers and undesirables frequenting saloons along Burnside. Not long after, the Parks Commission took over and created Portland's first supervised playground.

In recent years, the park has received some great artworks. Near Burnside stands a massive bronze elephant, based on a Shang Dynasty (China, circa 1200–1100 BC) wine pitcher, but supersized. An odd cast-bronze dog bowl set on black and white granite tiles is by William Wegman, the well-known dog photographer. A massive steel sculpture in front of the Pacific Northwest College of Art (PNCA) is by legendary sculptor (and PNCA alum) Lee Kelly.

In 2019, the park unveiled a revamped and expanded playground, now among the city's best. An additional park block, between Glisan and Hoyt Streets, is taking shape across from the PNCA. Soon, the southernmost block, marooned across Burnside and largely shunned, should be the new home to twenty or so food carts, recently evicted from their longtime home farther south to make way for a luxury hotel.

EXTEND YOUR VISIT

Check out the Oregon Jewish Museum and Center for Holocaust Education, the PNCA (newly installed in a cavernous former post office), and the many art galleries surrounding the park. On the first Thursday of each month, the PNCA and the galleries hold open studios. The Lan Su Chinese Garden is also just a few blocks away, as is the legendary Powell's City of Books.

7 LAN SU CHINESE GARDEN

Exquisite traditional garden in Portland's old Chinatown

Location: 239 NW Everett St.
Acreage: 1
Amenities: Garden, teahouse, gift shop, restrooms; note: entrance fee
Jurisdiction: Portland Parks and Recreation/nonprofit

Craftsmanship in stone, wood, water, and plants makes Lan Su an immersive experience. (Photo courtesy of Soren Jorgensen and Lan Su Chinese Garden)

GETTING THERE

BY CAR I-5 to exit 302A (Broadway-Weidler) westbound; cross the Broadway Bridge and go left onto NW Everett St.; four blocks to the garden. **BY TRANSIT** ★★★ MAX (Red or Blue Line) to Old Town/Chinatown; walk two blocks west on NW Everett St. **BY BIKE** ★★

The Lan Su Garden is one of Portland's cultural treasures and another must-see park. It fills a city block in the Old Town/Chinatown neighborhood, re-creating a traditional sixteenth-century (Ming Dynasty) private garden.

These gardens were designed to bring nature into the city—but not in a public way, as most American parks do. Rather, in Ming-era Chinese cities, a garden formed the center of a wealthy urbanite's walled compound, separated from the noisy, crowded, and potentially dangerous city by high walls. In this sense, Lan Su feels pretty authentic: it's surrounded by a district of nightclubs, bars, flophouses, and more than its share of transients. Entering the garden from the gentrifying but still gritty surroundings, you feel instantly transported to a very different time and place.

There are so many easy-to-miss details—the carved screens and doorways, the pattern of paving stones, the sightlines, the arrangement of plants—that you should consider taking a guided tour. These proceed through each courtyard, room, and terrace, slowly looping the central pond where a school of koi swims languidly beneath a bridge leading to an island pavilion. When the tour's over, stop at the teahouse to enjoy a traditional tea service and, if you're lucky, catch some live classical Chinese music.

Garden staff take great pride in the care that went into the garden's design and construction, which was a collaborative effort with Portland's sister city, Suzhou, in China's Jiangsu Province. Most of the garden structures are made of materials brought from China and assembled on-site by Suzhou artisans.

In addition to tours, the garden offers tai chi classes, calligraphy, and traditional dance demonstrations. A highlight is the Chinese New Year lantern viewing, where the garden glows by the light of hundreds of red lamps. Plan ahead, as it sells out.

8 PEARL DISTRICT PARKS

Varied trio of parks anchor a fashionable neighborhood

Location: NW 11th Ave. and NW Johnson St.
Acreage: 5
Amenities: Kid-friendly water feature (Jamison); restroom and fenced dog park (The Fields)
Jurisdiction: Portland Parks and Recreation

GETTING THERE

BY CAR I-405 to exit 2B (Everett/Glisan St.); east to NW 10th Ave.; left on 10th to NW Johnson St. for Jamison Square. **BY TRANSIT** ★★★ Portland Streetcar to NW 10th and Johnson. **BY BIKE** ★★

The Pearl District is fortunate to have three different but excellent parks: Jamison Square, Tanner Springs, and The Fields Park. It's worth visiting all three along the wooden boardwalk linking them.

Jamison Square, honoring local gallery owner and Pearl District champion William Jamison, is the neighborhood's heart. At its center is a shallow paved basin, sloping gently down from a lawn to a curving wall of terraced stone blocks. Water periodically emerges from the stones, slowly filling the basin. The design echoes the Portland Open Space Sequence, but in a more kid-friendly way—so much so that the park becomes a kiddie pool in summer, with kids running, splashing, and even snorkeling in the water as their parents lounge on blankets under the nearby trees.

Tanner Springs Park celebrates a vision of nature—rediscovered and restored—flourishing in the city.

This scene—happy kids enjoying the elements as adults picnic, sip coffee, and mingle—strikes me as the hallmark of a successful urban park. In researching this book I was therefore surprised to learn the fountain wasn't part of the original design. When local developers, building this neighborhood with affluent baby boomers in mind, saw the plans, they quailed at the thought of skateboarders taking over the basin.

To prevent this disaster—*young people using a park!*—they shrewdly added the water feature. Yet instead of ensuring the desired urbane, grown-up vibe, they unintentionally created one of Portland's biggest kid magnets. While I doubt anyone really regrets the outcome, grumbling about kids in fountains will never cease.

Two blocks north, Tanner Springs Park uses the design vocabulary of Jamison Square (slope, water, wall) to different ends. Tanner Creek once flowed from nearby hills into a shallow lake here. In the 1880s, the city filled the lake and routed the creek into a sewer pipe. The park is a memorial of sorts for the creek and lake, buried twenty feet below.

Walking down through the park, you travel from an "urban" place with lawn, benches, and street trees to a "natural" place with a creek, sedges, and wetland, sunken below and set off from the surrounding city. At the bottom end, a small wetland gathers the water along an undulating wall of steel beams, salvaged from the rail yards that once covered this spot. Along the back of the beams, ninety-nine tiles of fused glass depict the dragonflies, spiders, amphibians, and insects that likely inhabited this place before we put a city on top of it.

In a sense, the "nature" on display is artificial. Tanner Creek doesn't actually flow here, and the wetland is fed by recirculated water. The artifice is part of the point, though. This park invites you to consider how cities change the landscape, to wonder what's buried beneath our feet, and to dream a little about how we might live in a better balance with nature.

The Fields Park lies a block farther north, a large oval field bookended by a fenced dog park and an accessible play area. In contrast to Jamison and Tanner, The Fields is big, open, and focused on movement. The Pearl District's booming dog population finds much-needed room to run. Skateboarders set up improvised features. Joggers and walkers circle the oval, admiring views of the graceful Fremont Bridge. Kids keep busy at the play area, which has a sand pit, swings, and a web of steel rope ladders and bridges. Set off by a low fence and lined with benches, this is a great place to bring toddlers and others needing extra supervision.

9 COUCH PARK

Elegant, old park with a popular new playground

Location: NW 19th Ave. and NW Glisan St.
Acreage: 2.4
Amenities: Restrooms, picnic tables, dog off-leash area, accessible playground
Jurisdiction: Portland Parks and Recreation

GETTING THERE

BY CAR I-405 to exit 2B (Everett/Glisan St.); west on NW Glisan St. to the park at NW 19th Ave. **BY TRANSIT** ★★★ MAX (Blue or Red Line) to Providence Park; walk north four blocks. **BY BIKE** ★★

Couch Park anchors Nob Hill, the urbane district of boutiques and restaurants along NW 21st and 23rd Avenues. It's a neighborhood park, offering some lawn for the local dogs to run, picnic tables, and a new playground. Designed in partnership with Harper's Playground, a nonprofit that helps create "radically inclusive" play areas, it's one of Portland's best.

John Couch (that's pronounced "Cooch") arrived in Portland in 1839 and claimed land north of Burnside from the river to near here. To him we owe the North Park Blocks and the alphabetical order of streets. His daughter Clementine married one of Portland's leading merchants, who owned a mansion and estate on today's park. The school district later bought the property and built Couch School, now an alternative school called the Metropolitan Learning Center.

Big trees provide summer shade, a relief for the neighborhood's many early-twentieth-century apartments without air conditioning. Busy NW 21st Avenue, a block away, offers plenty of options for coffee or a lunch to enjoy at the park's picnic tables beneath cherry blossoms.

The main event, though, is the playground. For forty years, a beloved but worn wooden play structure stood here, gradually rotting in the rain. In 2014, Portland Parks and Recreation deemed it a safety risk and closed it, circling the structure with bright yellow "caution" tape. As it happens, there was a tax measure on the upcoming ballot that would fund park improvements across the city, many in underserved (and politically underpowered) outer East Portland. Was it a coincidence that *this* playground, located in an affluent and influential neighborhood, got the crime scene treatment right before the vote? We'll never know. At any rate, newspapers had a great photo op to highlight the deteriorating park system, voters approved the tax, and Portland parks got a big boost—Couch among them. Sometimes the ends *do* justify the means.

The new playground, lined with a soft surface and surrounded by a low fence, has slides, turf hills, climbing structures, and swings, accessible to a wide range of abilities. A highlight is the bundle of giant logs set on end to create a tepee structure. Brave kids struggle to climb this thing, with occasional success, despite their parents' cautionary calls. You may even be tempted to try it yourself.

10 WALLACE PARK

Neighborhood park with popular dog park and thousands of swifts!

Location: 1628 NW 25th Ave.
Acreage: 5.4
Amenities: Restrooms, picnic tables, play structures, fenced dog park, ball fields, basketball courts
Jurisdiction: Portland Parks and Recreation

GETTING THERE

BY CAR I-405 to exit 2B (Everett/Glisan St.); west on NW Glisan St.; right onto NW 24th Ave.; left onto NW Pettygrove St. to the park. **BY TRANSIT** ★★★ Bus 15 (Belmont/NW 23rd toward Thurman/Vaughn) to NW 23rd and Raleigh (stop 9031); walk two blocks west. **BY BIKE** ★★

Wallace Park was made for this: summer lounging on the magnificent lawn.

Wallace Park is lively and attractive, set in a charming Portland neighborhood of Craftsman homes and century-old apartment buildings at the base of the West Hills. If you're shopping or dining on nearby 23rd Avenue, consider a visit. And put it on your to-do list for September, when the swifts are here.

Swifts? It used to be a local secret, but now word is out that for a month or so in late summer, Vaux's swifts roost by the thousands in the massive steam chimney at Chapman School, adjacent to Wallace Park. At dusk they fill the sky, feeding on insects before swirling en masse into the chimney. It's a thrilling sight. The diminutive birds swoop, soar, and dive in prodigious numbers, following some mysterious law of coordinated movement. Often, a peregrine falcon or other raptor will disrupt the party, looking for a swift dinner. The swifts promptly mob it; spectacular aerial battles ensue.

Spectators lay out blankets and lawn chairs on the hill overlooking Chapman's soccer field to cheer the swifts and applaud lustily when the show ends at dark. It's become a civic event, curated by the Portland Audubon Society and carefully tracked online for "peak swift" (usually late September). Bring a picnic dinner; it will likely become one of your annual rituals.

There's more to Wallace Park, though. The fenced and bark-chip-lined dog park is one of the Portland's busiest and best. It's not uncommon to see fifty dogs in here, achieving canine self-actualization while their owners chat, gossip, and flirt. (I'm sure more than a few couples owe their relationship to this place.) Rounding out the park are some ball fields popular with Little League teams, basketball courts, a covered picnic area, and several good play structures.

A final detail: the park is home to an artwork called *Eleven Very Small Sculptures*, created by artist Bill Will in 1998. They are, well, very small. And hidden. I have yet to find all eleven, but will keep trying.

11 FOREST PARK

Portland's iconic urban wilderness

Location: Northwest Portland, from Burnside St. to Newberry Rd.
Acreage: 5172
Amenities: 80-plus miles of hiking, biking, and equestrian trails; restroom at Lower Macleay Park
Jurisdiction: Portland Parks and Recreation

GETTING THERE

There are many trailheads! For the Lower Macleay parking area: **BY CAR** I-405 to exit 3 (US 30); straight onto NW Vaughn St.; left onto NW 27th Ave.; right onto NW Upshur St. to the park. **BY TRANSIT** ★★★ Bus 15 (Belmont/NW 23rd to NW Thurman St.) to NW Thurman and 29th (stop 5839); continue toward bridge and look for stairs descending to Lower Macleay Park. **BY BIKE** ★★

Forest Park is Portland's nature mecca. There's no better place to hike, trail run, mountain bike, or just bathe in the deep calm of a Pacific Northwest forest. Entire books have been devoted to the park. I cannot do it justice here. Instead, I offer just a few observations:

- The park is enormous, stretching 9 miles along the Tualatin Mountains. It includes popular urban spots like Balch Creek and truly remote stretches among the fire lanes farther north. The Forest Park Conservancy, which helps the city maintain the trails and forests, maps nineteen trailheads.
- It's a huge forest! Paddling by in 1806, William Clark noted stands of Douglas-fir eight feet in diameter. Those giants fell to the axe long ago, but timber harvest ceased in the 1940s, and many trees are now approaching the century mark. This makes for magnificent gloom, especially on winter afternoons when the sun drops below the hills. Ravines cut down through the hillside; trails switch back and forth constantly as they follow the forest's contours. It's very easy to lose your sense of time and direction. That's part of the magic.

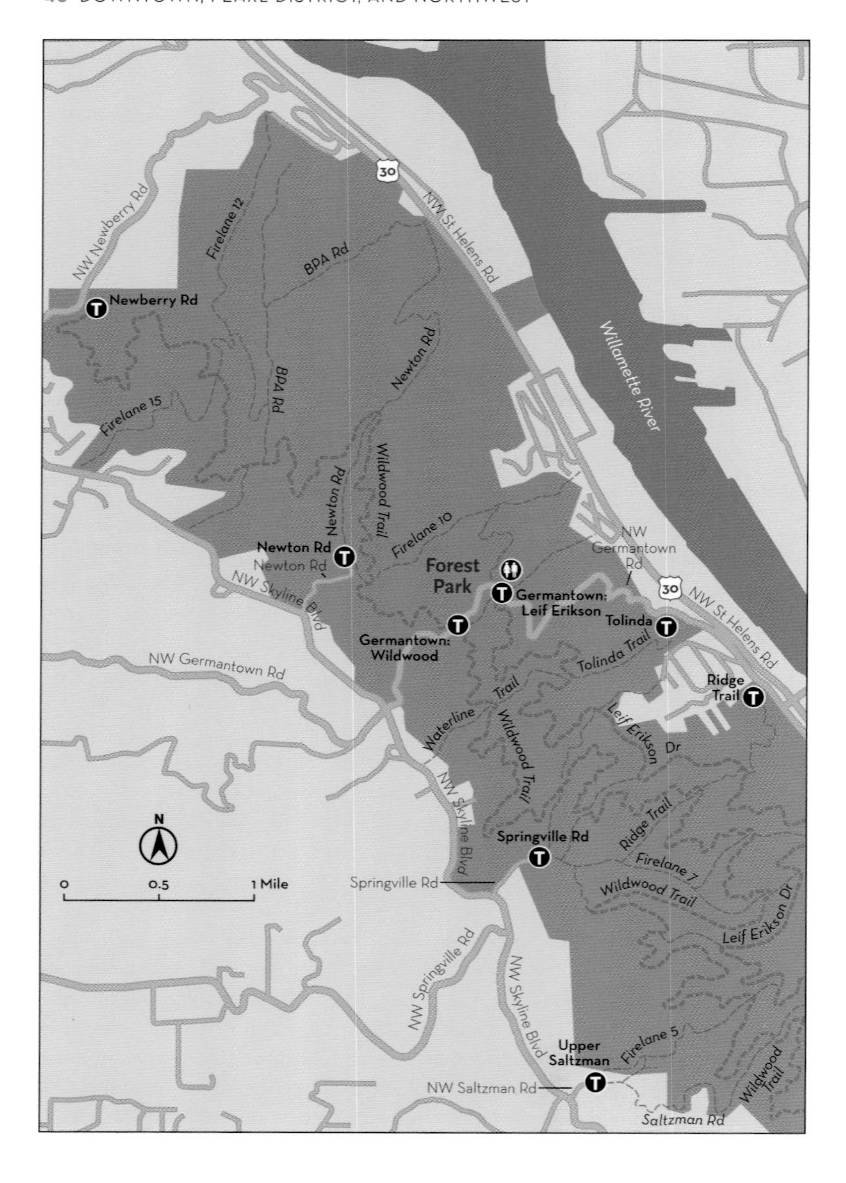
NW Newberry Rd
Firelane 12
BPA Rd
30
NW St Helens Rd
Newberry Rd
Newton Rd
BPA Rd
Willamette River
Firelane 15
Wildwood Trail
Newton Rd
Firelane 10
NW
Germantown
Rd
Newton Rd
Newton Rd
Forest
Park
Germantown:
Leif Erikson
NW Skyline Blvd
30
NW St Helens Rd
Tolinda
Germantown:
Wildwood
Tolinda Trail
NW Germantown Rd
Ridge
Trail
Trail
Waterline
Wildwood Trail
Leif Erikson Dr
NW Skyline Blvd
N
Springville Rd
Ridge Trail
Firelane 7
0
0.5
1 Mile
Springville Rd
Wildwood Trail
Leif Erikson Dr
NW Springville Rd
NW Skyline Blvd
Upper
Saltzman
Firelane 5
NW Saltzman Rd
Wildwood
Trail
Saltzman Rd

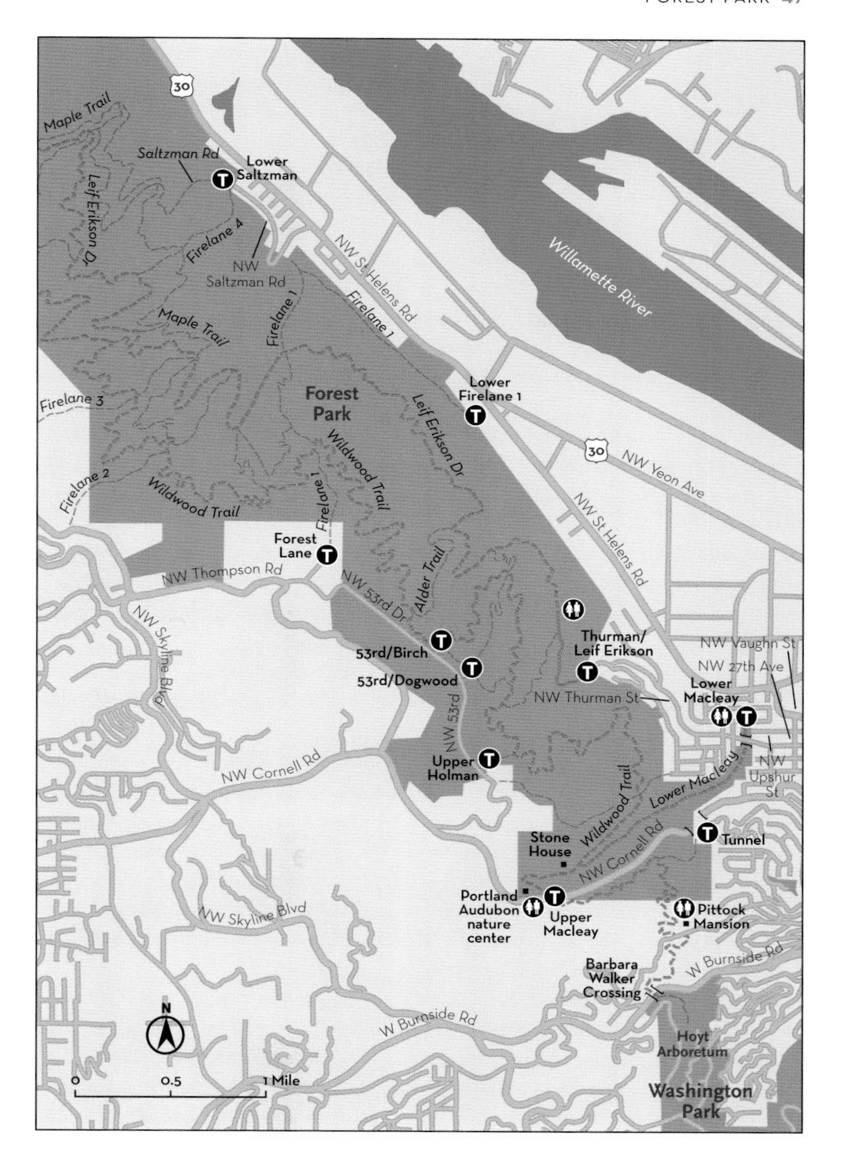

30
Maple Trail
Saltzman Rd
Lower Saltzman
Leif Erikson Dr
Firelane 4
NW Saltzman Rd
NW St Helens Rd
Willamette River
Firelane 1
Maple Trail
Firelane 1
Lower Firelane 1
Firelane 3
Forest Park
Leif Erikson Dr
Wildwood Trail
30
NW Yeon Ave
Firelane 2
Wildwood Trail
Firelane 1
NW St Helens Rd
Forest Lane
NW Thompson Rd
NW 53rd Dr
Alder Trail
NW Skyline Blvd
Thurman/ Leif Erikson
53rd/Birch
53rd/Dogwood
NW Vaughn St
NW 27th Ave
Lower Macleay
NW Thurman St
NW 53rd
Upper Holman
NW Cornell Rd
Lower Macleay
NW Upshur St
Wildwood Trail
Tunnel
Stone House
NW Cornell Rd
Portland Audubon nature center
Upper Macleay
Pittock Mansion
NW Skyline Blvd
Barbara Walker Crossing
W Burnside Rd
W Burnside Rd
N
Hoyt Arboretum
0
0.5
1 Mile
Washington Park

- Unless you *want* to get lost (which has its merits—just head downhill to Highway 30 and catch Bus 16 back to civilization), you'll need a map or trail guide. Portland Parks and Recreation has a good one online; the Forest Park Conservancy offers a more detailed version (see Resources).
- There are two major routes: the Wildwood Trail and Leif Erikson Drive. The Wildwood is Portland's premier trail, running 30 miles from Washington Park north to Newberry Road. Blue, diamond-shaped blazes mark it. Some of the best hours of my life have been spent running this undulating ribbon of green. Leif Erikson Drive runs parallel to and below the Wildwood, a wide and gently graded gravel road perfect for four-legged and/or two-wheeled outings. White concrete posts mark the way. Many fire lanes and spur trails connect Leif Erikson to the Wildwood, allowing for loops of nearly infinite distance and variety.

You really can't go wrong picking an area to explore. Bring water, an extra layer (it can get cold in those woods!), and a sense of adventure.

That said, I recommend starting with the Lower Macleay Trail, a justifiably popular route. It follows Balch Creek upstream for a mile, climbing three hundred feet, to reach Portland Audubon's nature center, where you can visit with birds recuperating at the wildlife care center. Along the way, you'll pass the Stone House, built in the 1930s by the Works Progress Administration as a public restroom. Now it's a romantic ruin.

Another of my favorites—and quieter—is the stretch of the Wildwood Trail between miles 18 and 23. Starting from the Springville Road trailhead, you can put together a loop ranging from 3 to 5 miles.

You'll likely notice invasive ivy choking some of the trees. This is an urgent concern, as much of the canopy is in decline as a result. In 2015, Portland Parks and Recreation announced a comprehensive plan to renew the park by stepping up invasive species control, whittling down the backlog of deferred maintenance, and building a proper visitor center. (Portland's flagship forest hardly has a bathroom—just a few portable toilets—let alone a place to welcome visitors and interpret the resource.) The city acquired land along Highway 30 and drew up a beautiful design. Now all they need is $20 million or so to build it.

Finally, it's worth noting that Portland's park system in a sense begins here. As far back as 1867, civic leaders eyed these forested slopes for a nature preserve. Their agitations led to the creation of a Municipal Park Commission in 1899. This in turn spurred landscape architect John Charles Olmsted's visit in 1903; his proposal for a system of parks, promenades, and trails established the vision Portlanders are still working to fulfill. It included "acquisition of these romantic wooded hillsides for

Early winter on the Lower Macleay Trail

a park or reservation of wild woodland character." Olmsted noted, "Some people look upon such woods merely as a troublesome encumbrance standing in the way of more profitable use of the land, but future generations will not feel so and will bless the men who were wise enough to get such woods preserved."

He continued:

> *Future generations, however, will be likely to appreciate the wild beauty and the grandeur of the tall fir trees in this forest park or reservation, as it would perhaps better be called, its deep, shady ravines and bold view-commanding spurs far more than do the majority of the citizens of today, many of whom are familiar with similar original woods. But such primeval woods will become as rare about Portland as they now are about Boston. If these woods are preserved, they will surely come to be regarded as marvelously beautiful.*

How fortunate we were to have such a foresighted visionary in our midst! And so . . . we ignored the suggestion. Instead, the city green-lighted clear-cutting and financed a road to spur residential development. Beset by landslides, the road proved very expensive. Dejected real estate speculators eventually gave up on their lots, which the county took in lieu of the delinquent property taxes. Forest thickened around the lonely road—now called Leif Erikson Drive.

Over the next decades, the park-in-waiting was logged, burned, and drilled for oil. Still the forest endured, and the voices in favor of preservation grew louder and more numerous. Finally, in 1948, after a determined campaign by the City Club of Portland, the city officially declared it a park.

12 HOWELL TERRITORIAL PARK

Beautifully preserved pioneer homestead on scenic Sauvie Island

Location: 13901 NW Howell Park Rd., Sauvie Island
Acreage: 120
Amenities: Picnic areas, historic house, portable toilet
Jurisdiction: Metro

GETTING THERE

BY CAR I-405 to exit 3 (US 30) at left; continue 9.5 miles and go right to cross the Sauvie Island Bridge; continue 1.2 miles on NW Sauvie Island Rd.; go right onto NW Howell Park Rd. **BY TRANSIT** ★ Bus 16 (Front Ave./St. Helens Rd.) to Gillihan

Rd. and Sauvie Island (stop 8437, the end of the line); walk a mile (careful, no shoulder) along NW Sauvie Island Rd. to the park. **BY BIKE** ★★★ Sauvie Island is a classic biking destination. Roads lack shoulders but are quiet and scenic. The approach on US 30 has a bike lane.

Howell Territorial Park is a great destination in its own right and a good launchpad to explore Sauvie Island, the nation's largest river island.

The park centers on a historic home, built in 1856 by one of the island's first American settlers. The Bybee House, named for its first owner, sits on a low rise overlooking Multnomah Channel and the green cloak of Forest Park. This view, from which nearly all signs of modernity are absent, conjures a sense of how beautiful, but lonely, this place must have felt then. Behind the home are several picnic shelters, set among magnificent old apple and pear trees grown from cuttings carried over the Oregon Trail. This is one of the best picnic spots anywhere in the region.

If the home is open, don't miss the chance to tour it. Plaques outside the house tell the story of Sauvie Island. Before Portland, before Fort Vancouver, before Lewis and Clark, the Multnomah people lived here, harvesting salmon from the Columbia and wapato—a starchy edible tuber that grows in shallow water—from the island's floodplain lakes. Prior to white settlement, it was likely the most populous place in the region anywhere downstream of Celilo Falls.

The Multnomah people kept the peace with the newcomers, trading furs for metal goods. Their openness proved their undoing, however, as trade exposed them to novel diseases. One epidemic, likely malaria, spread through the villages in the early 1830s and killed nearly everyone. Survivors fled the island, never to return. When the Bybee family arrived a few decades later, the island reputedly had only one resident: a French Canadian named Laurent Sauvé, managing a dairy farm for the Hudson's Bay Company.

These days, the island hums with the drone of tractors and the honking of geese. Summer attracts cyclists and beachgoers. Fall sees crowds visiting pumpkin patches and corn mazes. These aside, the island remains a quiet place, a world apart from busy Portland just a few miles down the road.

EXTEND YOUR VISIT

Sauvie Island has a lot to explore. Paddle on calm Multnomah Channel; good access is a mile away from Howell Territorial Park at NW Ferry Road. Beyond Ferry Road is the Wapato Access Greenway, where a trail leads to a picnic shelter and a 2-mile loop through wetlands along the channel. Farther afield, near the island's northern tip, are a series of popular Columbia River beaches along Reeder Road, most famously the clothing-optional Collins Beach. At road's end is the trailhead for the excellent 6-mile roundtrip hike to Warrior Rock Lighthouse. (Note: parking anywhere along Reeder requires a day pass from the Oregon Department of Fish and Wildlife, available online and at the Cracker Barrel Grocery by the Sauvie Island Bridge.)

13 PITTOCK MANSION

Ornate mansion and grounds with a superb city view

Location: 3229 NW Pittock Dr.
Acreage: 54
Amenities: Historic mansion with tours (entrance fee), viewpoint with benches and picnic tables, restrooms
Jurisdiction: Portland Parks and Recreation

GETTING THERE

BY CAR I-405 southbound to exit 2A (W. Burnside Rd.); right onto Burnside; after 1.7 miles, right onto NW Barnes Rd.; right onto NW Pittock Ave.; right onto NW Pittock Dr. to a parking area at left. **BY TRANSIT** ★★ Bus 20 (Burnside/Stark toward Beaverton) to Burnside and NW Barnes Rd. (stop 687); follow directions above. **BY BIKE** ★

Pittock Mansion commands a view of Portland fit for a king, or at least a plutocrat. Fortunately, this one is open to all.

Henry Pittock arrived as a young man on the Oregon Trail in 1853, ready for a new life. He found work as a typesetter at one of Portland's many fledgling newspapers and soon took over the shoestring operation. Over the following decades, Pittock methodically built the *Oregonian* into the newspaper of record while diversifying into paper mills, railroads, and real estate. He built his forty-six-room French Renaissance–style château in 1914 and presided over high society as one of Portland's richest men.

His time in the trophy home didn't last. The Spanish influenza pandemic of 1918–1919 claimed him. Pittock's heirs stayed in the mansion through the 1950s, but then left it vacant. When the Columbus Day Storm of 1962 damaged the building, real estate developers swooped in to finish it off and carve up the estate. Instead, citizens rallied, raised funds, and prevailed upon the city to buy it. Now the nonprofit Pittock Mansion Society (see Resources) manages it as a museum. The grounds are a city park.

From Pittock Mansion, the plutocrat's view of Portland

The mansion is worth seeing, ideally on a docent-led tour, as many of the architectural details are easy to miss. It offers a sense of what it was like to be very rich a century ago, with luxuries available only to the elite: thermostat-controlled central heat, refrigerator, elevator, central vacuum. Among the furnishings and artifacts, the mansion also hosts temporary exhibits focused on local arts, crafts, and history.

The mansion charges an entrance fee, but the grounds are free. Stroll among the gardens via a short, paved loop to a viewpoint. The paved path curves around a lawn, opening views back toward the mansion and across ravines dropping away to the north and south, to arrive at the grand vista east over the city. It's a classic: downtown buzzes in the foreground, Mount Tabor rises in the middle distance, and glorious Mount Hood looms over it all. Benches and picnic tables offer a place to rest and take in the view.

The path continues downhill, among roses and rhododendrons, dogwoods and magnolias, to pass the Gate Lodge, a secondary residence also open for tours. From here, head up a set of stairs to return to the mansion's main entrance or continue on the path to reach the parking area.

EXTEND YOUR VISIT

The mansion sits astride the Wildwood Trail, Portland's premier hiking route linking Forest Park to downtown and the West Hills. Walk south to cross the brand-new pedestrian bridge over Burnside Road, the Barbara Walker Crossing, to Hoyt Arboretum or go north to reach Macleay Park.

14 WASHINGTON PARK

Portland's flagship park high in the West Hills with views, trails, cultural attractions, and more

Location: West Hills between W. Burnside St. and US 26
Acreage: 410
Amenities: 25-plus miles of trails, accessible play area, accessible restrooms, paved paths, picnic tables and shelters, sports fields, outdoor amphitheater, tennis courts, cultural attractions
Jurisdiction: Portland Parks and Recreation

GETTING THERE

BY CAR US 26 to exit 72 (Zoo/Forestry Center), northbound (uphill) to the zoo parking area. Limited parking. Parking fee. **BY TRANSIT** ★★★ MAX (Blue or Red Line) to Washington Park; a free shuttle bus connects all park destinations. For the "traditional" entrance, exit MAX at Providence Park, walk south on SW 18th Ave., right onto SW Salmon St. to SW Park Pl. (three-quarters of a mile, uphill); or take Bus 63 along the same route. **BY BIKE** ★

Washington Park contains virtually every park experience: nature trails, monuments, cultural sites, views, kid attractions, and more. You'll find city and woods, solitude and crowds, human history and natural history. You could never do it justice in a day—nor can this description suffice. Consider this more invitation than overview. (Visit the park's website—see Resources—for additional information.) Also, strongly consider taking transit. The parking lot, though vast, often fills up.

The park dates to 1871, when cougars and bears roamed a forest wilderness above downtown Portland. City Park (as it was known then) took its current form from landscape architect John Olmsted's 1903 recommendations. It has the graceful, iron-and-stone aesthetic typical of Olmsted and the City Beautiful movement, which sought to harmonize a fractious and deeply unequal society through beautification. The park is a luxurious expanse of winding drives through woods and meadows opening on views across downtown to Mount Hood. It holds a captivating tension between the manicured and the wild.

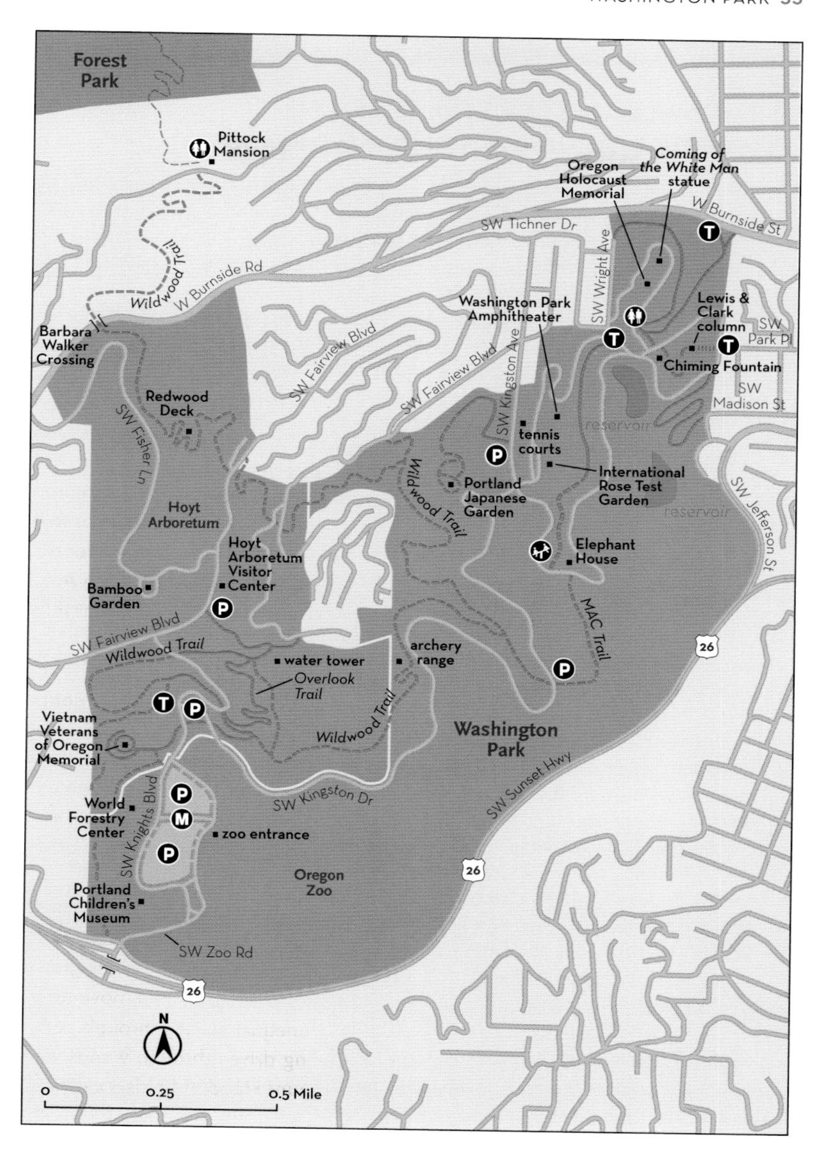
Forest Park
Pittock Mansion
Wildwood Trail
W Burnside Rd
Barbara Walker Crossing
SW Tichner Dr
Oregon Holocaust Memorial
Coming of the White Man statue
W Burnside St
SW Wright Ave
Washington Park Amphitheater
Lewis & Clark column
SW Park Pl
Chiming Fountain
SW Madison St
SW Fairview Blvd
SW Kingston Ave
Redwood Deck
SW Fisher Ln
tennis courts
reservoir
International Rose Test Garden
Portland Japanese Garden
Wildwood Trail
SW Jefferson St
Hoyt Arboretum
Hoyt Arboretum Visitor Center
Elephant House
Bamboo Garden
MAC Trail
SW Fairview Blvd
Wildwood Trail
water tower
archery range
Overlook Trail
26
Vietnam Veterans of Oregon Memorial
Wildwood Trail
Washington Park
SW Sunset Hwy
SW Kingston Dr
World Forestry Center
SW Knights Blvd
zoo entrance
26
Oregon Zoo
Portland Children's Museum
SW Zoo Rd
26
N
0
0.25
0.5 Mile

THE WILLAMETTE STONE: WHERE THE NORTHWEST WAS MAPPED

Viewed a certain way, the story of America is the story of *property*. We fought a Revolutionary War to secure property rights. We fought a Civil War to end the practice of holding human beings as property. And we fought for, bargained over, and outright stole the property of Native peoples under the banner of Manifest Destiny.

For *that* American dream to come true, however, it wasn't enough to take territory. Someone needed to transform the spoils of conquest into units to be bought and sold. For this, the American project depended as much on surveyors as on soldiers and pioneers.

In 1851, a surveyor general laid out the Oregon Territory's original survey lines—the east-west Willamette Baseline and the north-south Willamette Meridian. The Baseline ran as close as possible to, but south of, the Columbia River. (At that time, it was an open question as to who would own the future state of Washington—Britain or the United States.) The Meridian ran just west of Vancouver Lake to make the survey work a little simpler.

These two lines intersected at a little rock tucked in the woods above downtown Portland, not far from today's Washington Park. Here, the surveyor general hammered a cedar stake into the ground. A stone obelisk replaced the stake in 1885, lasting a century until vandals smashed it. Now a concrete pad, inlaid with a bronze plaque, marks where the stone once stood.

You can visit the spot at 253 NW Skyline Boulevard, where a mossy path leads 100 yards downhill into an anonymous patch of woods. There isn't much here to evoke the site's massive, if abstract and obscure, significance. Just a few benches.

And yet, the immense effort of surveying the Northwest's mountains, rivers, deserts, valleys, and coastlines began at this spot. It set the frame for the endlessly subdivided quadrilaterals—the sections, quarter sections, quarter-quarter sections, and so on—that constitute real estate from the Rockies to the Pacific and from Canada to California.

You'll probably start at the Washington Park MAX station, atop the nation's deepest rail tunnel, or the parking areas around it. That's fine, but consider starting instead at the "traditional" entrance on SW Park Place. This gives a better sense of the park's original orientation to the city. Here, terraced stairs lead up through formal gardens to a column honoring Lewis and Clark, where President Theodore Roosevelt personally laid the foundation stone in 1903. Nearby, Sacajawea, the Shoshone guide largely responsible for Lewis and Clark arriving on the West Coast alive, has her own place of honor. Her sculpture is by Alice Cooper, the first woman to have an artwork included in Portland's public sculpture collection. Famed suffragist Susan B. Anthony attended its unveiling.

As you pass Sacajawea, pause at the Chiming Fountain (built in 1891) and feel the city recede as the Douglas-firs close in. From here, a path leads uphill to the quietly devastating Oregon Holocaust Memorial. Just beyond is a 1904 statue of two American Indian men, staring toward an imagined wagon train of American settlers. It's titled *Coming of the White Man*. Intentional or not, the pairing of these two artworks, evoking two genocides a century and continent apart, serves to enhance their tragic power.

Farther uphill is the International Rose Test Garden, which has been earning Portland its nickname, City of Roses, since 1924. Over ten thousand roses bloom, surreally bright, against the backdrop of Mount Hood's white mantle. The betrothed vie for wedding permits here, possibly the most photogenic spot in Portland. An adjacent outdoor amphitheater hosts concerts in summer. Some of them are free: check the park's website (see Resources) for a calendar.

Just above the rose garden, the Portland Japanese Garden offers the most compelling reason to visit Washington Park. It considers itself the most "authentic" Japanese garden in North America. While I can't verify that, I *can* attest that its austere and meticulously tended spaces hold a power that's hard to describe and deeply moving. When out-of-towners want to visit a Portland attraction, I always put this atop the list.

SW Kingston Drive and the Wildwood Trail carry you higher still, through forest and meadow, to the Vietnam Veterans of Oregon Memorial. Here, a paved path spirals upward from a sunken plaza through a lawn ringed by giant Douglas-firs. Circling this idyllic amphitheater, the path climbs past black marble walls inscribed with names of the dead, year by year. It makes you want to cry and smile at the same time—so much beauty and solemnity intermingled.

Next is the World Forestry Center, a museum dedicated to the science, industry, and culture of forestry. Standing guard outside is Peggy the Train, a 1907 locomotive that hauled logs for a half century and now, in retirement, hosts hordes of children climbing on it.

Opposite the forestry center, the Oregon Zoo showcases Pacific Northwest species and globally significant wildlife. Though it dates to 1888, the zoo definitely doesn't *look* old-fashioned—it's wrapping up $125 million worth of voter-funded improvements and boasts beautiful new veterinary and education centers as well as refurbished elephant, rhino, primate, and polar bear exhibits, to name only a few.

At the south end of this complex, the Portland Children's Museum offers play-based learning for younger kids, with hands-on exhibits like a clay studio, maker space, role-playing theater, and a garden maze. The "Outdoor Adventure" area is especially popular.

Last but definitely not least is the 189-acre Hoyt Arboretum, which straddles SW Fairview Boulevard north of the Vietnam Veterans of Oregon Memorial. Along its 12 miles of trails are trees from around the world, with deciduous trees like oak, magnolia, and beech on the open slopes above the zoo and conifers in the ravines running down to Burnside Street. Start at the visitor center on Fairview to get a map and see what tours are scheduled. The arboretum is full of special places: a viewing deck deep in a sequoia grove, a woven steel orb (*Basket of Air* by sculptor Ivan McLean) floating above a bamboo grove, the partially paved Bristlecone Pine Trail winding among gingkos and pines in the park's quiet northwest corner. Hoyt deserves a full day's exploration.

Really, you could spend a week in Washington Park and not exhaust its possibilities. Beyond the areas I've mentioned, there are soccer fields and tennis courts, a mammoth play structure, a picnic shelter called the Elephant House (it did, in fact, once house elephants), and Portland Parks and Recreation's only archery range.

EXTEND YOUR VISIT

The Wildwood Trail begins here and continues north to Pittock Mansion and Forest Park. The bus network allows for a lot of one-way options.

15 COUNCIL CREST PARK

The best spot in the West Hills for views, with some interesting history

Location: 1120 SW Council Crest Dr.
Acreage: 44
Amenities: Picnic tables, dog off-leash area
Jurisdiction: Portland Parks and Recreation

GETTING THERE

BY CAR I-405 to exit 1C (6th Ave.) to southbound SW Broadway; from intersection with SW Lincoln St., follow SW Broadway Dr. 1.3 miles; left onto SW Greenway Ave.; after 0.6 miles, right onto SW Council Crest Dr. to the park. **BY TRANSIT** ★★

Atop the West Hills, Council Crest offers vistas unmatched elsewhere in the city.

Weekdays only, Bus 51 (Vista toward Council Crest) to SW Council Crest and Greenway (stop 1215); walk a quarter mile up SW Council Crest Dr. to the park. **BY BIKE** ★★ Steep but very scenic climb from downtown via Terwilliger (path) and Fairmount (road) Blvds.

At 1073 feet above sea level, the hill atop Council Crest Park offers views west over the Tualatin Valley and northeast across downtown Portland. It's just about the highest point in Portland and definitely the most scenic.

The view is a fitting reward for the many cyclists who grind up winding, mostly quiet streets from downtown, and for the hikers who trek up what might be the city's best urban nature trail from Marquam Nature Park. I recommend both approaches if you have time and (considerable) energy—but there's no shame in just driving up and wandering the grounds.

The view has been Council Crest's draw for over a century. Its current name dates from 1898, when the National Council of Congregational Churches met here, presumably to be closer to God. Only a few years later, theology and doctrine yielded to earthier pursuits when an amusement park opened here. Visitors boarded a trolley downtown for the twenty-minute ride uphill via giant wooden trestles spanning steep ravines.

The amusement park billed itself as "Dreamland of the Northwest" and probably lived up to the name. A scenic railway circled the park; adjacent to the railway, a miniature Columbia River stern-wheeler plied the waters of an elevated wooden canal. Nearby was the Crest Pavilion, reputedly Portland's most popular dance hall.

Popularity wasn't enough to save the park and its expensive trolley line from the Great Crash of 1929. The city acquired the site several years later and removed the rapidly deteriorating structures. Streetcar service ended in 1949, and Council Crest began its next chapter.

Now, the old railroad right-of-way is the circular park drive. Park anywhere along it and wander up the paved path to the central plaza, where stone pavers indicate the surrounding high points. (In researching this book, I learned that such "mountain finders" have a proper name: toposcopes. You're welcome.) A path lined with benches circles a water tower and continues down across a broad, sloping lawn to a sculpture of mother and child. Farther east and downhill is the spacious dog off-leash area, where you can put your pup through a hill-climbing workout.

Compared to the old days, there's not much to keep you here. I'll take it, though. The trees are enormous, the views are endlessly interesting, and the lawns invite dawdling with a book or a picnic. It's a quiet, graceful place in all seasons.

EXTEND YOUR VISIT

Use the bus to do an excellent one-way hike on the Marquam Trail to or from Marquam Nature Park.

16 MARQUAM NATURE PARK

Stillness reigns in a forested ravine a few blocks from downtown

Location: SW Marquam St. and SW Sam Jackson Park Rd., West Hills
Acreage: 205
Amenities: Hiking trails, portable toilet at trailhead
Jurisdiction: Portland Parks and Recreation

GETTING THERE

BY CAR I-405 to exit 1C (6th Ave.) to southbound SW Broadway; right onto SW 6th Ave., which becomes SW Terwilliger Blvd.; straight at stoplight onto SW Sam Jackson Park Rd.; right at sharp curve onto SW Marquam St. to the parking area. **BY TRANSIT** ★★★ Bus 8 (Jackson Park/NE 15th toward Marquam Hill) to SW Terwilliger and Sam Jackson (stop 5804); walk a quarter mile along SW Sam Jackson

Park Rd. to SW Marquam St. and the park. **BY BIKE** ★★★ SW Terwilliger Blvd. (path) from downtown.

Of the many forest parks in the West Hills, Marquam is my favorite for quiet. I'm not sure why or how, but these woods are especially tranquil, protected from ambient city sounds by steep ridges. Only the occasional lawnmower at work among the neighboring estates seems to intrude here. With steep trails and no amenities, the park draws only walkers, hikers, and trail runners, all pursuing their agendas in peace.

The park wraps around Marquam Hill, home to the veterans' hospital and Oregon Health and Science University, and fills Marquam Gulch, the ravine cutting down from Council Crest. SW Marquam Hill Road splits the park at its narrowest point, creating two halves. Each half has a loop trail with extensions and multiple trailheads, meaning you can put together loops as short as a mile or as long as 5 miles without backtracking. Transit connections at both ends of the park and atop Marquam Hill make it convenient for a one-way walk as well.

As with many of the city's natural areas, we have motivated citizens to thank. Judge Philip Marquam, recently arrived from the California gold fields, bought the hill and gulch in 1857, when ancient forests still grew on the upper slopes. Judge Marquam hired surveyors to lay out a neighborhood in the gulch. They must have never actually visited the spot, as they proposed streets that utterly disregarded the impossible topography. Needless to say, the neighborhood wasn't built. Marquam sold all of the gulch's timber; by the end of the century, loggers had completely denuded it. An open landfill, described by a contemporary as "a fetid marshy dumping ground for garbage, dead dogs and cats," filled the gulch's lower reaches. It was a no-man's-land, more or less.

Yet as the city inexorably grew, homes sprang up around the gulch. In 1923, fed up with the dump's stench, angry neighbors marched on City Hall. Money was found to fill it in, creating today's Duniway Park just downhill from Marquam Nature Park. The gulch's forest slowly grew back. By the 1960s, continued growth brought developers to the gulch with a more viable development proposal. Concerned neighbors mobilized, fought the plans, and bought the land, creating Marquam Nature Park in 1983 and eventually turning it over to the city.

EXTEND YOUR VISIT

The Marquam Trail connects up to Council Crest and forms the walking portion of the 4T Trail, a marked loop that uses trolley, train, trail, and tram for a multimodal grand tour of the West Hills. (See Resources for more.)

17 ELIZABETH CARUTHERS PARK AND SOUTH WATERFRONT GREENWAY

Chic urban spaces for a chic neighborhood

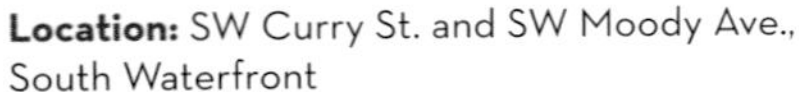

Location: SW Curry St. and SW Moody Ave., South Waterfront
Acreage: 2.1 (Caruthers), 4.4 (Greenway)
Amenities: Paths, splash pad, restrooms (Caruthers); promenade and river access point (Greenway)
Jurisdiction: Portland Parks and Recreation

GETTING THERE

BY CAR I-5 southbound to exit 299A (OR 43/SW Hood Ave.); continue on SW Hood Ave. under the freeway; left onto SW Macadam Ave.; right onto SW Curry St. to reach Caruthers Park. **BY TRANSIT** ★★★ Portland Streetcar (N./S. lines) to SW Moody and Gaines. **BY BIKE** ★★★ Willamette Greenway from downtown and points south.

Elizabeth Caruthers Park anchors the South Waterfront neighborhood. A few blocks east, the South Waterfront Greenway fronts a scenic stretch of the Willamette River opposite Ross Island. Neither park quite counts as a destination unto itself, but together they make good stops on a walking tour of this ever-evolving neighborhood.

Caruthers Park is among Portland's most stylish. Seating areas set amid a network of paths and plantings occupy the north end. The design is formal, with low plantings that use color and variable height to create a sense of separation. A modest spray feature and some artfully stacked logs provide kid amenities without compromising the sophisticated vibe.

In the middle of the park, a great lawn extends up an artificial hill, which provides a vista over the park and lends it a sense of drama. At the south end, boardwalks wind among Oregon grape, bear grass, and other native plants surrounding a western red cedar that will someday tower over this end of the park, adding welcome shade. With good lighting and open sightlines, the park is also a great place to visit after dark.

A few steps to the east, the South Waterfront Greenway opens up a quarter mile of river frontage that for decades was inaccessible, polluted, and undesirable. Now cleaned and with the shoreline restored, it's an appealing place for a riverside walk.

(It will be even better when eventually connected to sections of riverfront paths to the north and south.)

My favorite element here is a sculpture by the artist Buster Simpson, called *Cradle* (2014). Steel cables secure massive stumps, uprooted and laid on their sides, to concrete anchors. Reminiscent of the wood structures installed in rivers across the Pacific Northwest to re-create lost salmon habitat, the sculpture evokes both the grief and the hope in our quest to keep these fish from extinction.

Down the path, a series of curved steel retaining walls suggest giant salmon struggling upriver to spawn, their dorsal fins piercing the water's surface. Above them are gleaming white Adirondack chairs that beckon you to greet the sunrise over Ross Island in style. A smaller path leads down through the riprap, providing a launch for canoes, kayaks, and stand-up paddleboards.

For now, the greenway ends abruptly at an old shipyard, where for a century the Zidell family built and launched the barges that still carry potash, sand, wheat, and other commodities up and down the Columbia River. It's a reminder of how recently South Waterfront was an industrial zone—or, to be precise, mostly a postindustrial wasteland. Following a century of sawmills, warehouses, and factories, the area had largely emptied by the 1960s. Rail lines, highways, and residential development on the nearby higher ground isolated the riverfront and gradually drove industry elsewhere.

Polluted and severed from downtown by I-5, South Waterfront languished for decades. It was nobody's first choice to redevelop. Yet in the 1990s, Portland's planners recognized the city needed to grow up and not out, and the South Waterfront presented that rarest of opportunities: a blank slate. They dreamed up a city-within-a-city, denser than any other in the region, connected to downtown by a streetcar.

Though slowed by the Great Recession in 2008, the neighborhood has developed pretty much as planned: walkable, shiny, and green. If you haven't seen it in a while, come and check the progress—maybe on a spring weekend when Caruthers Park is in bloom and the farmers market fills the sidewalks with people.

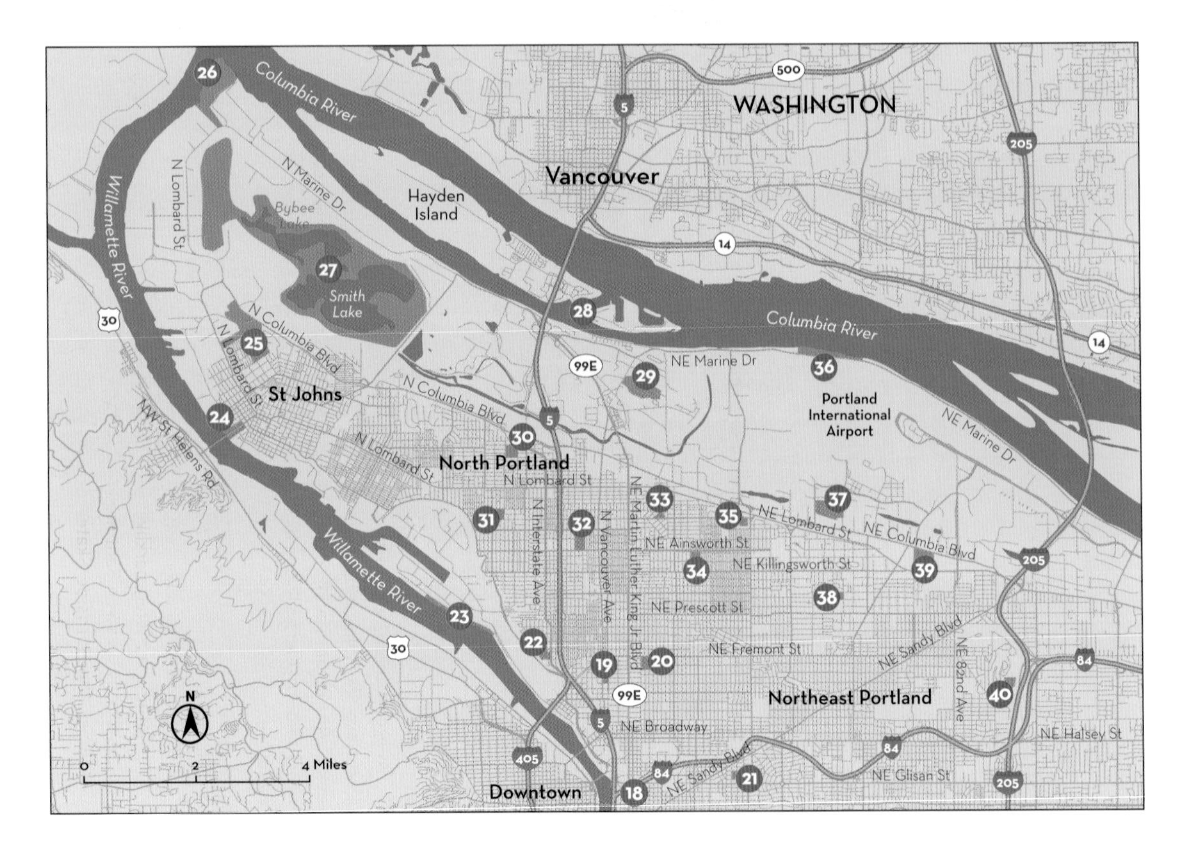
WASHINGTON
Vancouver
Hayden Island
Columbia River
Willamette River
N Lombard St
N Marine Dr
Bybee Lake
Smith Lake
N Columbia Blvd
St Johns
NW St Helens Rd
North Portland
N Interstate Ave
N Vancouver Ave
NE Martin Luther King Jr Blvd
NE Marine Dr
Portland International Airport
NE Lombard St
NE Columbia Blvd
NE Ainsworth St
NE Killingsworth St
NE Prescott St
NE Fremont St
NE Sandy Blvd
NE 82nd Ave
Northeast Portland
NE Broadway
NE Halsey St
NE Glisan St
Downtown
0
2
4 Miles
N
500
5
205
14
30
99E
405
84
18
19
20
21
22
23
24
25
26
27
28
29
30
31
32
33
34
35
36
37
38
39
40

NORTH AND INNER NORTHEAST PORTLAND

18 BURNSIDE SKATEPARK

The Valhalla of skateparks

Location: SE 2nd Ave. underneath the Burnside Bridge
Acreage: 0.5
Amenities: Loud music (maybe)
Jurisdiction: None!

GETTING THERE

BY CAR I-5 northbound to exit 300 (SE Water Ave.); left onto Water Ave.; left onto SE 2nd Ave.; five blocks to the park. Limited street parking. **BY TRANSIT** ★★★ Bus 20 (Burnside/Stark) to NE Grand (stop 704) or Portland Streetcar (A/B Loops) to Burnside; walk one block to NE Couch St. and follow pedestrian paths to 2nd Ave.; park is under bridge at left. **BY BIKE** ★★★ Via Eastbank Esplanade.

With all due respect to artisanal coffee shops and the TV show *Portlandia*, the place to see what *actually* makes Portland great is the Burnside Skatepark. There's nothing remotely parklike about it, unless you're thinking about *Paranoid Park* (the creepy Gus Van Sant movie filmed in it).

And yet, the Burnside Skatepark is hallowed ground in the world of street skating. Just about every city in America now has a skatepark as a marquee park amenity. Burnside was the first, and in proper Portland fashion, it's a DIY affair. Located beneath the Burnside Bridge, the park is semi-sheltered from the rain and, until recently, safely isolated from the sort of people who might object to the graffiti and blasting of hardcore or hip-hop.

In the late 1980s, this was mainly a place to score heroin or for the homeless to escape the rain, with nothing around except warehouses and the train tracks. Then some local skaters realized the banked wall on the bridge foundation was rideable. This was a city-owned no-man's-land, so they skated more or less unmolested by the law. Soon, someone enhanced the bank with a little concrete. Then a little more concrete. And so on until, in 1990, the skatepark took shape.

There were no plans for building skateparks then, nor any companies doing it professionally. Burnside took shape by trial and error, achieving fame along the way for its difficulty and for the skill and passion of its riders. Generations of pro skaters have come to pay their respects. You should too.

Not that you should skate it. While the locals tolerate visitors, it's considered poor etiquette to clog up the bowls and ramps by repeatedly wiping out—which is likely, given how big the features are. I include the skatepark in this book mostly as a place to see a unique feature of Portland and to be inspired by the beauty and grace of expert-level skateboarding.

Although still "unofficial," Burnside Skatepark is now a Portland institution and an illustration of how times change. In 2015, when a new apartment tower rose next door, the tallest and possibly fanciest one east of the Willamette, there was much angst about the skatepark's fate. Fortunately, the building's developer was savvy enough to recognize the skatepark, with its frisson of urban grit, as a brand-enhancing amenity. The skatepark survived, deprived of some sunlight by the neighboring behemoth but enhanced with artificial lighting, courtesy of the developer.

It's still an incredible place to skate—or so I've been told, as I'm *way* too scared to try it.

19 DAWSON PARK

Witness to Portland's Black history and heart of a fast-changing neighborhood

Location: N. Williams Ave. at N. Stanton St.
Acreage: 2.1
Amenities: Basketball court, play equipment, picnic tables and shelter, public art, restrooms, splash pad
Jurisdiction: Portland Parks and Recreation

GETTING THERE

BY CAR I-5 to exit 302A (Broadway-Weidler); north on N. Williams Ave. a half mile to the park. **BY TRANSIT** ★★★ Bus 4 (Fessenden toward St. Johns) to N. Williams and Morris (stop 6364). **BY BIKE** ★★

Dawson Park is a haven of green along busy Williams Avenue, a bit formal, but also cozy. Elms, maples, and Douglas-firs ring a central lawn. A recently refurbished and accessible playground welcomes kids, especially little ones. Picnic tables host locals waging epic chess and dominoes matches. A gleaming cupola sits atop a gazebo.

A plaza adjacent to the lawn includes a splash pad, ringed by polished stones inscribed with vignettes of the park's past. They include the day in 1968 when a young presidential candidate named Robert F. Kennedy chose Dawson Park for his Portland campaign rally.

That last detail hints at the park's history as a site of struggle and resilience. This is the Albina neighborhood, where Portland's legacy of racial exclusion and misguided redevelopment has played out most egregiously.

The town of Albina incorporated in 1887 near today's Broadway Bridge. It soon merged with the neighboring cities of Portland (across the river) and East Portland, its growth tied to the nearby Union Pacific rail yards. A working-class district, Albina welcomed generations of newcomers: Irish, Germans, and Scandinavians, and then, in the early twentieth century, African Americans.

The influx of Black residents picked up during World War II, when Portland's shipyards promised work and a chance to escape discrimination in the South. After the war, many Blacks settled in Albina, in part because real estate agents and lenders colluded to ensure Blacks could buy homes only here. The silver lining to this illegal redlining was that Albina became a vibrant Black enclave, home to churches, jazz clubs, and small businesses.

In the 1950s, city leaders took up the national enthusiasm for urban renewal, which often entailed demolishing older neighborhoods to build shopping centers and freeways. Unsurprisingly, Albina's modest homes and Black-owned businesses were targeted as a "blighted" area ripe for renewal. The city razed Albina's core along Broadway—including the Hill Block Building, home of the cupola now in Dawson Park—to build Memorial Coliseum and its ocean of parking. Not long after, I-5 plowed through, displacing even more residents and saddling those left with a legacy of air pollution.

Finally, in the 1970s, the city cleared many of the blocks around Dawson Park for a planned expansion of Emanuel Hospital. The expansion never happened. The blocks stood vacant and weed-choked for three decades, until Portlanders rediscovered the charms of historic, close-in neighborhoods—and real estate developers cashed in. Today, new apartments, coffee shops, pubs, and boutiques line Williams Avenue, largely benefiting the newcomers. Meanwhile, many Blacks have left the neighborhood.

This vexed history only makes Dawson Park more special, though. It remains a gathering place where many former residents come to reconnect. To its credit, when Portland Parks and Recreation recently renovated Dawson Park, it sought out former residents and engaged them in the design process to ensure they continue to feel welcome.

20 IRVING PARK

Attractive and historic park in the city's "streetcar suburbs"

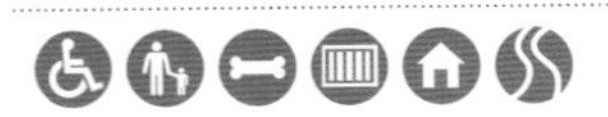

Location: NE Fremont St. and NE 7th Ave.
Acreage: 16
Amenities: Basketball courts, dog off-leash area, ball fields, picnic areas, playground, splash pad, tennis courts, restrooms, paved paths
Jurisdiction: Portland Parks and Recreation

GETTING THERE

BY CAR I-5 to exit 302A (Broadway-Weidler); east on Weidler; left onto NE Martin Luther King Jr. Blvd.; right onto NE Fremont St.; one block to the park. **BY TRANSIT** ★★★ Bus 6 (Martin Luther King Jr. Blvd.) to NE Fremont (stop 5910); walk east on Fremont one block. **BY BIKE** ★★

Like an old Portland foursquare Craftsman home, Irving Park is elegant, expansive, and a bit worn, but full of charm and history. In the 1880s, streetcar lines spread northward from Albina through land Captain William Irving had claimed a generation earlier. New neighborhoods popped up along the routes. The closest of these, Irvington, was fanciest, with large lots and homes set far back from the street. Prosperous merchants and lumbermen built mansions. Many still stand.

A great open space marked the neighborhood's northern edge. It was a farm, then a horse track, and at one time even a camp for Oregon National Guard troops en route to the Spanish-American War. In the 1920s, it found new purpose as Irving Park.

The horse track is now a great field, teeming with Little League matches and pickup games of Ultimate Frisbee. On the higher ground, groves of sycamore and red oak invite you to spread a picnic beneath their branches. At the park's

A quintessential Portland park, Irving Park has timeless appeal.

northwest corner, excellent basketball courts (some covered and lit) host one of Portland's more dynamic basketball scenes, with ballers at all hours.

At the park's south end, beyond the restrooms and the dog off-leash area, are a playground and a splash pad—both recently refurbished—and tennis courts. A paved path rings the park, lit by antique wrought-iron fixtures. With such a mix of activities and spaces, the park is often lively, yet rarely crowded, and appealing in all seasons.

Another dimension to Irving Park—harder to perceive now than in years past—makes it special. The park has always straddled a social divide, between comfortable Irvington to the south and humbler neighborhoods to the north. By the 1960s, this had become a racial divide as well, thanks to discriminatory redlining and "urban renewal" (see Dawson Park).

Decades of oppressive policing and malign neglect by city leaders left many younger members of Portland's Black community frustrated. Tensions boiled over in July 1967. Local activists planned a festival in Irving Park to feature famed Black Panther Eldridge Cleaver. It drew over a hundred, mostly young, people—and an intense police presence. Cleaver did not appear, tensions rose, and soon rocks and fists flew and the police moved in.

By nightfall, hundreds of protestors were in the streets confronting an even larger number of police officers. Reports of smashed storefronts along nearby Union Avenue (now Martin Luther King Jr. Boulevard) and firebombs prompted Governor Tom McCall to put the Oregon National Guard on notice. It was all over within forty-eight hours, but the "Irving Park Riot," like so much urban unrest in 1967, marked a turning point in Portland. Portlanders are still struggling to overcome our city's legacy of institutionalized racism and displacement.

You may or may not choose to dwell on this while strolling Irving Park's shady, quiet paths. Either way, this is as good a neighborhood park as you'll find anywhere.

21 OREGON PARK

Big trees delight in this classic neighborhood space

Location: NE Oregon St. and NE 29th Ave.
Acreage: 3.8
Amenities: Accessible restrooms, picnic area, basketball court, play structure, paved paths
Jurisdiction: Portland Parks and Recreation

GETTING THERE

BY CAR I-84 eastbound to exit 1 (NE 33rd Ave.); right onto NE 33rd Ave.; right onto NE Sandy Blvd.; left onto NE 29th Ave. **BY TRANSIT** ★★★ Bus 19 (Woodstock/Glisan toward Gateway) to NE Glisan and 30th Ave. (stop 2106); walk one block north. **BY BIKE** ★★

With a name like Oregon Park, you might think this is a major park. No. It's a little neighborhood affair: some trees, a lawn, a basketball court, and a play structure. It just happens to be next to Oregon Street. In a sense, I guess, it merits the name. Like our state, it's modest, green, sometimes dreary, and often nearly perfect.

This park is low-key. The play structure is dated but well maintained. The lawn in the northwest corner hosts impromptu Frisbee games and small picnics. The basketball court sees regular pickup games that in my experience are more relaxed than at places like Irving Park or Laurelhurst Park. Even on a sunny day, you're not likely to feel crowded here.

The main reason you might cross town for Oregon Park is twofold. First, it lies just off NE 28th Avenue, one of Portland's best restaurant rows, quieter and less trendy than Alberta and Division Streets but just as good.

Second is the trees. Oregon is one of those parks, like Alberta, where the trees alone justify its existence. Sweetgums, with their distinctive five-pointed leaves and spiky seedpods, enclose the park along its perimeter, welcoming you across an invisible threshold. Sycamores spread delicate green light across the basketball court. Douglas-firs circle the playground as if to watch over and protect the young souls within.

There's something thrilling about these great trees. They cast an ancient, patient aura over the park, an aura somehow heightened and distilled by virtue of its confinement within two city blocks. A deeper wild hides in these trees, unnoticed by most of the Frisbee players, hoopsters, and tire-swing spinners, but waiting patiently there nevertheless for anyone who seeks it.

22 OVERLOOK PARK

Spacious bluff-side park with great views

Location: 1599 N. Fremont St.
Acreage: 11
Amenities: Restrooms, picnic shelters, sports fields, dog off-leash area, play structure, jogging track
Jurisdiction: Portland Parks and Recreation

GETTING THERE

BY CAR I-5 to exit 303 (Swan Island); westbound on N. Going St.; left onto N. Interstate Ave.; after a half mile, right onto N. Fremont St. **BY TRANSIT** ★★★ MAX (Yellow Line) to Overlook Park. **BY BIKE** ★★

Overlook Park perches on a bluff above the Union Pacific rail yards in North Portland, just off Interstate Avenue. It's easy to reach by transit—you practically step out of the MAX train into the park—and makes a great walking or biking destination from the nearby Mississippi neighborhood via the Failing Street pedestrian bridge.

Burning off some steam after a bike ride to Overlook Park

As the name suggests, the park has views over the river and downtown. Portland's heritage as a river and rail town—gateway to the Pacific Northwest—fills the foreground. The massive Union Pacific rail yards' din filters up to the park; the industrial lands on the Willamette River's far bank hum with activity. Behind them looms the dense green wall of Forest Park in the Tualatin Mountains, sharply contrasting the natural with the human. To the left, all of downtown and its many bridges stretch to the horizon. This view alone is worth a visit, especially if you don't spend much time in North Portland.

The park is also good for picnics, with tables set amid trees near the bluff's edge. (In a city of parks with impressive trees, Overlook holds its own. Some of the trees along Overlook Boulevard and the bluff are true giants.) An elegant stone picnic shelter is available for reservations. Nearby are a play structure and a miniature basketball court—great for one-on-one games. Opposite the restrooms, the dog off-leash area has more picnic tables and an equally compelling view.

The rest of the park is a broad field with a south-facing grassy slope leading up to Overlook Boulevard, ideal for afternoon sunbathing. Atop the slope, wander a few hundred yards along North Melrose Drive to the historic Overlook House. Mrs. Elvira Raven spent decades cultivating gardens around this handsome Tudor-style home before gifting it to the city in 1951. It's now a community center and popular wedding venue, managed by the Friends of the Overlook House, and is open for weekly tours (see Resources).

EXTEND YOUR VISIT

Just beyond the Overlook House is Mocks Crest, at the end of Skidmore Street. It's one of the city's premier sunset-viewing spots. On warm summer nights, romance is always in the air.

23 McCARTHY PARK

Magnificent river beach hides in plain sight at Portland's industrial city-within-a-city

Location: 4385 N. Channel Ave.
Acreage: 7.5
Amenities: 1-mile paved path, beach, picnic tables
Jurisdiction: Port of Portland

GETTING THERE

BY CAR I-5 to exit 303 (Swan Island); continue west on N. Going St., which becomes N. Channel Ave. and then N. Lagoon Ave.; left onto N. Commerce St. and again onto N. Channel Ave.; first right to reach McCarthy Park parking area. **BY TRANSIT** ★★ MAX (Yellow Line) to Killingsworth; then Bus 72 (Killingsworth/82nd Ave. toward Swan Island) to N. Channel Ave. and Ballast (stop 1042); backtrack a short distance to McCarthy Park trailhead. **BY BIKE** ★★

Question #1: Have you ever been to Swan Island? My guess is that many Portlanders will answer no. That's not surprising, as this charmless landscape of office parks and warehouses has only one road in and out. If you don't work here, you have no reason to be here. Except that . . .

Question #2: Did you know Swan Island has one of the city's best beaches? It's called Lindbergh's Beach after the famous aviator, who visited in 1927 on a victory tour following his epochal transatlantic flight. An orphaned stretch of the Willamette River Greenway runs a mile alongside the beach, with viewpoints, benches, and picnic tables. This is McCarthy Park, a first-rate riverfront amenity that its owner, the Port of Portland, seems intent on keeping secret from the rest of us. No longer!

Congratulate yourself upon locating the obscure parking area, then set off toward the river on a paved path. A spur leads down to the beach; the main path curves left to parallel it past some interpretive signs. Beyond the signs and a second beach-access spur, the path arrives at the gleaming North American headquarters of Daimler Trucks, where a plaza along the path offers a spot to admire the building, the beach, and the concatenation of industry on the Willamette's opposite bank.

The path continues past Daimler to a second plaza with two picnic tables and, eventually, to a junction. A left turn here leads under an arch back to Swan Island's streets. The arch matches the shape and dimensions of Portland's billion-dollar Big Pipe, the recently installed megapipe that (mostly) prevents sewage from overflowing into the river. Continuing straight, you reach a third beach-access point and then . . . a dead end. Someday, it is to be hoped, this path will continue through the Union Pacific rail yards to the Rose Quarter. Not yet.

Backtrack and pick your beach spot. The beach is broad and often strewn with driftwood, which creates cozy zones for a picnic or lounging. Some of these spots, it's true, host "campers" living on the margins of society. On recent visits, though, I've found none. In any case, leave them in peace. There's plenty of room.

The river is mostly shallow along this beach, making for relatively safe swimming and wading. (Note: the Willamette downstream of the Fremont Bridge is a Superfund site, with nasty PCBs lurking in river sediments. Swimming and wading are not going to hurt you, but eating resident fish like carp or bass will.)

Are you wondering why a rectangular peninsula is called Swan Island? It was indeed an island once, separated from wetlands beneath Mocks Crest—where present-day Willamette Boulevard runs—by a narrow river channel. Sandbars routinely formed upstream of Swan Island, hindering navigation. In 1927, the Army Corps of Engineers solved this by filling the channel and fusing Swan Island to the mainland. Enlarged by dredge spoils, the "improved" Swan Island began a new career as Portland's first airport, and later a World War II–era shipyard. After the war, the neighboring wetlands were filled, and today's industrial landscape took shape.

EXTEND YOUR VISIT

Launch a canoe or kayak from the nearby Swan Island boat ramp along North Basin Avenue and enjoy one of Portland's more interesting paddles. You'll pass Vigor Industrial's shipyards and dry docks—where Caribbean cruise ships, naval destroyers, and the occasional oil-drilling rig get repaired—and then the steep, wooded slopes of Waud's Bluff, where in April of 1806, William Clark turned his boat around after exploring the lower reaches of the Willamette River.

24 CATHEDRAL PARK

Winding paths and a river beach beneath the soaring St. Johns Bridge

Location: N. Edison St. and N. Pittsburg Ave.
Acreage: 21
Amenities: Accessible restroom, canoe launch and dock, dog off-leash area, paths, picnic tables
Jurisdiction: Portland Parks and Recreation

GETTING THERE

BY CAR I-405 north to exit 3 (US 30) at left; 4.6 miles on US 30/St. Helens Rd., then left for St. Johns Bridge; go right onto N. Syracuse St., right onto N. Burlington Ave., and right onto N. Edison St. **BY TRANSIT** ★★★ Bus 16 (Front Ave./St. Helens Rd. toward St. Johns) to N. Philadelphia and Ivanhoe (stop 4440); follow the sidewalk along N. Philadelphia downhill to the park. **BY BIKE** ★★

I've always revered this stylish park as a masterpiece of the City Beautiful era, when parks like Laurelhurst and Mount Tabor defined Portland. Only while researching this book did I learn it actually dates to 1980! Whoops. Some history is in order.

Chinookan-speaking peoples lived and fished for generations in this area prior to European settlement. William Clark spent a night here in 1806 on his brief reconnaissance up the Willamette River. In 1847, James John settled here and eventually laid out the town site that would bear his name. (The "saint" part stems, I think, from John's bequest of his estate to fund a school.)

In the early twentieth century, the St. Johns riverfront developed shipyards, ironworks, a woolen mill, and the first electric-powered lumber mill in the United States. The bridge went up in 1931. Industry gradually declined as the modern port developed farther downriver. There was talk of a riverside freeway.

In the early 1970s, residents floated a different idea: an "ecology" park planted with native trees. The city obliged, and in May 1980, just as Mount St. Helens was blowing its top, the park opened. In retrospect, it seems like a no-brainer to put a park under Portland's most beautiful bridge, with its four-hundred-foot-tall gothic towers and slender steel suspension cables. Yet, as with so many parks, in Portland and elsewhere, what seems obvious now only exists because someone—some people—saw the potential and worked tirelessly to make it real.

As you descend the path from Edison Street, the arched bridge columns frame views across the river to Forest Park. Past an outdoor stage and across North Crawford Street, a small memorial garden tucked among trees features a Wall of History

Bridge above, river below, Forest Park beyond: Cathedral Park's setting is dramatic.

telling the park's story. Somewhere in this wall, its location secret, is a time capsule that was placed in 1980. It will be retrieved in 2030. Mark your calendar.

On the park's central lawn along the river, a sculpture entitled *Drawing on the River* (2008, by Donald Fels) suspends thirty-foot-long bands of woven steel from pillars resembling ship hulls. The bridge looms overhead, lofty and monumental, with all the grace and drama of an actual cathedral.

The beach is great for swimming. (Yes, this stretch of the Willamette River is a Superfund site, but contact with the water is fine. Just don't eat resident fish.) If you don't want to get wet, wander out along the dock at the end of North Albany Street. This is also a good place to launch a canoe or paddleboard.

EXTEND YOUR VISIT

A paved path leads a short distance south to the city's Water Pollution Control Laboratory, a beautiful building with a demonstration rain garden.

25 PIER AND CHIMNEY PARKS

A magnificent forest, a giant dog park, and more at these expansive parks

Location: N. Lombard St. and N. Bruce Ave. (Pier); 9360 N. Columbia Blvd. (Chimney)
Acreage: 85 (Pier), 18 (Chimney)
Amenities: Accessible play area and restroom, picnic tables and shelters, skatepark, disc golf course, ball fields, basketball and tennis courts, splash pad, outdoor pool, paths, fenced dog park
Jurisdiction: Portland Parks and Recreation

GETTING THERE

BY CAR I-405 northbound to exit 3 (US 30) at left; continue 4.6 miles; left at the stoplight to St. Johns Bridge; over bridge, left onto N. Lombard St.; three-quarters of a mile to the park at right. **BY TRANSIT** ★★★ MAX (Yellow Line) to Lombard; then Bus 75 (Cesar Chavez/Lombard toward St. Johns) to Pier Park (stop 10697). **BY BIKE** ★★★ Via Marine Drive Path/40-Mile Loop.

When you've visited enough of Portland's parks, you eventually start wondering which stand of Douglas-firs (*Pseudotsuga menziesii*) is the greatest of all. Many of Portland's older parks have them. They are native to this region and grow to enormous size, easily topping two hundred feet. Planted as ornamentals a century ago, they have grown, in some parks, to become legitimate forests.

Hills, dales, and champion trees make Pier Park seem even bigger than it is.

Pier Park is a strong contender for the Douglas-fir championship title. Aside from a few baseball fields and a skatepark, most of it is a giant grove, with many trees so tall it's hard to tell where they end. They compete for light and shed their lower limbs. As a result, the park's forest feels open, with clear sightlines and grass in many places. There is joy to be found just wandering among the trees, watching the sunlight or rain filter down through their branches.

(If you see other wanderers looking a little more intent, they're likely using Pier Park's disc golf course, reputed to be the city's best.)

Beyond trees and discs, Pier Park's third claim to fame is its skatepark, with huge features that make my bones hurt just looking at them. There is a street course with big rails and tricky transitions, and several bowls, the largest of which connect via a twenty-foot-diameter *full* pipe. This is not for amateurs!

Like so many good things in Portland, the skatepark is a story of grassroots activism. At the turn of the millennium, the Burnside Skatepark was the only high-quality skatepark in town. Recognizing a need for more, Portland skaters banded together to advocate that Pier Park's existing skatepark, poorly designed and underutilized, be renovated with bond funds approved by voters in 2002. When neighborhood politics got tough and the city got squirrelly, skaters took matters into their own hands and raised the money to build the skatepark themselves. The city eventually got on board and, after seeing how immensely popular it proved to be, adopted a plan calling for nineteen city-funded skateparks across the city.

Chimney Park lies across rail tracks from Pier Park, connected via a pedestrian bridge. Joggers and walkers in Pier Park often head to Chimney to extend their loop, but most Chimney Park users come for the giant fenced dog park. If that's you, access it from Columbia Boulevard and park next to the old city incinerator.

Across Columbia Boulevard is the former St. Johns Landfill, decommissioned in 1991 and now being transformed into something like a native grassland. Eventually it will open to the public and provide another reason to explore this fascinating corner of Portland. When it does, the trail through Chimney and Pier (part of the currently disjointed 40-Mile Loop) will become far more popular with cyclists as well.

26 KELLEY POINT PARK

Forest paths and beaches where the Willamette and Columbia Rivers meet

Location: N. Marine Dr. and N. Lombard St.
Acreage: 105
Amenities: Accessible restroom, paths, picnic tables, canoe launch
Jurisdiction: Portland Parks and Recreation

GETTING THERE

BY CAR I-5 to exit 307 (MLK Jr. Blvd./Marine Dr.); west on Marine Dr.; park entrance is at right after 4.5 miles. **BY TRANSIT** ★ MAX (Yellow Line) to Expo Center; weekdays only, transfer to Bus 11 (Rivergate/Marine Dr.) to N. Marine and Pacific Gateway Blvd. (stop 9459); walk a mile along N. Marine Dr. and N. Kelley Point Park Rd. to the park. **BY BIKE** ★★★ Via Marine Drive Path.

Kelley Point is one of my absolute favorite places in Portland. My family has a tradition of visiting each spring. When the park's bottomland forests of cottonwood, birch, alder, and ash sprout new growth, our beach season begins. We picnic along the Columbia and admire the great river rolling on by.

This is not where you might look for a great park, hidden in a seemingly endless landscape of warehouses, distribution centers, car lots, and junkyards. Yet when you've almost run out of land heading west on Marine Drive, a little road branches off at right into a forest. At road's end, a short path leads to a beach where the two great rivers of our region meet. This is Kelley Point.

There are two parking areas: the first is best for reaching the Columbia Slough and trails leading to a beach on the Willamette. This part of the park is rarely busy.

From the second parking lot, a paved path leads past restrooms and a great lawn where dogs often frolic. At the north end of the lawn, benches face a beautifully framed view of the Columbia. Kelley Point, with a ramshackle picnic area, is just beyond.

Here you can often actually see the two rivers come together, blending hues: Cascades and Coast Range water greeting Canadian glacial melt and Rocky Mountain runoff. The quiet shores of Sauvie Island and the floodplains around Vancouver Lake stretch toward the horizon. Massive container ships pass within hailing distance en route to and from the adjacent port terminals. It's a unique and captivating scene.

Where the waters meet: the Willamette and Columbia Rivers at Kelley Point

It's also a relatively recent one. The city dumped massive quantities of fill here in the early twentieth century to make a port. Before that, this spot was an island surrounded by sloughs and wetlands.

Despite being wet and remote, in 1828 it captured the imagination of Oregon's original booster, a Massachusetts schoolteacher named Hall Jackson Kelley. Like many of his generation, Kelley read the recently published journals of Lewis and Clark with intense interest. Unlike most, however, Kelley took up the cause of settlement with uncommon zeal.

Unburdened by any firsthand knowledge of the Oregon Territory, Kelley fixated on this spot, which to judge from his map looked destined by geography for greatness. He didn't realize it was often underwater.

From Massachusetts, Kelley promoted his colony to anyone who would listen, including the United States Congress, and finally decided to lead the settlement himself. He arrived in Oregon in 1834, delirious with malaria and nearly broken by the rigors of his transcontinental journey. He spent the winter as an unwelcome guest at Fort Vancouver and caught a ship home the following spring, never to return.

Back home, Kelley continued churning out pamphlets and books extolling the territory he hardly knew. When the Oregon Trail opened in the 1840s, many migrants carried Kelley's compelling—if not always accurate—pamphlets with them. In 1926, a group of Portlanders petitioned the federal government to name the site of Kelley's would-be metropolis after him.

Note: Portland Parks and Recreation prohibits swimming at Kelley Point's Columbia River beach due to the swift drop-off and unpredictable currents. Plenty of people disregard this stricture, but be advised.

EXTEND YOUR VISIT

Consider canoeing, kayaking, or stand-up paddleboarding the placid waters of the Columbia Slough from the boat launch here. If you time the tides correctly, you can drift the slough's mellow current in both directions.

27 SMITH AND BYBEE LAKES

Wetland and lake complex invites paddlers and birders

Location: 5300 N. Marine Dr.
Acreage: 2000
Amenities: Restrooms, picnic shelter, accessible trail, canoe launch
Jurisdiction: Metro

GETTING THERE

BY CAR I-5 to exit 307 (MLK Jr. Blvd./Marine Dr.); west on N. Marine Dr.; 2.2 miles to the park entrance on the left. **BY TRANSIT** ★★ MAX (Yellow Line) to Expo Center; weekdays only, transfer to Bus 11 (Rivergate/Marine Dr.) to the 5300 block (stop 9202) at the park entrance. **BY BIKE** ★★★ Via Marine Drive Path.

Smith and Bybee Lakes form a vast, watery expanse sheltering migratory birds and ocean-bound salmon. They also offer a chance of solitude for city dwellers. Ringed by warehouses and industrial facilities in far North Portland, they practically hide in plain sight.

As a park, they mostly offer two things to do: watch birds and paddle. If you're not looking for one of those options, it's best to treat Smith and Bybee not as destinations unto themselves, but rather as a rest stop during a ride along some or all of the 40-Mile Loop, Portland's classic bike trail. (See Resources for guides with more on this and other urban cycling options.)

If you *are* looking to watch birds and other wildlife, follow the approximately 1-mile, wheelchair-accessible Interlakes Trail to several viewpoints across the lakes. Though I like birds well enough, I lack the patience for proper birding and tend to stick to the exciting, easy-to-identify ones: eagles, osprey, hawks, and the like. For this, winter is a good time. The big birds are out fishing, and the lack of foliage makes them easier to spot. Spring and fall are good for migratory birds like willow flycatchers and marsh wrens, and lake denizens like western painted turtles, river otters, and beavers.

To go paddling, visit in spring. April through June the lakes are highest, access is easiest, and wildlife is plentiful. The Metro Regional Government manages lake levels via a water-control structure, keeping spring levels high to benefit fish and waterfowl and reduce the spread of invasive reed canary grass.

After salmon have left the lakes for the Pacific, Metro opens the structure. The lakes then connect to the Columbia Slough, their levels rising and falling with the tidal-influenced slough. Metro recommends a depth of at least ten feet for optimal paddling. (If you come later in the season, prepare to navigate stretches of algae and mud.) You can find a link to the relevant river gauge at Metro's website (see Resources).

Paddling affords a closer view of the lakes' astounding ecological productivity. In good conditions, you can float placidly among half-drowned willow thickets along the margins of forests with cottonwood, ash, alder, and maple. In side channels and sloughs you might encounter dense mats of pond lilies, paddle-grabbing duckweed, and (if the land is dry enough) fields of reed canary grass. All around are burrows, warrens, and dens for critters large and small. Given how wet and otherwise inaccessible the lake margins are, you can easily feel as though you have stumbled upon a primeval corner of the earth.

28 LOTUS ISLE PARK

A postage stamp–size slice of history hidden among the Columbia's houseboats

Location: N. Tomahawk Island Dr., Hayden Island
Acreage: 1.7
Amenities: Accessible play area, picnic tables, beach
Jurisdiction: Portland Parks and Recreation

GETTING THERE

BY CAR I-5 to exit 308 (Hayden Island); east on N. Tomahawk Island Dr. a half mile to the park. **BY TRANSIT** ★★ Bus 6 (Martin Luther King Jr. Blvd.) to N. Hayden Island Dr. and Tomahawk Island Dr. (stop 13629); backtrack to N. Tomahawk Island Dr. and walk a half mile to the park. **BY BIKE** ★★

Lotus Isle Park isn't much of a park: an acre and a half of grass and trees, with a decent play structure and a nice little beach. Come not for the amenities but for the ambiance, because this is an odd place.

First of all, it's on Hayden Island, a strange land of marinas, big-box stores, and chain restaurants. Second, the park is so inconspicuous I'll bet even some island residents don't know about it. This is a strong contender for the title of Portland's Most Obscure Park.

Find a quiet weekend, midday, when the Interstate Bridge's normally apocalyptic traffic congestion is at an ebb, and spend some time exploring. Maybe even ride your bike here—an easier task than you might think. Or bring a paddle craft and explore the calm waters of the North Portland Harbor, aka Hayden Slough, the narrow river channel separating Hayden Island from the rest of Portland.

From the park's entrance, a paved path leads a short distance to a play structure. Nearby, a rough trail leads steeply down to a crescent beach tucked behind houseboats in calm water. The paved path continues past the play structure several hundred yards to a meadow, ringed with benches under the shade of maples. From here, views across the channel reveal row upon row of houseboats, a veritable floating city.

THE MILLION-DOLLAR PLEASURE PARADISE

Portlanders of a certain age remember halcyon days at Hayden Island's Jantzen Beach Amusement Park. From its debut in 1928 to its eventual demise in 1970, "the Coney Island of the West" welcomed thirty million visitors. It inaugurated a new era in mass entertainment—and spawned competitors.

Right after the debut of Jantzen Beach, a group of Portland investors who owned the sandbar just upstream sensed opportunity. They loudly announced plans to open a competing megapark virtually next door to Jantzen Beach. This was almost certainly an empty threat, designed to help the investors unload otherwise worthless property at a markup to the Jantzen Beach owners, who would presumably want to shut down competition. Jantzen's owners didn't bite, however, and the investors felt obliged to back up their hype.

Thus did 128-acre Lotus Isle Amusement Park open in 1930, the "Million-Dollar Pleasure Paradise," with more than forty rides and picnic space for fifteen thousand. For a short time, it stole Jantzen Beach's thunder. With its hundred-foot-tall neon sign in the shape of the Eiffel Tower, visible from Portland, Lotus Isle was a massive hit.

The park's gargantuan Peacock Ballroom (capacity: 6600) hosted top entertainers and the world's first walkathon. Events like Jell-O Week ("Nine Big Days of Fun and Frolic" with a demonstration of the "Latest Fashions in Food," presented by Miss Pauline Edwards of the General Mills Corporation) celebrated a distinctly modern consumer culture. A weeklong Mardi Gras party opened with a logrolling competition and ended with the crowning of Miss Portland. The carnival rides, pleasure boats, swimming beaches, and midway thronged with crowds.

Yet Lotus Isle seemed cursed from its beginnings. Just as the park was being built, the stock market crashed, ushering in the Great Depression. A few months into the first season, a young boy drowned at the park. The next day, Lotus Isle's principal investor committed suicide.

The following spring, a low-flying plane crashed into the park, destroying a building and spooking one of the park's main attractions, a circus elephant named Tusko. He escaped his enclosure and spread further carnage. His reign of terror ended only when troops from the National Guard arrived and recaptured him. The damage he caused was never repaired.

In the summer of that same year, the Peacock Ballroom burned down and rumors of arson swirled. By the end of 1932, Lotus Isle was bankrupt.

Its owners set a match to the place and walked away. The land sold at auction and was eventually redeveloped into the marinas you see today. Like Jantzen Beach Amusement Park, since replaced by a depressing shopping mall, Lotus Isle left few marks on the land. Those rotting pilings are all that remain of its legacy. From the bench at Lotus Isle Park's little promontory, your eye can follow the line they trace to a spot on the opposite bank, where the Lotus Isle Depot once received park visitors arriving in droves on the interurban streetcar. It's quiet now.

Tusko's story is worth a book in itself. After he was brought from Thailand to New York as a juvenile, his circus career took a wrong turn when he escaped his keepers in 1922 and rampaged through the Skagit River Valley farm town of Sedro-Woolley, north of Seattle. By the time he arrived at Lotus Isle, his reputation as "America's Meanest Elephant" was well established. Not long after Tusko's mishap at Lotus Isle, his owner took him to the Oregon State Fair in Salem and quietly abandoned him there. The state fair organizers, balking at the expense of feeding Tusko, foisted him off on the county sheriff. Residents of Salem publicly debated what to do with the troubled elephant; glue factories and canned food came up as potential solutions. Finally, the sheriff managed to auction Tusko for $200, which barely covered the cost of feeding him. After changing hands several more times, Tusko landed in Seattle, where he was kept in such dismal conditions that Seattle's mayor confiscated him. Tusko lived out his final years in Woodland Park Zoo, content at last, before dying of a blood clot in 1933. His bones reside at the University of Oregon's Museum of Natural and Cultural History.

In the foreground, you'll spot a line of rotting pilings marching toward the Portland shore. These are all that remain of the interurban streetcar line that once connected Vancouver, Washington, to Portland via the little neighborhood of Bridgeton. (Yes, there was once "light rail" to Vancouver! Not such a radical idea after all.)

In 1915, the interurban rail company opened a beach park here, drawing tens of thousands of summer visitors. At the time, the site was a giant sandbar, separated from Hayden Island by a narrow channel. In the early 1930s, the infamous Lotus Island Amusement Park (see sidebar) briefly flourished here. In later decades, the Port of Portland filled the channel to make way for marinas. Through a quirk of fate, this sliver of land ended up in the city's hands as an accidental park. It's been a quiet place ever since—and a perfect perch from which to soak up Portland's under-the-radar houseboat scene.

29 COLUMBIA CHILDREN'S ARBORETUM

Little-known grove tucked among industry and wetlands in the Columbia Slough

Location: 10040 NE 6th Dr.
Acreage: 29
Amenities: Path, portable toilet
Jurisdiction: Portland Parks and Recreation

GETTING THERE

BY CAR I-5 to exit 307 (MLK Jr. Blvd./Marine Dr.); follow Marine Dr. eastbound 1.3 miles; right onto NE 13th Ave.; right onto NE Meadow Dr.; left onto NE Meadow Ln. **BY TRANSIT** ★★ Bus 6 (Martin Luther King Jr. Blvd.) to NE Vancouver Way and Freightliner (stop 9438); walk right onto NE 6th Ave. and continue a quarter mile; past a fenced bus parking area, turn right into the park. **BY BIKE** ★★

Like Lotus Isle Park, this is one of Portland's most obscure. That's not to say it's unknown or unloved—to the contrary, its history is a story of community care and investment—but the location is practically top secret. To reach the park, you leave the street grid and enter a vortex of warehouses, industrial facilities, and drainage channels, with a few subdivisions sprinkled in at random. The park entrances are inconspicuous, to say the least: one hides behind a bus barn, the other at the end of a narrow gravel lane that looks like someone's driveway.

So why come here? It's a sentimental favorite, I guess. The park is small and lacks amenities, but like Whitaker Ponds Nature Park, it hints at how marvelous the Columbia Slough once was.

The park occupies a sliver of the land once called Switzler's Lake, where landscape architect John Olmsted urged the city to establish a major park. He noted that "no other form of park has ever proved so attractive and so useful to the masses of the people as the meadow park, particularly when there can be associated with it long reaches of still water as a landscape attraction and for boating purposes." Though the Children's Arboretum is too small to meet Olmsted's vision, it is just large enough to help you imagine how things might have been.

From the parking area on Meadow Lane, a packed gravel path leads a quarter mile through woods to a meadow and then forks. One branch leads north over a slough to exit at NE 6th Avenue; the other disappears into woods to emerge near the bus barn.

Autumn sun and fun in the central meadow of the Children's Arboretum

Double back along the park's southern end to find a small side channel (known as the "moat") and a restored wetland. You can see the entire place in twenty minutes, so don't hurry. If the weather is good, linger in the meadow, lie down, and stare at the sky. (Really, you should do this in *every* park, but especially here. Remember that feeling from your childhood?)

Speaking of childhood, you may wonder about the name. When World War II brought an influx of shipyard workers to this hitherto rural area, schools were needed in short order. The city built Columbia School nearby and planned a second one for this site. Then the Vanport Flood struck in 1948, ravaging neighborhoods up and down the Columbia Slough. The expected growth never came.

Instead, the school district turned the land over to Columbia School's students, who planned and built a community garden, park, and arboretum. Their goal was to plant the state tree from each of the fifty states. Columbia School closed in the late 1970s, and the project faded. In 1999, the land transferred to Portland Parks and Recreation, which plans to improve parking and add a proper restroom.

30 KENTON PARK

Roomy neighborhood park with new play structures in a historic neighborhood

Location: N. Argyle St. and N. Brandon Ave.
Acreage: 12
Amenities: Accessible restroom, accessible play area, basketball court, picnic tables, fields, splash pad
Jurisdiction: Portland Parks and Recreation

GETTING THERE

BY CAR I-5 northbound to exit 306A (Columbia Blvd.); right onto N. Columbia Blvd. to cross under freeway; soft left at stoplight onto N. Argyle St. via N. Interstate Pl.; continue three blocks to the park. **BY TRANSIT** ★★★ MAX (Yellow Line) to Kenton/N. Denver Ave.; walk one block west on N. Argyle St. **BY BIKE** ★★

Kenton Park is a tree-lined square of green near the Kenton neighborhood's historic main street, North Denver Avenue. This is pretty much a neighborhood park, but you should visit to enjoy the excellent play area (installed in 2018) and explore a corner of Portland that still flies under the radar.

You can enter the park from just about anywhere, but a good place to start is on the path leading from Brandon Avenue at Willis Boulevard. It curves through the park, with views of Mount St. Helens north over the sunken T-ball field.

The path goes to a brightly colored, soft-surface play area. Stacked logs, a climbing structure with a slide, swing sets, a series of low obstacles, and a splash pad keep kids of every ability and age busy. A restroom and picnic tables are nearby. If you have kids, plan to spend some quality time here.

When done at the park, wander down Willis Boulevard to Denver Avenue and admire Kenton's old downtown. Kenton was once the end of the road to the Columbia River Ferry, which crossed the mighty river from Vancouver, Washington. Kenton's calling card is now the giant Paul Bunyan statue along Interstate Avenue, but its true heritage is . . . meat!

In 1908, the Swift Company built stockyards and a livestock exchange (now the Expo Center) on the floodplain below Kenton. This soon became the biggest such market in the Pacific Northwest, drawing crowds to the annual Pacific International Livestock Exposition. Out-of-town traders stayed at the elegant Kenton Hotel, awaiting the cattle drives up North Greeley Avenue from the Albina rail yards. Swift Company executives lived in handsome concrete homes along Denver Avenue. Many of these distinctive houses remain.

Kenton declined after the war. The meatpacking industry left town, the livestock expositions ceased, and the Kenton Hotel, abandoned, became an eyesore. The specter of "urban renewal" loomed as Kenton stumbled through the closing decades of the twentieth century. Fortunately, it never lost its identity. The residents saved the hotel and turned it into apartments. Now bars, restaurants, and a farmers market line Denver Avenue. As in so many old Portland neighborhoods, signs of revival are everywhere.

31 ARBOR LODGE PARK AND HARPER'S PLAYGROUND

Neighborhood park with Portland's first, and maybe best, inclusive playground

Location: N. Bryant St. and N. Delaware Ave.
Acreage: 8.7
Amenities: Accessible playground and restroom, fields, dog off-leash area, picnic tables, tennis courts
Jurisdiction: Portland Parks and Recreation

GETTING THERE

BY CAR I-5 to exit 304 (Rosa Parks Way); continue west on N. Rosa Parks Way three-quarters of a mile; right onto N. Delaware Ave.; one block to the park. **BY TRANSIT** ★★★ Bus 35 (Macadam/Greeley toward University of Portland) to N. Greeley and Bryant (stop 2185); the park is east of N. Greely around the corner on N. Bryant St. **BY BIKE** ★★

Five-year-old Harper Goldberg tried to use the play structure at Arbor Lodge Park, but her walker got stuck in the bark chips. As a kid with mobility limitations, she had nowhere to play. So her parents set out to do something about it.

That was 2009. By 2012, with help from Portland Parks and Recreation and an army of volunteers, Harper's parents cut the ribbon on a new kind of playground, one they called "radically inclusive."

Harper's Playground is the main reason to visit Arbor Lodge Park. It's superb, a truly accessible—and fun—place for kids of all ages and abilities. It's also beautiful, incorporating trees, native plants, boulders, and sculptural seating elements into the design. The vivid colors in vogue at other newish Portland playgrounds are eye-catching, but seem destined to fade into something less joyous. By contrast, Harper's restrained aesthetic complements the park's quiet neighborhood ambience. You feel you're still in a *park*, not at a carnival.

Harper's parents could have declared victory and enjoyed their kid's playground. Instead, they formed a nonprofit dedicated to making inclusive play available to every child. In the years since, the organization, which is also called Harper's Playground, has worked to build an inclusive playground in every quadrant of the city. So far, they have first-rate playgrounds to their credit at Dawson, Couch, and Gateway Discovery Parks. Learn more at www.harpersplayground.org.

The rest of Arbor Lodge Park is pleasant, if unremarkable. As one of Portland's very few parks entirely free of pesticides and herbicides, it's an especially nice place to roll in the grass. And you'll likely see more birds, bats, and mason bees here than at most neighborhood parks.

EXTEND YOUR VISIT

Stroll through "downtown" Arbor Lodge (at North Greeley Avenue and North Rosa Parks Way) for coffee or lunch, then check out the city views from Willamette Boulevard. Just south of Ainsworth, Willamette does a 180-degree turn above a semi-wild gully known as the "Dog Bowl." This is an ideal spot for sunset watching and dog running. (You might even spot a coyote, so keep your dog close!)

32 PENINSULA PARK AND ROSE GARDEN

Grand old park with formal rose gardens

Location: N. Rosa Parks Way and N. Albina St.
Acreage: 16
Amenities: Rose garden, restrooms, paths, playground, splash pad, picnic tables and shelters, sports fields, tennis and basketball courts, community center with seasonal outdoor pool
Jurisdiction: Portland Parks and Recreation

GETTING THERE

BY CAR I-5 to exit 304 (Rosa Parks Way); continue east on N. Rosa Parks Way three blocks. **BY TRANSIT** ★★★ Bus 4 (Fessenden) to N. Albina and Ainsworth (stop 71) and the park. **BY BIKE** ★★

Peninsula Park is a contender for the "most elegant" superlative. Like many of Portland's parks from the early twentieth century, it embodies the grace and dignity associated with landscape architect Frederick Law Olmsted and the City Beautiful movement. Peninsula Park takes the aesthetic a step further than most, with an unusually formal layout centered on its magnificent rose garden.

Since the rose garden is the park's true calling card, you should start there. It dates to 1909 and was the city's first public rose garden. (This was an era when rose gardens were a top park priority. No city could hold its head high without one.) Peninsula Park hosted the annual rose show until supplanted by the International Rose Test Garden at Washington Park, established in 1917. Fortunately, Peninsula Park's garden survived changing tastes and fluctuating neighborhood fortunes. In

Last of the bloom at Peninsula Park Rose Garden on a late summer evening

2012, rose lovers formed the Friends of Peninsula Park Rose Garden to renovate the garden in time for its one-hundredth birthday.

For the full effect, descend the stairs from Ainsworth. (The two-acre garden, once a gravel pit, is below street grade.) Wander among the more than five thousand roses arranged parterre-style around a fountain. Admire the fine brickwork, the antique lamps, and the gazebo. Squint a little and you can imagine the Palace of Versailles just beyond. There's no place in Portland like it.

The rest of the park has plenty to offer as well. Symmetrical paths arc from the rose garden around a central meadow doubling as a sports field. The paths converge at a plaza in front of the Peninsula Park Community Center, the city's oldest. Nearby, a grove of Douglas-firs shades an eclectic playground and splash pad. The main climbing structure features a tube, perhaps twenty feet long, suspended about six feet off the ground. Little ones crawl through it and squeal with delight; older kids try to balance on top, enjoying a whiff of danger. I know of at least one nine-year-old who still loves it.

33 WOODLAWN PARK

Intimate, charming park in a historic neighborhood center

Location: NE 13th Ave. and NE Dekum St.
Acreage: 7.6
Amenities: Amphitheater, basketball courts, climbing structure, picnic tables, play structure, accessible restrooms, spray feature
Jurisdiction: Portland Parks and Recreation

GETTING THERE

BY CAR I-5 to exit 304 (Rosa Parks Way); continue east on N. Rosa Parks Way to NE Martin Luther King Jr. Blvd.; go left, then immediately right onto NE Dekum St.; continue five blocks. **BY TRANSIT** ★★★ Bus 8 (Jackson Park/NE 15th toward Dekum) to NE Dekum and Claremont (stop 1275). **BY BIKE** ★★

Woodlawn Park is definitely a neighborhood place: lawns dotted with picnic tables, a modest play area, and some basketball courts. That's about it. The park is special, though. It's as if someone took a much grander park, like Laurelhurst, and shrank it down to just a few acres.

Entering from Dekum Street, you pass a basketball court edged by low stone walls. Descending alongside the central lawn to a ponderosa-ringed play area, you feel you've moved deep into a sylvan grove. The play area and splash pad extend underneath NE Claremont Avenue, which flies over the park like a miniature viaduct. It's an uncommonly appealing space.

The park is also worth visiting for the neighborhood. Woodlawn started as a farming village on the outskirts of Albina. When a rail line opened in 1888, connecting the Stark Street Ferry dock in East Portland to the Vancouver Ferry dock on Hayden Island, it ran right through the village. Developers Frank Dekum and Richard Durham laid out the unusual street pattern around the streetcar tracks, which ran diagonally from Union Avenue (today's Martin Luther King Jr. Boulevard) to end at Woodlawn's station, now the site of Woodlawn Park.

Businesses clustered around Durham Avenue and Dekum Street: grocery stores, butchers, a bakery, a doctor, even a nickelodeon. For a time, Woodlawn was among the liveliest of the streetcar suburbs. With the demise of streetcars,

Woodlawn Park's cozy play area, perfect for younger kids

Woodlawn turned more residential and then became isolated and somewhat downtrodden as urban renewal tore apart nearby neighborhoods.

More recently, a new wave of Portlanders has discovered Woodlawn, taken by its leafy streets, old homes, and short commutes to downtown. The upside of this gentrification is the revival of Woodlawn's historic center, now thick with cafes, shops, and pubs. Come on a farmers market day and buy a picnic lunch to enjoy in the park. It's about as concentrated a dose of Portland charm as you'll find.

34 ALBERTA PARK

Big trees and covered courts invite visits to this neighborhood gem in all seasons

Location: NE Killingsworth St. and NE 19th Ave.
Acreage: 17
Amenities: Baseball field, covered basketball courts, bike polo, dog off-leash area, running path, play equipment, picnic tables, tennis court, restrooms
Jurisdiction: Portland Parks and Recreation

GETTING THERE

BY CAR I-5 to exit 303 (Killingsworth St./Swan Island); continue east on NE Killingsworth St. to NE 18th Ave. **BY TRANSIT** ★★★ Bus 8 (Jackson Park/NE 15th

toward Dekum) to NE 15th and Killingsworth (stop 6795); walk three blocks east.
BY BIKE ★★

When you've had your fill of boutiques and restaurants on NE Alberta Street, head a few blocks north to unwind at Alberta Park. The park is a big rectangle of forest and lawns fronted by elegant older homes, an elementary school, and a fire station where friendly firefighters occasionally invite kids to tour the engines inside.

Many Portland parks have big Douglas-firs, but Alberta Park *really* has them: 242, according to a tree survey Portland Parks and Recreation recently completed, plus some grand fir, Pacific silver fir, and ponderosa pine. Volunteers mapped all 335 of the park's trees; the bureau used this information to create a fascinating online story map and tree guide. Using a smartphone, you can wander the park and spot individual specimens. (Some other leafy Portland parks have likewise been mapped. Check out the Resources section for more information.)

These trees provide shelter from wind and rain in the winter, thanks to the umbrella of fir boughs holding up the sky above. They're even better in summer; just set foot in the park on a hot day and you'll feel the temperature drop ten degrees from the surrounding neighborhood. (Ever heard of the urban heat island effect? That's when cities become unnaturally hot due to all the paved surfaces absorbing heat. Places like Alberta Park are the city's natural air conditioners, spreading cool and clean air beyond their boundaries.)

Come for the trees, but stay for the amenities. This is a true year-round park. A wood chip–covered path ringing the park offers mostly mud-free jogging in all weather. A dog off-leash area, nestled among the firs, has room for even the biggest dogs and is nicely situated near the play structure and basketball court, making it feasible to exercise all your animals at once. (This was a big draw when my son was a toddler.)

Speaking of basketball courts, Alberta Park has one of the best. I've spent more than one rainy midwinter afternoon shooting hoops under the court's enormous roof. You'll nearly always find dry conditions. Nearby, the excellent tennis court along 19th Avenue sees a lot of action. Meanwhile a second, much dingier court along 22nd Avenue hosts another Portland institution: bike polo.

Though Seattle gets credit for inventing the sport, bike polo soon took root in Portland. Teams of three riders using DIY mallets (usually a ski pole attached to some PVC pipe) tangle over a small ball in slightly anarchic fashion, mixing elements of street hockey with medieval jousting. Like other Portland hipster institutions—think Zoombombing, Adult Soapbox Derby, World Naked Bike Ride—bike polo is oddly ageless. (Tattoos, cheap beer, and fixed gears never go out of style.) It's also a ton of fun to watch.

Perhaps the best thing about Alberta Park is how well its amenities blend with the wooded setting. You don't have to go far into the park to feel you've entered a forest. Portland Parks and Recreation recently converted an acre in the park's center to a "nature patch," planting thousands of native understory plants and leaving logs to rot in place as habitat for bugs and squirrels. The nature patch concept is rolling out across Portland parks, designed to support native pollinators while reducing maintenance costs associated with mulching and mowing.

EXTEND YOUR VISIT

Check out the Ainsworth Linear Arboretum along NE Ainsworth Street at the park's north end. You'll find a guide to the street's sixty-plus different species, many uncommon in Portland, on the Portland Parks and Recreation website (see Resources).

35 FAUBION SCHOOL PLAYGROUND

Action-packed playground at an innovative school

Location: NE Dekum St. between NE 29th Ave. and NE 32nd Ave.
Acreage: 1
Amenities: Playground
Jurisdiction: Portland Public Schools

GETTING THERE

BY CAR I-5 northbound to exit 305A (US 30 Bypass/Lombard St. E.); right onto Lombard St. for 2.5 miles; right onto NE 32nd Ave.; right onto NE Dekum St. **BY TRANSIT** ★★★ Bus 17 (Holgate/Broadway toward Saratoga and 27th) to NE 27th and Dekum (stop 7240); walk two blocks east on Dekum. **BY BIKE** ★★

School playgrounds in Portland vary wildly in age, quality, and upkeep. Many are worth a visit, but only one makes the grade for this book: Faubion School. For decades, Faubion was a run-of-the-mill school in a diverse but economically precarious neighborhood. What it had going for it was its location next door to Concordia University, a Lutheran college.

Years of collaboration between college and school culminated in 2017, when Portland Public Schools completed a ground-up reconstruction of Faubion School. The sleek new Faubion hosts an innovative education partnership called "3toPhD" putting a preschool, a health clinic, a fresh food hub, and college classrooms under the same roof as Faubion's students. As of this writing, the program's future is, unfortunately, in doubt, as Concordia abruptly closed in 2020 after 125 years educating Portlanders.

What will happen next remains to be seen. What *you* should see is the amazing playground this partnership helped to create. Like most Portland schoolyards, it is open to the public outside of school hours. Four turf-lined equipment clusters, separated by a wide path with seating for the grown-ups, appeal to a range of ages. Between the equipment's vivid colors and the turf's synthetic green glow, the place is eerily cheery. Natural vegetation is lacking, but the upside is that you can have fun here even in a downpour.

Among the many attractions are several climbing structures, a rope pyramid, saucer swings, a covered court, and—seemingly the crowd favorite—two zip lines capable of producing real thrills without jarring your spine.

Given how much fun this playground is, expect to share it. If the crowds start to overwhelm, head to the adjacent sports field, where you'll find a running/walking track, an expanse of grass, and maybe some quiet.

36 BROUGHTON BEACH

Well-kept, broad beach on the Columbia River with swimming and room to roam

Location: NE Marine Dr. at NE 33rd Dr.
Acreage: 33
Amenities: Swimming beach (no lifeguard), restrooms
Jurisdiction: Metro

GETTING THERE

BY CAR I-5 to exit 307 (MLK Jr. Blvd./Marine Dr.); follow Marine Dr. east 3 miles to the park entrance at left. **BY TRANSIT** ★ Bus 70 (12th/NE 33rd toward Sunderland) to NE Sunderland and 33rd Dr. (stop 11171); walk north on 33rd; go right to join the Marine Drive Bike Path to Broughton Beach (1.4-mile walk). **BY BIKE** ★★★ Via Marine Drive Path.

Broughton Beach is a wide, long strip of Columbia River frontage tucked behind the airport. It's a busier and less "natural" stretch of river than at Sauvie Island or Frenchman's Bar, but what it lacks in green it makes up for in size and convenience.

Winter at Broughton Beach means no swimming, but also no crowds.

Old-timers who associate the beach with trash, parties, and dissolution should take note: Metro, the agency that manages Broughton Beach, has spiffed it up significantly. There is now adequate parking, a ranger frequently on-site, and regular beach cleanings.

Still, this is not a natural area. The beach backs up to the levee along Marine Drive, beyond which is the Portland International Airport. Incoming jets fly low overhead, and you can't quite escape the sound of cars buzzing past. Still, the view of Mount Hood is spectacular, and in summer, the water is downright inviting. With a gently sloping bottom and relatively soft sand, the river access is fun for kids, and their parents won't need to panic. That said, the Columbia is not to be trifled with. Broughton Beach is pretty safe thanks to the shallow bottom and the wing dams, those lines of closely spaced pilings that stretch out from shore. They force the current to the center of the river, helping scour the bottom and maintain a shipping channel. Water behind the wing dams tends to be calm. Nevertheless, it's a good idea to stay near the shore and wear a personal flotation device.

From the parking lot, you can wander up the beach about three-quarters of a mile. A few trees near the halfway point offer the only shade. The beach's eastern end is low and especially wide. There's plenty of room for kids and dogs to run and play in the shallows. (Dogs are supposed to stay on leash . . . you've been warned.)

Don't count nature out entirely. You stand a good chance of spotting an osprey or a cormorant diving for its dinner, or even a sea lion heading up to the salmon buffet at Bonneville Dam.

EXTEND YOUR VISIT

Take a walk, jog, or ride a bike on the Marine Drive Path, which runs along the Columbia all the way to the Sandy River.

37 WHITAKER PONDS NATURE PARK

Pocket wilderness in the Columbia Slough

Location: NE 47th Ave. near NE Columbia Blvd.
Acreage: 26
Amenities: Viewing dock, trail, gazebo, canoe launch
Jurisdiction: Portland Parks and Recreation

GETTING THERE

BY CAR I-5 northbound to exit 305A (US 30 Bypass/Lombard St.); right onto E. Lombard St. for 2.7 miles; exit right for NE 42nd Ave.; bear left to cross over Lombard; cross NE Columbia Blvd. onto NE 47th Ave. and continue a quarter mile to the park entrance at right. **BY TRANSIT** ★★ Bus 75 (Cesar Chavez/Lombard toward St. Johns) to NE Columbia Blvd. and 47th (stop 13472); walk a quarter mile north on NE 47th Ave. to the entrance. **BY BIKE** ★★

Whitaker Ponds Nature Park is a postage-stamp remnant of the wetlands, meadows, and forests that once filled the Columbia Slough, sheltering salmon on their ocean-bound journey.

Throughout Portland's early years, only a handful of settlers penetrated the slough's watery expanse. When landscape architect John Charles Olmsted visited in 1903, the area was still largely wild. He recommended the city create "a great meadow reservation . . . to preserve the beautiful bottom land scenery" here.

Things didn't turn out that way. Soon after Olmsted's visit, landowners along the slough formed an association to dike and drain the area. They built a levee along the Columbia River in 1919, shutting off its life-giving floods, and shunted the slough's water into pipes and ditches. They also filled and paved over wetlands to make way for today's industrial landscape. Impervious surfaces now cover more than half of the slough's watershed.

Still, the slough offers a measure of refuge to wildlife and even a few brave fish—in spite of the motor oil draining from junkyards, the shipwrecked shopping carts, and the dismal riprap. It's a testament to resilience. That may be why it inspires so much love, and why groups like the Columbia Slough Watershed Council (see Resources), headquartered at Whitaker Ponds, work so hard to restore it. Volunteers estimate they have pulled more than two thousand old tires out of the ponds.

I like Whitaker Ponds best in late spring, when the trees have leafed out but the ponds still hold plenty of water. From the parking lot, follow a short paved path to a viewing dock on the west pond. Bring binoculars and, depending on the time of day and season, you will likely spot turtles, egrets, osprey, beavers, and more. This is a small area, but it's the best habitat around, so there's always something going on.

A trail heads right past a gazebo, often used by the watershed council for classes, to loop the west pond. The quick half-mile walk goes between the ponds and along a stretch of Whitaker Slough, an arm of the Columbia Slough. From the trail, the ponds seem almost primordial; the heron taking flight at the sound of your step looks as if it has been there since the dinosaurs.

EXTEND YOUR VISIT

Whitaker Slough is a great, calm place to paddle. The confluence area, where Whitaker Slough meets the main Columbia Slough, is especially nice. There's a canoe launch just north of the west pond a few hundred yards from the parking area.

38 KᴴUNAMOKWST PARK

A sweet little park with new play features

Location: NE Alberta St. at NE 52nd Ave.
Acreage: 2.4
Amenities: Accessible play area and restroom, picnic shelter, playground, skatepark, splash pad
Jurisdiction: Portland Parks and Recreation

GETTING THERE

BY CAR I-84 eastbound to exit 1 (NE 33rd Ave.); left onto NE 33rd Ave. for 1.5 miles; right onto NE Prescott St.; left onto NE 52nd Ave.; two blocks to the park. **BY TRANSIT** ★★ MAX (Red or Blue Line) to Hollywood; transfer to Bus 75 (Cesar Chavez/Lombard toward St. Johns) to NE 42nd and Alberta St. (stop 7505); walk ten blocks east on NE Alberta St. **BY BIKE** ★★

Working the "skate dot," one of Portland's beginner-friendly skate parks, at K^{h}unamokwst Park

It's pronounced "KAHN-ah-mockst." The name comes from Chinook *Wawa*, a trade language that people up and down the Columbia River have spoken for millennia. The word means "together." Built in 2015, K^{h}unamokwst is the first park in the city's history to have an indigenous name and the first developed park in the long-neglected Cully neighborhood.

Come to celebrate these firsts and, more to the point, have some fun. The park designers packed many kid amenities into a small space; most are universally accessible. So throw the kids in the bike trailer with a picnic and plan to spend a few hours here. (If you're there without snacks and they get hangry, you'll find great ice cream and pizza along nearby 42nd Avenue.)

Like many of Portland's newer parks, K^{h}unamokwst's design centers on a paved oval path circling a great lawn. At one corner, a pair of picnic tables overlook a modest rain garden and a small skatepark. While plenty of skaters slay this park, it's mellow by design and welcomes beginners.

South of the lawn, a bark-chip play area has climbing rocks and a ramp-accessed tower. A single Douglas-fir stands watch, casting precious shade. Next door is a cluster of rocks with a hand pump and a spray jet, a fun but low-key water feature. Swings on a barrier-free soft surface round out the play offerings. A sheltered picnic area and restroom provide the basic comforts.

Being new, the park lacks the sylvan gravitas of Portland's best older parks. It makes up for this by being bright and cheery, and—so far—well maintained. Cully waited too long for this park, but at least it got a good one.

39 CULLY PARK

Grassroots energy has transformed a landfill into a dynamic park for a diverse neighborhood

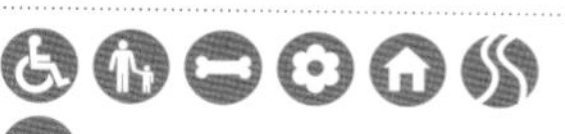

Location: NE 72nd Ave. near NE Killingsworth St.
Acreage: 25
Amenities: Accessible restrooms and play area, fenced dog park, community garden plots, fitness course, picnic areas, fields, Native Gathering Garden
Jurisdiction: Portland Parks and Recreation

GETTING THERE

BY CAR I-205 to exit 23B (US 30 Bypass/Killingsworth); stay right for Killingsworth; right onto NE 72nd Ave. to the park. **BY TRANSIT** ★★ MAX (Red, Green, or Blue Line) to 82nd Ave.; transfer to Bus 72 (Killingsworth/82nd toward Swan Island) to NE Killingsworth and 72nd (stop 3212); walk north a quarter mile on NE 72nd Ave. to the park. **BY BIKE** ★★

Like many areas farther east, Northeast Portland's Cully neighborhood developed outside of the city, with little thought paid to sidewalks and parks. Residents have long contended with poor transit access, a lack of open space, and an abundance of polluted brownfields. And they've waited a long, long time for a full-scale park. Thankfully, that park is finally here.

For decades, Cully Park was a gravel mine. When the gravel played out, it became a landfill. Then its owners went bankrupt and dumped the area on the state. The city acquired it in 2000, promising residents a park. When the master plan was finally complete it 2008, it pegged development costs at north of $20 million, thanks largely to the complexities of building a park on a landfill actively belching methane. Then the Great Recession struck that same year, busting the city's budget. The park seemed to slip out of reach.

Community members were not deterred, though. They formed a partnership called, bluntly, "Let Us Build Cully Park." They begged, badgered, and bullied the city to build the park or get out of the way. They raised millions, tweaked the park design based on close consultation with local residents, and built a lot of the park

Newish Cully Park has big views, a generous play area, and lots of room to roam. (Photo by Matthew Scotten)

themselves. After some initial resistance, Portland Parks and Recreation came around and championed the partnership. The park finally opened in 2018 to a chorus of praise.

Thanks to the design limitations imposed by the landfill, the park is light on trees but long on views across the Columbia River to Mount St. Helens. Although squarely in the city, you can almost taste a hint of sea air rolling in on the river fog. The park is still raw, but as the vegetation grows in and the final design elements fall into place, its appeal will only grow.

Key draws are the park's expansive, fenced dog park, a paved jogging path with fitness stations, and a playground. The latter is truly impressive, no doubt thanks to having been designed largely by children. Nature play elements like basalt blocks and actual trees (which, if they survive in this exposed spot, will provide great climbing opportunities) mix with active features like a climbing net, slide, spinner, and suspension bridge. I've seen plenty of kids, my own included, go feral with joy.

Cully Park also has beautifully terraced community garden plots, a welcome addition to this part of the city.

Perhaps the best element of all is the Native Gathering Garden, where from a circle of basalt blocks on a raised mound, rows of boulders radiate in the cardinal directions and toward Mount St. Helens and Mount Hood. The garden's plants are culturally significant to the people who have always lived here, including Chinookan peoples along the Columbia and the Kalapuyans of the lower Willamette Valley. Tribal members harvest these plants at the appropriate time and in the appropriate way. (Please respect these traditions—admire the garden, but don't harvest plants yourself.) Spiraling paths connect the mound to a second circle edged with massive tree poles. These spaces exist to acknowledge indigenous connections to the land and create a venue for ceremonies, events, workshops, and other gatherings. In short, they celebrate the present and the future as much as the past.

All of this makes Cully Park a hopeful place. Don't miss it.

EXTEND YOUR VISIT

Just across NE Columbia Boulevard—and perhaps one day connected by a pedestrian bridge—is Colwood Park, formerly an eighteen-hole golf course now repurposed with nine holes and an ambitious restoration project along Whitaker Slough.

40 JOSEPH WOOD HILL PARK

The best view in East Portland

Location: NE Rocky Butte Rd.
Acreage: 2.4
Amenities: Paths, monument
Jurisdiction: Portland Parks and Recreation

GETTING THERE

BY CAR I-84 eastbound to exit 4 (NE 68th Ave.); straight onto NE Halsey St.; left onto NE 92nd Ave.; right onto NE Rocky Butte Rd. **BY TRANSIT** ★ MAX (Blue, Red, or Green Line) to Gateway Transit Center; transfer to Bus 24 (Fremont/NW 18th toward Providence Park) to NE 92nd and Russell (stop 8115); walk up NE Rocky Butte Rd. (three-quarters of a mile and 125 feet of elevation gain). **BY BIKE** ★★ Road to the butte is steep but quiet and scenic.

Rocky Butte is the hill overlooking the tangled interchange of I-205 and I-84 in East Portland. Like its peers—Mount Tabor, Powell Butte, Mount Talbert, and others—it's an extinct volcano. Joseph Wood Hill Park is at the summit, a broad lawn set atop magnificent stone ramparts. From below, it almost looks like a ruined hilltop castle somewhere in Tuscany. From the top, the views are awesome.

Park anywhere along Rocky Butte Road, which loops the summit. Walk up a steep gravel path on the south or a graceful set of stone steps on the north. On top are a few trees, an oval path of bright red pumice, and a monument to Mr. Hill.

There isn't much to do here except admire the view, but that alone is worth the trip. On a clear day you can see far up the Columbia River Gorge, across the broad plains of southwest Washington, and over all of central Portland.

The butte owes its superior view to the Missoula Floods, which scoured Eastern Washington and littered the Willamette Valley with bits of Montana mountaintops. These Ice Age floods rushed down the Columbia River Gorge to drown the Portland area under four hundred feet of water, repeatedly blasting Rocky Butte's east side to its hard volcanic core.

This geologic legacy made the butte a convenient place to quarry very hard basalt. The rocks showed up in Portland landmarks like the old Henry Weinhard's brewery on Burnside near Powell's City of Books, and the magnificent old Portland Hotel that stood on what is now Pioneer Square.

For a time, the butte was also home to the Pacific Northwest's most elite military prep school, The Hill Academy, established downtown by Joseph Wood Hill in 1901, moved here in 1931. The school enjoyed the rare privilege of nominating one student to West Point each year until it closed in 1959. Later, its grounds became part of what is today Portland Bible College and its parent ministry, Mannahouse—indicated by the enormous white domes just north of the park.

The elaborate stonework ringing Joseph Wood Hill Park is a legacy of the Works Progress Administration (WPA), which put unemployed men to work during the Great Depression. The military academy, which owned most of the butte, granted land and access to Multnomah County, which used the federal largesse to pay an army of stonemasons and laborers to build the road and faux fortress. Like other WPA sites around the Pacific Northwest, it reflects care and craftsmanship that now seem lost to history.

EXTEND YOUR VISIT

Visit the National Sanctuary of Our Sorrowful Mother, better known as The Grotto. It's a Catholic shrine built into a cave in the side of Rocky Butte. The shrine is interesting, but the intimate botanical garden on top of the cliff above the cave is the real draw. It's a short drive or, if you prefer, a pleasant

Wy'East (also known as Mount Hood) in all its spring glory, from atop Rocky Butte

1.5-mile walk from Joseph Wood Hill Park. If walking, follow the park road north to find a trail branching off opposite the bible college entrance. Follow the trail downhill through woods between the butte and I-205. You'll pass rock climbers—and likely some transient campers—to arrive at NE Skidmore Street. The Grotto entrance is a few blocks west.

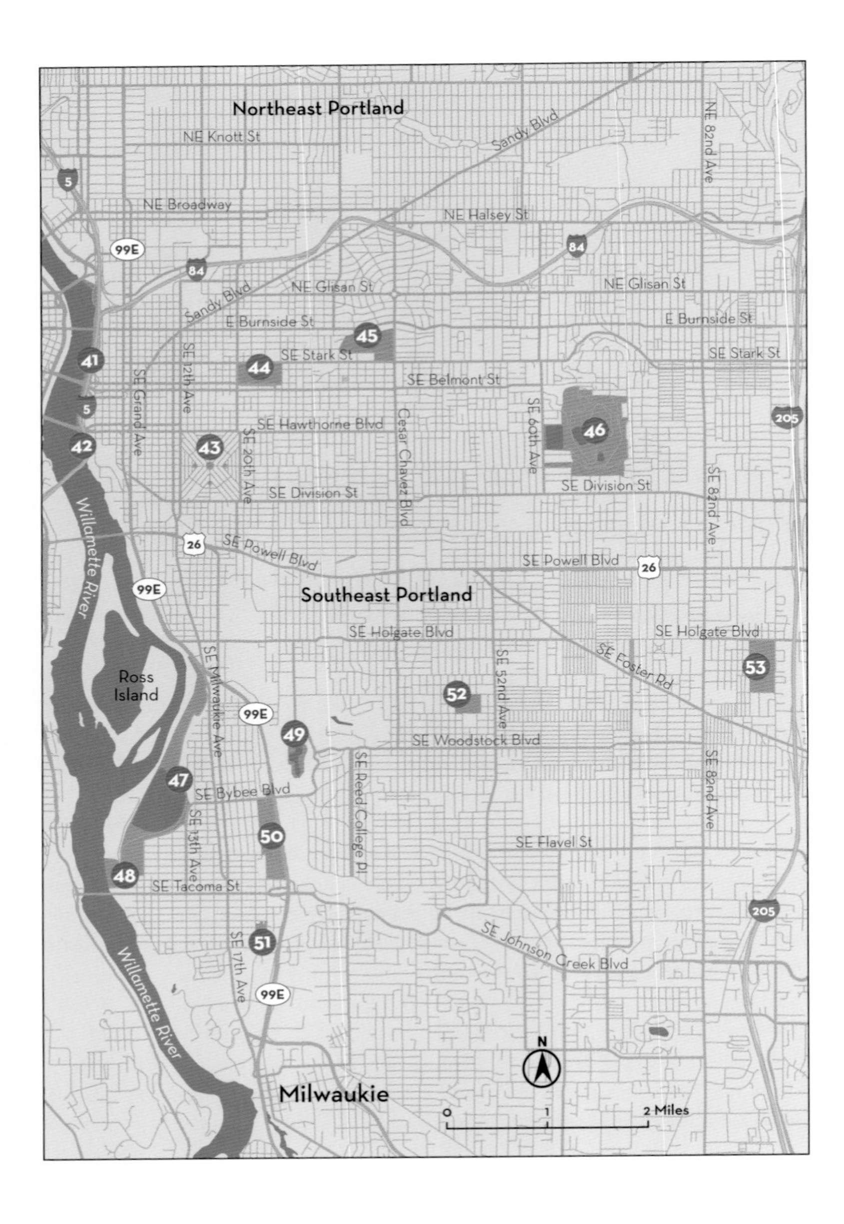
Northeast Portland
NE Knott St
Sandy Blvd
NE 82nd Ave
5
NE Broadway
NE Halsey St
99E
84
NE Glisan St
Sandy Blvd
E Burnside St
45
SE Stark St
44
41
SE 12th Ave
SE Grand Ave
SE Belmont St
5
SE Hawthorne Blvd
Cesar Chavez Blvd
SE 60th Ave
46
205
42
43
SE 20th Ave
SE Division St
SE 82nd Ave
Willamette River
26
SE Powell Blvd
SE Powell Blvd
99E
Southeast Portland
SE Holgate Blvd
SE Holgate Blvd
SE Foster Rd
53
Ross Island
SE Milwaukie Ave
SE 52nd Ave
52
99E
49
SE Woodstock Blvd
SE Reed College Pl
47
SE Bybee Blvd
SE 13th Ave
SE 82nd Ave
50
SE Flavel St
48
SE Tacoma St
205
SE 17th Ave
51
SE Johnson Creek Blvd
99E
Willamette River
N
Milwaukie
0
1
2 Miles

INNER SOUTHEAST PORTLAND

41 EASTBANK ESPLANADE

Linear park with river access and close-up views of downtown

Location: SE Water Ave. and SE Hawthorne Blvd.
Acreage: 11
Amenities: 1.5-mile paved path, benches
Jurisdiction: Portland Parks and Recreation

GETTING THERE

BY CAR I-5 northbound to exit 300 (SE Water Ave.); right onto SE Water Ave.; right onto SE Madison St. to the parking area underneath the bridge. Parking fee. **BY TRANSIT** ★★★ Buses 2, 6, 10, or 14 to Hawthorne Bridge (stop 2641); backtrack on sidewalk two blocks, following signs for the esplanade. **BY BIKE** ★★★ Via Springwater Corridor and Willamette Greenway.

Vera Katz Eastbank Esplanade traces the Willamette River's eastern shore from the Hawthorne Bridge to the Steel Bridge. It's a fantastic place to walk, run, ride, or just linger over views of Portland's skyline. I've jogged the 4-mile loop

connecting the esplanade to Tom McCall Waterfront Park so many times I feel I know every step—and I still look forward to it.

Waterfront Park honors Tom McCall, the Republican governor who did so much to make Oregon a livable, green, and progressive place. The esplanade honors a Portland mayor who did much the same. Among Vera Katz's many accomplishments as mayor (1993–2005), seeing the esplanade from concept to completion may have been the biggest. To find room for a path along a riverfront obliterated by riprap and crowded by a freeway, she navigated a thicket of zoning, environmental, fiscal, and logistical hurdles that might have defeated a less committed and less skilled leader.

Starting at a plaza between the Hawthorne Bridge and the Portland Fire Bureau dock, the path heads north to a long deck, cantilevered over the water. Under the shade of a cedar, a bronze Vera sits on a low wall, greeting passersby.

Beyond, the path narrows as I-5 edges closer. Though park designers did an excellent job screening out the monster freeway, its noise is inescapable. After a quarter mile, a ramp spirals upward to exit the path at the Morrison Bridge. Past the bridge, the esplanade splits at a pinch point into a narrow concrete path that parallels an elevated walkway. These two branches soon reunite. A short distance later the esplanade leaves terra firma altogether, diving under the Burnside Bridge on a quarter-mile floating walkway, past a dock. The Human Access Project (see Audrey McCall Beach) has exciting plans to convert it to a swimming dock.

After returning to land, the esplanade continues to the Steel Bridge, where engineering genius (and $10 million) has made it possible to cross the Willamette near river level. This is no small feat! The bridge, built in 1912, is unique in that its lower deck (for freight trains) can be raised and lowered independently of the upper deck (for cars and light rail). The esplanade essentially "hangs" from the lower deck, following it up and down. Its midspan view over the Willamette is one of my favorites—especially in winter, when high flows bring the swirling, dark waters tantalizingly close to your feet.

Sculptures and interpretive signs line the path, creating a portrait of the bustling, dynamic industrial waterfront that once stretched from Albina to the Brooklyn neighborhood south of Powell Boulevard.

EXTEND YOUR VISIT

Though it changes names, the esplanade continues south under the Hawthorne Bridge to pass Audrey McCall Beach, the Oregon Museum of Science and Industry, and the Tilikum Crossing Bridge to reach Springwater on the Willamette.

OPPOSITE: *The Eastbank Esplanade leads upstream toward the Hawthorne Bridge.*

42 AUDREY McCALL BEACH AND THE DOCK

Ground zero for the nascent downtown river swimming scene

Location: East bank, south of the Hawthorne Bridge
Acreage: 1
Amenities: Swimming beach and dock—that's it
Jurisdiction: Portland Parks and Recreation/ Human Access Project

GETTING THERE

BY CAR I-5 northbound to exit 300 (SE Water Ave.); right onto SE Water Ave.; right onto SE Madison St. to parking area underneath bridge. Parking fee. Walk a quarter mile south on the Eastbank Esplanade to the beach and dock. **BY TRANSIT** ★★★ Buses 2, 6, 10, or 14 to Hawthorne Bridge (stop 2641); backtrack on the sidewalk for two blocks, following signs for the esplanade, and walk a quarter mile south. **BY BIKE** ★★★ Via Springwater Corridor and Willamette Greenway.

Audrey McCall Beach is the creation of the Human Access Project (HAP), a jolly and slightly provocative band of river lovers working to "transform Portland's relationship with the Willamette River" (see Resources). They asked, "Why does Portland ignore its river?" By way of an answer they noted that (a) Portlanders don't realize the bad old days of raw sewage are gone and the river is safe for swimming; and (b) they lack suitable places to access the water.

To address both issues, HAP has sponsored an annual event called the Big Float, celebrating our connection to the urban Willamette. They have also worked to create proper swimming beaches. They are heroes of mine, both because of how they've improved this city and because of how deftly they've cajoled city leaders into accepting and even adopting their agenda.

To my mind, Audrey McCall Beach is HAP at its best. This lovely gravel crescent stretches from the Hawthorne Bridge to the Dock (more on that in a minute). For as long as I can remember, this beach was a dismal pile of riprap and trash, passed over and ignored by commuters on the bridge. That all changed a few years ago, when HAP worked with volunteers (including local inmates) to remove nineteen tons of concrete, old steel cables, and who knows what else from the river.

When you visit, bring some sort of water shoe. The gravel is largish, tough on feet, and hot in the summer. And though HAP and others take good care of the beach, like all such places in Portland it sees some use by folks who don't prioritize public hygiene. Believe me, though, it's a truly pleasant spot, and the swimming is, indeed, good.

A BRIDGE FOR THE PEOPLE

The Tilikum Crossing Bridge, built in 2015, connects Inner Southeast Portland to the South Waterfront neighborhood. As most Portlanders have heard by now, Tilikum is the largest car-free bridge in the United States and reputedly the nation's *only* bridge with light rail, bus, bike, and pedestrian access. As such, it's an icon of Portland's green self-image.

Portland of late has done some soul-searching about how much it deserves this image. Increasing traffic congestion, declining affordability, a homelessness crisis, a history of structural racism finally coming to light—these challenges force Portlanders to acknowledge that our vaunted "livability" is in doubt and that Portlanders' access to this livability is and long has been grossly inequitable.

These considerations likely loomed over the citizen commission tasked with naming the bridge. Their choice, Tilikum, comes from Chinook *Wawa*, an indigenous lingua franca used by traders up and down the Columbia. It means "people," "tribe," or "relatives." Thus, Tilikum Crossing is—or aspires to be—the "Bridge of the People."

In my view, it merits the beautiful name. And while not technically a park, it deserves mention in this book because it's one of the city's best new public spaces. The bridge has fourteen-foot-wide pedestrian and bicycle lanes on both sides, creating plenty of room to ramble. Around the bridge's twin 180-foot towers, the pedestrian lanes widen to create viewpoints with short interpretive passages etched into the bridge railing. Views take in downtown, Ross Island, South Waterfront's gleaming towers, and—best of all—the wide and deep Willamette River itself.

MAX trains and streetcars periodically rumble past, but in between, a great and eerie silence prevails. This must be one of the quietest places in the central city. That fact alone justifies a visit.

The bridge also has a great work of art, by artists Anna Valentina Murch and Doug Hollis. One hundred seventy-eight LED lights project onto the bridge's cables and piers, shifting color according to the river's speed, height, and water temperature. It's a brilliant visualization of the river's subtle, constant fluctuations. I now find myself eager to check the bridge color whenever I'm downtown after dark.

Next to the beach is one of Portland's most interesting summer scenes: the Dock. This public dock, accessible from the Eastbank Esplanade, was built for rowers, dragon boat racers, and recreational paddlers. In recent years, the young and beautiful have started taking it over on hot days, sunbathing and frolicking in the river.

It's no stretch to call this Portland's Riviera, at times a giant floating party. Though I often feel old here, I love lounging on the Dock and plunging midstream into the Willamette. It's an easy swim to Audrey McCall Beach and under the Hawthorne Bridge, which looms spectacularly high when seen from river level. If you're a halfway competent swimmer (keep in mind, there are no lifeguards here), I urge you to visit and see the city from a new perspective.

43 LADD CIRCLE PARK AND ROSE GARDENS

Picture-perfect gardens in what just might be Portland's most beautiful neighborhood

Location: SE Ladd Circle
Acreage: 1.6
Amenities: Rose gardens, benches
Jurisdiction: Portland Parks and Recreation

GETTING THERE

BY CAR I-5 northbound to exit 300 (SE Water Ave.); straight onto SE Yamhill St.; right onto SE Martin Luther King Jr. Blvd.; left onto SE Clay St.; right onto SE Ladd Ave. to Ladd Circle. **BY TRANSIT** ★★★ Bus 14 (Hawthorne) to SE Hawthorne and 16th (stop 2603); walk south to Ladd Circle. **BY BIKE** ★★

If you asked two groups to define the perfect neighborhood, with professional city planners in one and average Americans in the other, the Venn diagram of their overlap would probably resemble Ladds Addition. Its unconventional street layout, eclectic architectural styles, towering street trees, and elegant rose gardens exude charm and welcome.

At the neighborhood's center is Ladd Circle, two hundred feet across with ornamental plantings and a few park benches. It may not sound like much, but there are few better places to soak up the joie de vivre of Portland on a summer day. Cyclists stream around the circle, following a major bike route connecting Southeast Portland to downtown. Musicians often gather in the circle for jam sessions and impromptu performances—I've even seen a string quartet there on several occasions.

The neighborhood is named for William Sargent Ladd. A successful merchant, banker, real estate investor, and early Portland mayor, he chose (against his surveyor's advice) to develop his Southeast Portland farmland with a circular park and diagonal streets. The diagonals converge at four diamond-shaped plots of land, each equidistant from Ladd Circle, where in 1909, Portland's first park superintendent, Emanuel Mische, established rose gardens. Volunteers now tend the three thousand–plus plants.

The four gardens each feature rows of formally planted and meticulously maintained roses, with a pair of benches in the middle, perfect for a tête-à-tête. The north garden is my favorite, fronted by a grandiose manor at its north end and the imposing St. Sharbel Maronite Church on the south.

The rose gardens have a unique feel. They are unequivocally public spaces. Yet when I'm in them, I feel a bit like I'm loafing in the front yard of a well-to-do but tolerant neighbor. They are refined and democratic at the same time.

I recommend you make a circuit of the four gardens, sampling the many rose varieties on display. Then, spend a languid summer evening hour in Ladd Circle, feeling the warm light fade.

EXTEND YOUR VISIT

Set aside an hour or two to wander Ladds Addition and get royally lost—you'll be amazed how easy that is. Admire the century-old Craftsman homes, cute 1920s bungalows and fourplexes, and the occasional 1960s ranch house. Venture onto side streets and into the narrow alleys. Amid a happy maze of diagonal streets and odd angles, you may soon lose track of direction. Some of Ladds's streets have trees so large they blot out the sky, further adding to the pleasant disorientation. When the streets spit you out into the surrounding city, turn around and plunge back in. Sooner or later, you'll end up back at Ladd Circle.

44 LONE FIR CEMETERY

Giant trees and weathered headstones at the city's oldest cemetery

Location: SE 26th Ave. between SE Stark St. and SE Belmont St.
Acreage: 30
Amenities: Paved paths, historical tours
Jurisdiction: Metro

GETTING THERE

BY CAR I-5 northbound to exit 300 (SE Water Ave.); left onto SE Water Ave., which becomes SE Stark St.; continue to SE 26th Ave.; cemetery entrance is on 26th

Glorious trees and three centuries of history at Lone Fir Cemetery. (Photo by Alyssa Koomas)

at right. **BY TRANSIT** ★★★ Bus 15 (Belmont/NW 23rd toward Gateway) to SE Belmont and 26th Ave. (stop 13043); walk two blocks north on 26th. **BY BIKE** ★★

Needless to say, Lone Fir Cemetery isn't a park. Yet when it comes to peace, quiet, and glorious trees, it outdoes most parks in town, with many fine places to roll out a picnic blanket and commune with the living and the dead. I like to think the people buried here welcome our company.

When the cemetery opened in 1855, there really *was* only one tree. That lone fir (it still stands, near the cemetery's oldest, northwestern section) presided over a field just recently cleared of ancient forests. The field's previous owner, James Stephens, had come from Kentucky with his father, Emmor. The senior Stephens soon died upon arrival in Oregon, and James buried him near that lone fir.

In 1854, Stephens sold the farm to a man named Colburn Barrell, on condition that Barrell maintain Emmor's grave. Only weeks earlier, a steamship of which Barrell was part owner had exploded at the dock in Canemah, above Willamette Falls, killing twenty-four of its fifty passengers. Among the dead was Barrell's business partner, Crawford Dobbins. A grief-stricken Barrell transferred Dobbins's remains from a downtown graveyard to a plot near Emmor, setting aside ten acres around the one fir tree as the Mount Crawford Cemetery.

Over the next decade, the cemetery expanded to its current size. In 1866, it became the Lone Fir Cemetery. With a proper burial ground finally available to provide the deceased with a suitably sylvan repose, Portlanders emptied the city's makeshift downtown graveyards and moved their kin here.

Until the River View Cemetery opened in 1882, Lone Fir was Portland's *only* cemetery. As such, it received people from all walks of life. Portland's founder, Asa Lovejoy, is buried here, as are several mayors. So too are criminals and members of the demimonde. (One of the more prominent stones, erected by bereaved clients, honors a famed prostitute.) I recently learned that a first cousin of Vincent van Gogh also resides here. An alcoholic who may also have suffered from epilepsy, Hendrik van Gogh stole his father's fortune, escaped to America, and died in Portland a year later under mysterious circumstances.

Many graves are unmarked. Anonymous inmates of the Oregon Hospital for the Insane, once located at present-day SE 12th and Hawthorne, lie here. (James Hawthorne, founder of the hospital, was ahead of his time in taking a compassionate view of mental illness. He's not buried here, but a monument honors him.)

Others among the unnamed were Chinese laborers, single men who came to work and died far from family. Many of them ended up in the cemetery's southwest corner, forgotten. Later, a Multnomah County office building stood above them. In 2004, the county decided to sell the land for redevelopment, prompting concerns that human remains might still lie underneath. When archeological investigations confirmed this, the sale was called off and the site was thrown into limbo. The building has since been razed and now sits empty. Metro, which manages Portland's pioneer cemeteries, is working with the Lone Fir Cemetery Foundation to create a memorial garden here, honoring these men and the largely unacknowledged role they played in building the city.

The cemetery contains so many stories. Visit the Friends of Lone Fir Cemetery website (see Resources) to learn more, join a walking tour, or volunteer.

Finally, take time to wander. There's drama here—in the quintet of giant sequoias now obscuring the grave they once marked, in the eerily dilapidated Macleay family mausoleum, and in the quotidian sorrows and joys of lives long and illustrious, short and tragic, or simply forgotten. So will it be, sooner or later, for all of us.

45 LAURELHURST PARK

The most romantic park in the city: refined, urbane, and natural

Location: SE Oak St. and SE 37th Ave.
Acreage: 27
Amenities: Picnic areas, paths, pond, dog off-leash area, restrooms, play equipment, basketball and handball courts
Jurisdiction: Portland Parks and Recreation

GETTING THERE

BY CAR I-84 eastbound to exit 2 (NE Cesar Chavez Blvd.) southbound for 1 mile; right onto SE Oak St. **BY TRANSIT** ★★★ Bus 20 (Burnside/Stark toward Gresham Transit Center) to E. Burnside and SE Floral (stop 701); walk south on SE Floral Pl. to SE Ankeny St.; left to reach the park entrance. **BY BIKE** ★★

Laurelhurst is my neighborhood park and hands down my favorite. I'm grateful I need only walk ten blocks to arrive at a place that goes toe-to-toe with Manhattan's Central Park.

The key to Laurelhurst's charm is its topography. William S. Ladd, the former mayor who developed nearby Ladds Addition, owned several hundred acres in what is now Inner Southeast Portland. At a particularly lovely spot on his property was a spring-fed pond where Ladd watered his cattle and locals cooled off in summer. In 1911, Portland's visionary park director, Emanuel Mische, acquired the pond and surrounding acres for a park. His Olmsted-inspired design blended nature (big trees and native plantings) with artifice (clever sightlines, a deepened and widened pond) in subtle ways that reveal themselves gradually. Having visited Laurelhurst Park on average of once a week for a decade, I'm still discovering new details.

The park is really two: Mische's magical assemblage of paths, meadows, and groves, and a more prosaic annex across SE Oak Street. The latter has a play structure, a lumpy soccer field, excellent (and busy) tennis and basketball courts, a small dance studio, and a defunct wading pool waiting interminably for its replacement. The real draw, though, is north of SE Oak Street in the main park.

From the SE 37th Avenue entrance, a curving, paved path leads past charmingly ramshackle horseshoe pits on the right and the Broad Meadow—given over to dogs in winter—at left. At the path's bottom, you reach Firwood Lake and the Children's Lawn. People gather here to partake of serenely silent tai chi sessions, spontaneous capoeira jams, cosplay sword fights, baby boot camps, and silent discos (yes, it's a thing).

Beyond the Children's Lawn are restrooms and branching paths leading east through the Concert Grove (great for shady picnics) and west up Rhododendron Hill. Both paths eventually return you to the 37th Avenue entrance. The outermost loop is just about a mile—great for running and easy biking.

On those first warm evenings of spring, when the dogwoods explode in white, cherry blossoms line the paths in lurid pink, and the pale grass erupts from the ground with pent-up energy—and when Portlanders emerge from their winter holes to resume public life—there's no place I'd rather be.

46 MOUNT TABOR PARK

The premier eastside park: trails, views, history, and more on a local volcano

Location: SE 60th Ave. and SE Salmon St.
Acreage: 197
Amenities: Visitor center, accessible play area and restrooms, basketball and tennis courts, dog off-leash area, paved paths, trails, picnic tables and shelter, playground, amphitheater
Jurisdiction: Portland Parks and Recreation

GETTING THERE

BY CAR I-84 eastbound to exit 3 (58th Ave.); left onto NE Glisan St.; right onto NE 60th Ave.; after three-quarters of a mile, left onto SE Belmont St.; right onto SE 69th Ave.; right onto SE Park Dr.; right into parking lot. **BY TRANSIT** ★★★ Bus 15 (Belmont/NW 23rd toward Gateway) to SE 69th and Yamhill (stop 7853); walk right onto SE Yamhill St.; after two blocks veer left onto a path into the park. (Buses 2 and 71 provide additional access points.) **BY BIKE** ★★ Great ride to the summit on quiet roads.

Atop Mount Tabor, look for a giant, branching maple tree near the northern end of the summit meadow. I was married here. I'm but one of many Portlanders with strong and deep ties to this place.

Mount Tabor's dark, conifer-clad slopes loom over Southeast Portland like a sky island in the surrounding ocean of asphalt. On rainy winter mornings, when the bohemians of Hawthorne Boulevard still slumber, mist clings to these trees with a wildness belying their urban setting. In this generally flat and occasionally

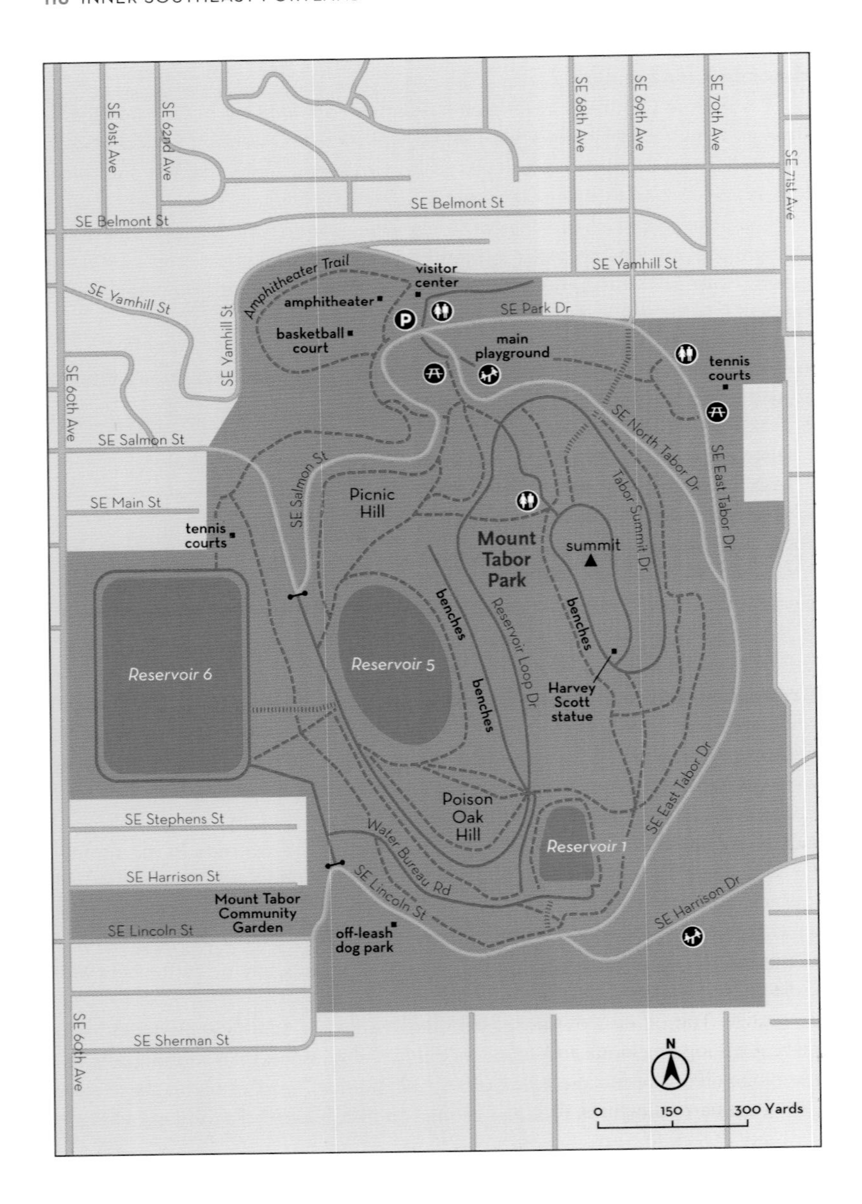
SE 61st Ave
SE 62nd Ave
SE 68th Ave
SE 69th Ave
SE 70th Ave
SE 71st Ave
SE Belmont St
SE Belmont St
SE Yamhill St
SE Yamhill St
SE Yamhill St
Amphitheater Trail
visitor center
amphitheater
basketball court
SE Park Dr
main playground
tennis courts
SE 60th Ave
SE Salmon St
SE Salmon St
SE North Tabor Dr
SE East Tabor Dr
Tabor Summit Dr
SE Main St
Picnic Hill
tennis courts
Mount Tabor Park
summit
benches
benches
benches
Reservoir Loop Dr
Reservoir 6
Reservoir 5
Harvey Scott statue
Poison Oak Hill
SE Stephens St
Water Bureau Rd
SE East Tabor Dr
Reservoir 1
SE Harrison St
SE Lincoln St
SE Harrison Dr
Mount Tabor Community Garden
SE Lincoln St
off-leash dog park
SE Sherman St
SE 60th Ave
N
0
150
300 Yards

dreary corner of Portland, the park is a beacon, reminding us that nature has pride of place in our city.

The park has soft-surface trails, paved paths, roads closed to motor vehicles, and roads open to vehicles but that are lightly traveled. You can spend days exploring. There's a lot to do here, but simply walking is best. (You can bike, too, but be ready for stiff climbs. The top is a good four hundred feet above the surrounding neighborhoods.)

The visitor center is a great place to start. Here you'll find restrooms, park info, and likely a volunteer with the Friends of Mount Tabor Park. This citizen group has mapped three walking loops at 1, 1.7, and 3 miles in length. Pick up a map or visit their website (see Resources) to learn more, make a donation, and volunteer.

From the visitor center, head south to a picnic shelter and playground set among widely spaced, enormous Douglas-firs. Nestled in the mountain's shoulder, it offers summer shade and some shelter from bitter east winter winds. This is a play area where you'll be happy to let kids linger and wander.

Up a short path is Mount Tabor's summit, reached by flights of steps and also a loop road closed to cars. On a nice day, the summit meadow is among the best spots on the planet to toss a Frisbee or unroll a picnic blanket. Openings in the trees afford views east to Mount Hood. On the west side, perfectly placed benches overlook SE Hawthorne Boulevard, which stretches westward to disappear at the foot of downtown skyscrapers gleaming in the afternoon light.

Paths and trails lead down from the summit in every direction. Head east toward additional picnic areas and secluded tennis courts overlooking the Montavilla neighborhood, or south toward the extensive dog park (where hills tire even the strongest pups) and an obscure playground. Venture west down the main slope via trails paralleling Salmon Street past Picnic Hill, or along Reservoir Loop Drive as it loops around Poison Oak Hill. This is one of the park's prettiest spots, the name notwithstanding.

On the park's western slope are several large reservoirs, encircled by paths graced with antique lampposts. For over a century, these reservoirs stored drinking water, gravity-fed from Bull Run Lake on Mount Hood. In the early 2000s, the Environmental Protection Agency decreed that Portland's open reservoirs be covered or decommissioned. The latter happened here; the gleaming pools are now merely decorative. They're not entirely useless, though. The paths circling the reservoirs make great jogging loops and are usually lit at night. And the stairs connecting the reservoirs offer a perfect place to punish your quads.

As the name suggests, this park is a mountain. To be precise, a dormant volcanic butte. (Okay, to be *really* precise, a cinder cone.) It's one of the Boring Volcanic

Snow day at Mount Tabor's excellent sledding hill

Field geologic features (see Mount Talbert Nature Park). The cinder cone's central vent—from which lava, gas, and rocks spewed, gradually building up the hill—is visible behind the visitor center. Look for oddly porous red and black rocks in the amphitheater near the basketball court.

This is a mere sampling of what Tabor offers. Visit in August to watch the famed Adult Soapbox Derby, a true "Keep Portland Weird" event, where the brave and/or inebriated race full-sized, homemade soapbox cars of varying quality down a hill too steep for safe travel. Visit in deep winter for clear views and a chance of urban snow. Try riding or running to the top, a Portland fitness rite of passage. Or just wander the park's quiet corners. Even on the balmiest days, you can find solitude somewhere.

47 OAKS BOTTOM WILDLIFE REFUGE

Birds and trails in an urban wetland

Location: SE Sellwood Blvd. and SE 7th Ave.
Acreage: 163
Amenities: Nature trails (approximately 2 miles)
Jurisdiction: Portland Parks and Recreation

GETTING THERE

BY CAR SE McLoughlin Blvd./OR 99E southbound to SE Bybee Blvd. westbound; Bybee Blvd. becomes SE 13th Ave.; right onto SE Sellwood Blvd. (becomes SE 7th Ave.); right into Sellwood Park. (Parking also available at North Woodlands and South Refuge trailheads.) **BY TRANSIT** ★★★ Bus 99 (Macadam/McLoughlin) to SE Tacoma and 7th (stop 5676); walk north on SE 7th Ave., then left at Spokane St. to South Meadow trailhead and Springwater Corridor. North Woodlands trailhead: Bus 19 (Woodstock/Glisan toward Mount Scott) to SE Milwaukie and Mitchell (stop 3935) and park entrance. **BY BIKE** ★★★ Via Springwater Corridor.

Oaks Bottom is a floodplain wetland tucked between the Sellwood neighborhood and the Willamette River. On its trails you stand a good chance of spotting bald eagles, coyotes, and Portland's official bird, the long-legged great blue heron. That this wetland exists at all is a story worth retelling, because it helped kick off Portland's modern greenspaces movement.

Wetlands once lined the lower Willamette River's floodplain. The Central Eastside, Swan Island, the Pearl District—all were shot through with creek bottoms and "swamps" that threatened malaria and inhibited settlement. One by one, we filled them in, creating an orderly riverbank lined with docks and indusry. The habitat vital for birds, mammals, and especially salmon disappeared.

Well into the 1970s, after Earth Day and momentous legislative achievements like the Endangered Species Act and Clean Air Act, many people—even conservationists—saw little natural value in urban places like Oaks Bottom. Not Mike Houck. As a young biology teacher, he watched with dismay as many of his conservation colleagues focused on distant wild places when there was so much work to do close to home. So he convinced the Portland Audubon Society to hire him with a title of his own invention: Urban Naturalist.

The city had already filled in a good chunk of Oaks Bottom. The southern end was an old city dump; the northern end received spoils from the I-405 freeway

Winter riding above Oaks Bottom, with views to downtown and the West Hills

construction. New plans called for filling the remaining wetlands and building museums, a yacht harbor, and a motocross course, all linked to the bluff top by an aerial tram.

Mike wasn't having it. He spearheaded a grassroots campaign that included some "guerrilla" conservation: at one point, Oaks Bottom sprouted mysterious, handmade signs saying "wildlife refuge." This and other advocacy actions, combined with pressure from the neighborhood association and other supporters, prompted the city to abandon development plans and, eventually, declare Oaks Bottom Portland's first official wildlife refuge. Mike went on to found the Urban Greenspaces Institute and campaign tirelessly for nature in the city. He's still at it. We owe him a debt of gratitude every time a peregrine soars over a downtown bridge or a heron squawks along the riverbank.

You can access the refuge from Sellwood Park, where a trail leads down from the parking lot to the South Meadow (aka the old dump), now being restored as an oak savanna and grassland. Connect here to the Bluff Trail, which loops the wetland. The trail passes among young cedars and over footbridges with periodic views of the wetland. Above it looms a giant mural of a great blue heron (another Mike Houck brainchild) adorning the side of the Portland Memorial Mausoleum. According to Mike, it's the largest hand-painted mural in North American.

SPRINGWATER ON THE WILLAMETTE

The Springwater Corridor is Portland's best-known and much loved rail trail, stretching 21 miles from the Central Eastside to the country hamlet of Boring. One of the trail's best stretches is its first 3 miles, commonly called Springwater on the Willamette. It is essentially an extension of the Eastbank Esplanade, but with a different character. The esplanade is urban and lively; Springwater on the Willamette is quiet and natural, running several miles along a branch of the Willamette called Holgate Channel.

Beginning in the industrial landscape of Inner Southeast Portland near the Tilicum Crossing Bridge, the path runs beneath the Ross Island Bridge and then abruptly changes character. Traffic noise disappears behind a high bluff as the path follows the river's wooded bank. Benches and picnic tables offer views of downtown and Ross Island. Around the 1-mile mark, you pass the Ross Island lagoon on the opposite bank. Here, the Ross Island Sand and Gravel Company mined gravel for a century. Mining ceased in 2001. Conservationists are working to get what's left of the island into public ownership as a natural area.

Beyond, the path enters woods along Oaks Bottom Wildlife Refuge. Around the 2-mile mark, a junction offers detours east into Oaks Bottom and west to the river. The main path continues over a new culvert, aka "the salmon subway," connecting Oaks Bottom to the river. There is often wildlife around here: the city's wildlife camera has recorded otters, beavers, mink, and more.

Around the 2.5-mile mark, a trailside observation deck provides elevated views over the Oaks Bottom wetland. This is a great spot for bird-watching. A short distance farther, a side path leads to Oaks Amusement Park and a second access trail to the wildlife refuge. At 3 miles, the path reaches a trailhead at SE Spokane Street and Sellwood Riverfront Park. Sellwood Park and charming downtown Sellwood are just uphill.

Two notes of caution: First, you may encounter unhoused people camping in the woods along the trail. Please remember these folks are doing the best they can in the midst of a housing crisis. Second, be considerate of your fellow park-goers. When I bike the path, I'm all too easily irked by pedestrians obliviously chatting, shooting selfies, and swerving across the path to admire a bird. When I walk it, I'm equally prone to vilify the aggro bicyclists threatening to mow me down in their single-minded, joyless pursuit of exercise or their destination. In other words . . . I can relate to both sides. This path happens to be an excellent walking trail *and* an excellent biking route. There's just not quite enough room for everyone.

After passing through an ash-dominated woodland, the trail reaches a junction. From here, check out the short interpretive loop around Tadpole Pond, then head uphill to a trailhead along Milwaukie Avenue, or downhill to a railroad underpass, where you can join the Springwater on the Willamette path (see sidebar).

Part of what makes this walk so nice is the variety of forest types. Some areas have typical floodplain forest trees, like cottonwood, alder, ash, and willow. Other areas, slightly higher and better drained, have Oregon white oak and madrone. The wetland itself constantly changes with the seasons.

For years, the parks bureau regulated water levels in the wetland with a small dam, trying to mimic a natural river connection. In 2018, the city installed a huge new culvert underneath the Springwater Corridor and constructed a new channel through the wetlands. Now with a *real* connection to the Willamette, Oaks Bottom is set to become a regular home for juvenile salmon migrating downstream.

48 SELLWOOD AND SELLWOOD RIVERFRONT PARKS

Big trees, views, and Portland's best beach—for humans as well as dogs

Location: SE Sellwood Blvd. and SE 7th Ave.
Acreage: 25
Amenities: Restrooms, play structure, basketball and tennis courts, sports fields, horseshoe pits, seasonal outdoor pool, beach with dock, dog off-leash area
Jurisdiction: Portland Parks and Recreation

GETTING THERE

BY CAR SE McLoughlin Blvd./OR 99E southbound to SE Bybee Blvd. westbound; Bybee Blvd. becomes SE 13th Ave.; right onto SE Sellwood Blvd. (becomes SE 7th Ave.); right into Sellwood Park. **BY TRANSIT** ★★★ Bus 99 (Macadam/McLoughlin) to SE Tacoma and 7th (stop 5676); walk north on SE 7th Ave. two blocks to Sellwood Park. **BY BIKE** ★★★ Via Springwater Corridor.

These two parks are basically one, upper and lower, separated by a rail line and the Springwater Corridor. The riverfront park draws people from all over Portland, while the main park is more of a neighborhood destination. Both merit a visit.

Sellwood Park sits on a bluff at the edge of the Sellwood neighborhood. If you don't know Sellwood, check out its main street along 13th Avenue, lined with restaurants, cafes, and shops. All around it are picture-perfect, leafy streets with classic old Portland homes.

The park is a few blocks west. It has a great playground and a seasonal pool especially suited to little kids. Venture along the park's north edge to Sellwood Boulevard, where you'll find benches and a magnificent view over Oaks Bottom and downtown. Views are limited within the park itself thanks to the immense Douglas-firs, thick enough here to create welcome summer shade.

To visit Sellwood Riverfront Park, go downhill past restrooms and tennis courts to SE Grand Avenue. You will pass tiny Oaks Pioneer Church, the oldest intact church building in Oregon. It dates to 1851. The church was built from a house owned by Lot Whitcomb, Oregon's first shipping tycoon and the founder of Milwaukie. The church narrowly escaped demolition thanks to determined preservationists and was moved here in 1969. It's now a popular wedding venue.

Head right on SE Spokane Street to cross the Springwater Corridor, then go right on SE Oaks Park Way to reach the riverfront park. (You can, of course, also drive here. Beware, the parking lot regularly fills on summer weekends.) A paved path circles a broad and often muddy dog off-leash area. Beyond, gravel trails lead to a beach and a small natural area. Dogs need to stay on leash in the natural area, where Portland Parks and Recreation is restoring a degraded floodplain forest.

At the beach, dogs run free. Indeed, Sellwood Beach is second only to the Sandy River Delta for canine self-actualization. It stretches about a half mile downstream, offering ample running room. In summer it's also one of Portland's best swimming beaches, with a gradual drop-off and only a little current. You might think that frolicking dogs and sand-digging toddlers would be a bad mix. Though I'm sure it could happen, over many years of bringing a kid and a dog I've never seen a serious conflict.

EXTEND YOUR VISIT

Check out adjacent Oaks Amusement Park (open seasonally) for an old-fashioned carny vibe and a vintage roller rink at the West Coast's oldest amusement park. For a more natural experience, head to Oaks Bottom Wildlife Refuge.

49 CRYSTAL SPRINGS RHODODENDRON GARDEN

Rhododendrons explode with color on a fairy-tale island

Location: 5801 SE 28th Ave.
Acreage: 9.5
Amenities: Paved paths, trails, visitor center with tours, accessible restrooms; note: entrance fee
Jurisdiction: Portland Parks and Recreation

Gorgeous at any time, Crystal Springs glows in spring with rhododendron blossoms.

GETTING THERE

BY CAR SE McLoughlin Blvd./OR 99E south to SE Bybee Blvd. eastbound/Reed College; east on Bybee Blvd. three-quarters of a mile; left onto SE 28th Ave.; garden entrance is at left. Limited parking. **BY TRANSIT** ★★★ Bus 19 (Woodstock/Glisan toward Mount Scott); bus follows alternating routes—ask driver for stop nearest the park, either SE 28th and Martins (stop 7286; walk north on 28th) or SE Woodstock and 32nd (stop 6402; walk west on SE Woodstock Blvd., then right onto SE 28th Ave.) **BY BIKE** ★★

Portland is blessed with a perfect climate for growing big trees and flowering plants. In a city where even humble side yards bloom with a vengeance, it takes a lot for a botanical garden to stand out. Crystal Springs does so. In my highly nonscientific ranking of Portland's gardens, I put it second only to the Japanese Garden for sheer beauty and ambience. (Leach Botanical Garden and Elk Rock Garden are a close third and fourth.)

Prime time at Crystal Springs is spring—specifically April and May—when the more than 2500 rhodies, azaleas, and related plants blossom. It's worth braving the inevitable crowds at this time of year, especially on Mother's Day. (If possible, arrive by bike or transit.)

A paved path leads downhill from the entrance to a causeway over Crystal Springs Lake. A trail goes right to loop a small lawn tucked among cedars, firs, maples, and many, many rhododendrons. Across the causeway, the path winds around another, somewhat larger lawn highly sought after for weddings. The path runs alongside the lake in places, where geese gather for handouts.

The garden isn't that big and takes only a few minutes to traverse. Take your time and enjoy the many benches set among stone walls, alongside paths, and overlooking the water.

To me, rhododendrons are icons of the western Cascade Mountains. They grace the understory of old-growth forests as readily as they do city yards, stitching together the wild and the cultivated with grace and harmony. They can be leggy, bushy, or treelike, depending on sun exposure; gnarled and petite or lush and gigantic, depending on elevation; showy or restrained, depending on . . . well, I'm not honestly sure. (I've seen wild rhodies on Mount Hood as exuberantly colorful as any cultivar at Crystal Springs. Go figure.) Perhaps your curiosity will be sparked and you'll join the Friends of Crystal Springs Rhododendron Garden (see Resources) to learn more and enjoy free admission year-round.

EXTEND YOUR VISIT

Wander across 28th Avenue to visit Reed College's elegant campus. It straddles a surprisingly deep little canyon holding Reed Lake, fed by the Crystal Springs. When I first saw the lake in the early 1990s, it was a stinking swamp. Reed students and city workers have since restored it, improving oxygen levels and fish habitat. Amazingly, salmon now spawn here.

50 WESTMORELAND PARK

Big park with a restored creek and Portland's best nature play area

Location: SE Bybee Blvd. and SE 22nd Ave.
Acreage: 42
Amenities: Accessible restroom, nature play area, paths, sports fields, basketball and tennis courts, picnic tables, play structure, bowling green, casting pond
Jurisdiction: Portland Parks and Recreation

GETTING THERE

BY CAR SE McLoughlin Blvd./OR 99E south to SE Bybee Blvd. westbound exit; the park is straight ahead. **BY TRANSIT** ★★★ MAX (Orange Line) to Bybee; cross over SE McLoughlin Blvd. to the park. **BY BIKE** ★★

Westmoreland Park is another great green spot in the Sellwood-Moreland neighborhood, with Crystal Springs Creek meandering through wetlands and past an exceptional nature play area.

A lot of the park is dedicated to field sports; the northwestern corner is where most readers of this book will want to focus. For a long time, this section was a soggy lawn, littered with goose droppings, surrounding a fetid pond. The creek ran arrow-straight through an artificial rock-lined channel devoid of vegetation. In the late 1990s, it repeatedly flooded, inundating picnic and play areas. The city recognized that something needed to be done and set about reimagining the area.

The transformation has been amazing to watch. In 2015, workers drained the duck pond, restored half a mile of the creek channel, and planted thousands of native plants. The word "restored" does not do it justice, though. With help from the Army Corps of Engineers, the city built a brand-new stream, complete with meanders, logs, pools, and riffles.

A paved path enters the reinvented park from Bybee Boulevard, paralleling the newly natural creek past picnic areas. A spur path leads to a viewing platform over the wetlands. Opposite, a boardwalk arcs along a bend in the creek. At the wetland's southern end, a small ramp provides access to the water. It's often crowded with gleeful splashing kids and their hovering parents.

Beyond the creek access is the park's crowning glory: the nature play area. I can't help but choke a bit on the fact we need to spend large sums of money re-creating the opportunities for rock scampering, tree climbing, and general going-feral adventures kids used to experience for free. Alas, it seems that *actual* nature is either too hard to come by or, ostensibly, unsafe.

Griping aside, this nature play area is awesome. Huge logs, fastened together and jammed full of sticks, invite fort building. Boulder piles of varying heights and perched logs provide climbing thrills for larger kids. For little ones, there's a sand pit with a seasonal water feature. If you have a kid under the age of eight or so, visit this park!

Past the nature play area is a giant rectangular casting pond. I don't often see people using it, but when a good fly fisher is out practicing, it's a beautiful sight to behold. Beyond are basketball courts and sports fields, including Sckavone Stadium, where semipro baseball teams compete.

I often wondered why the city once thought a park consisting of soggy lawns covered in duck poop and ringing a stinking, algae-choked pond was a good idea. Only while researching this book did I learn the pond once had a recreational purpose. Westmoreland Park was another creation of the Works Progress Administration (WPA), the New Deal–era jobs program that built Timberline Lodge. This park's features were labor-intensive by design, to employ as many people as possible. (WPA workers excavated the casting pond, nearly four acres large and several feet deep, *by hand.*) The duck pond was designed as a "model yacht lagoon." I don't know how strong the demand for model yachting ever was, but I guess this was a design solution for a place bound to be wet thanks to the creek. Only later did the geese, ducks, and algae take over.

51 JOHNSON CREEK PARK

Pocket natural area where two creeks converge

Location: SE 21st Ave. and SE Clatsop St.
Acreage: 4.5
Amenities: Accessible restroom, play structure, picnic tables, paths
Jurisdiction: Portland Parks and Recreation

GETTING THERE

BY CAR SE McLoughlin Blvd./OR 99E southbound; just past the Tacoma St. exit, turn right onto SE Umatilla St.; left onto SE 21st Ave.; two blocks to the park. **BY TRANSIT** ★★ MAX (Orange Line) to SE Tacoma/Johnson Creek; follow signs to the Springwater Corridor; cross SE McLoughlin Blvd.; right onto SE 19th Ave. at SE Ochoco St.; right onto SE Marion St. to reach the park (three-quarter-mile walk). **BY BIKE** ★★★

Crystal Springs Creek emerges from a canyon on the Reed College campus, clear and cold, to flow a few miles into Johnson Creek. The two creeks meet at this little park, a semi-hidden gem. On multiple visits I've rarely seen many people, mostly just neighbors walking their dogs or pushing a kid on the swings. Even when Westmoreland Park, a few blocks away, bustles with activity, Johnson Creek Park is serene. Perhaps I've just missed the busy days—or I'm about to ruin a well-kept secret. Either way, I think this place is worth crossing town to visit. If you are biking the Springwater Corridor, definitely make the short detour to come here.

A path runs through the park near SE 21st Avenue, passing restrooms and a playground. A side path leads across Crystal Springs Creek via a footbridge to a meadow. Split-rail fences and native plantings ring the meadow in a not very successful attempt to steer visitors clear of sensitive riparian areas. The meadow is lovely, intimate and secluded, surrounded by the sounds of flowing water. Find a patch of grass or a picnic table and linger.

Green returns to Johnson Creek Park after a long, wet winter.

You *can* access the creeks at a few places—though please do so tenderly. In the heat of summer, when you want to dip a toe (and are not likely to disturb many fish anyway), head to a little gravel beach on Johnson Creek. Squint a little and you can imagine you are deep in a forest somewhere.

Keep in mind, in winter this place can be wet, or even partially underwater. (It is a confluence, after all.) These creeks can really rage at high water—especially Johnson Creek. Use caution with little ones.

52 WOODSTOCK PARK

Mellow and inviting—a classic Southeast neighborhood park,

Location: SE 47th Ave. and SE Steele St.
Acreage: 14
Amenities: Accessible play area and restroom, dog off-leash area, paths, playground, ball fields, tennis courts
Jurisdiction: Portland Parks and Recreation

GETTING THERE

BY CAR US 26/SE Powell Blvd. eastbound to SE Cesar Chavez Blvd.; go right and continue 1 mile; left onto SE Steele St.; eight blocks to the park. **BY TRANSIT** ★★★ Bus 19 (Woodstock/Glisan toward Mount Scott) to SE Woodstock and 49th (stop 6419); walk five blocks north on SE 50th Ave. to the park. **BY BIKE** ★★

Woodstock is an archetypal neighborhood park, like Irving, Wallace, or Oregon: a big square of giant trees, sweeping paths, play equipment in varying states of repair, and fields. Nearly every neighborhood in Inner Portland has one of these parks. I could just as easily have included places like Creston Park at SE 43rd Avenue and Powell Boulevard, with its dual dog parks and outdoor pool, or Albert Kelly Park, just off the Beaverton-Hillsboro Highway in Southwest Portland, with its mammoth oaks and recently daylighted creek. Each is a neighborhood anchor and cause for celebration.

So, why Woodstock? I'm not sure. Another sentimental favorite, I guess. This was the first Portland park I ever saw, as a teenager visiting my older brother at nearby Reed College. Having grown up in a much newer and rough-hewn town, I was struck by the big trees and the sense of ageless calm. Woodstock Park had, and has, a leafy, spacious, and peaceful feel that, to me, is the essence of Portland.

As with Creston and Albert Kelly Parks, Woodstock's best asset is its tree canopy. The requisite Douglas-firs mingle with massive maples, beeches, and a few dogwoods, which add autumn color, an open feeling in winter, and spring blossoms.

The big trees surround a central lawn, mostly used as a dog off-leash area. Picnic tables line its edges. In the southwestern corner, a merry-go-round, swings, and a dated but serviceable climbing structure cater mostly to younger kids. Farther east are equally utilitarian ball fields and tennis courts.

Find a picnic table, have a seat, and watch the pups frolic. Maybe bring a coffee from one of the fine purveyors along nearby Woodstock Boulevard, a quietly hip strip running from about 40th Avenue to 50th Avenue. The street, like the park, is deep Southeast Portland: mellow, a little quirky, and with a few rough spots not yet polished into the steel and glass taking over much of the central city.

53 LENTS PARK

Community park, with a renovated play area, in a diverse neighborhood on the rise

Location: SE 92nd Ave. and SE Steele St.
Acreage: 38
Amenities: Accessible play area and restrooms, sports fields, basketball and tennis courts, dog off-leash area, picnic tables, community garden plots, half-mile jogging path
Jurisdiction: Portland Parks and Recreation

The accessible play area at Lents Park welcomes kids of all ages.

GETTING THERE

BY CAR I-205 to exit 17 (SE Foster Rd.) westbound; right at stoplight onto SE 92nd Ave.; park is at left after a third of a mile. **BY TRANSIT** ★★★ MAX (Green Line) to Lents/Foster; walk north on I-205 pedestrian path to SE Steele St.; cross 92nd to the park (one-third-mile walk). **BY BIKE** ★★★ Via I-205 Path and SE Steele St.

Lents is an outer Southeast neighborhood finally overcoming the wounds inflicted on it by the construction of I-205 in the early 1980s. Established in 1892 as a farm town supplying produce to Portland via the Springwater line, Lents nearly died when the eastside freeway plowed right through its heart. Until recently, the post-freeway town center at Foster Road and 92nd Avenue was a depressing mix of vacant lots and dilapidated storefronts. The neighborhood never gave up, though, and revitalization has come at last.

Lents Park is the neighborhood's true center. Start at the main entrance at 92nd Avenue and Steele Street. This area was a gravel quarry long ago and is lower than the rest of the park. It feels cozy, hemmed in by trees and a low hill. Plans will soon be implemented for a formal entrance with a grand stone staircase ascending to the main part of the park.

For now, focus on the adjacent play area, which like most new Portland playgrounds is garish, highly accessible, and a lot of fun. The climbing rock is a highlight, offering a real challenge to younger climbers and a coveted summit from which to regard the surrounding playground mayhem.

Beyond the play area, a paved path leads past community garden plots to reach the main level, which has basketball courts, tennis courts, and some very popular soccer fields. On weekends, there are seemingly constant pickup soccer games, rain or shine. Farther north is an artificial turf soccer field mostly used by league teams. A soft-surface jogging path circles the fields. Flat and largely sheltered by trees, it's an especially nice spot to walk or run.

At the park's north end is Walker Stadium, home to the Portland Pickles baseball team (and its farm team—the Gherkins, of course). Check out the game schedule at www.portlandpicklesbaseball.com.

EXTEND YOUR VISIT

Head south a few blocks along 92nd Avenue to visit Lents Town Center. On Sunday mornings, June through November, check out the Lents International Farmers Market. It is modest, but unique among Portland markets with its focus on fruits and vegetables specific to Lents's diverse cultural traditions.

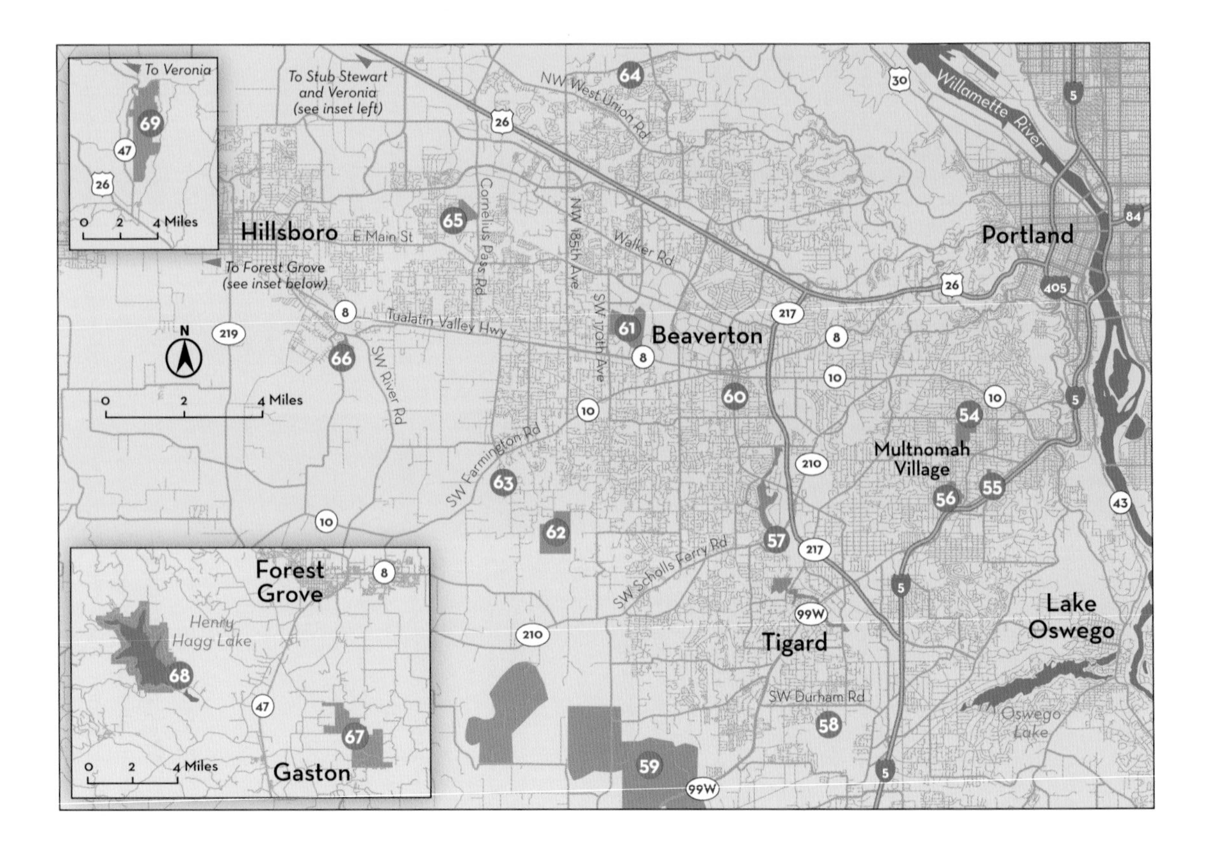

To Veronia
69
47
26
0 2 4 Miles
To Stub Stewart and Veronia (see inset left)
64
NW West Union Rd
30
Willamette River
5
26
Hillsboro
E Main St
65
Cornelius Pass Rd
NW 185th Ave
Walker Rd
Portland
84
To Forest Grove (see inset below)
405
8
Tualatin Valley Hwy
217
219
N
61
Beaverton
66
SW River Rd
SW 170th Ave
0 2 4 Miles
10
60
54
SW Farmington Rd
Multnomah Village
210
63
55
56
43
62
57
SW Scholls Ferry Rd
Forest Grove
Henry Hagg Lake
68
47
67
0 2 4 Miles
Gaston
99W
Tigard
Lake Oswego
SW Durham Rd
58
Oswego Lake
59

THE WEST SIDE: SOUTHWEST PORTLAND, BEAVERTON, TIGARD, AND HILLSBORO

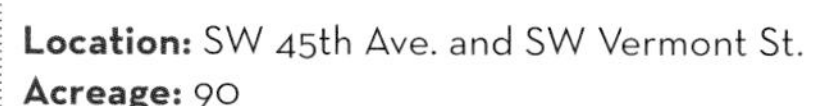

54 GABRIEL PARK

Megapark with everything you'd want for a day in Southwest Portland

Location: SW 45th Ave. and SW Vermont St.
Acreage: 90
Amenities: Accessible play area and restroom, sports fields, basketball, tennis, and volleyball courts, dog off-leash areas, paved paths and trails, picnic tables, skatepark, community center
Jurisdiction: Portland Parks and Recreation

GETTING THERE

BY CAR I-5 southbound to exit 296B (Multnomah Blvd.); right onto SW 45th Ave.; after a half mile, right onto SW Vermont St.; right into park. **BY TRANSIT** ★★ Weekdays only: Bus 1 (Vermont) to SW 45th and Nevada (stop 9328) and park entrance. Weekends: Bus 44 (Capitol Hwy./Mocks Crest toward PCC Sylvania) to

SW 36th and Capitol Hwy. (stop 10865); walk north on SW 36th Ave.; left onto SW Caldew St. to enter the park (three-quarter-mile walk). **BY BIKE** ★★

Gabriel Park is hands down one of Portland's best and most varied community parks. If it weren't located across the West Hills in the (to me) terra incognita of Southwest Portland, I'd visit more often.

I can credit my first adventures with a map and compass to Gabriel Park. (This used to be a favorite outdoor classroom for the Mazamas, the Portland mountaineering club. It's an older sibling to the upstart group farther north, The Mountaineers.) I can also thank—blame?—the place for my son's obsession with skateboarding. It was at Gabriel's stellar skatepark that he first saw real skateboarding.

Those are just two of many reasons you might want to visit. Also consider the park's community center—Portland's best—and not one, but *two* fenced dog parks. There is also an extensive trail network.

A good place to start is the entrance off 45th Avenue, with parking, restrooms, tennis and volleyball courts, and that skatepark: ten thousand square feet of bowls, ramps, and tricky-looking walls.

From here, you can wander north over low hills toward the community center, or east to the playground along Vermont Street. The equipment is nothing special, but the setting is great: tucked in the trees below street grade, it feels more serene and spacious than most playgrounds.

Heading in the opposite direction from the 45th Avenue entrance, you pass between tennis courts to enter the woods, where a tributary of Fanno Creek flows through the park. The stream neatly bisects the park into a more "active" northern half and a quieter southern half. One of Gabriel Park's best features is the way it uses the rolling, gently sloping terrain to maximum advantage. It has many "rooms" and continually varied sightlines, making it feel even bigger than it is.

South of the creek, you emerge from woods to a secluded linear meadow with the winter dog park and the community garden. At this point, the road feels far away and even a committed urbanite can start to appreciate the allure of Southwest Portland, with its tree-clogged, sidewalk-less neighborhood lanes, its discontinuous street grid, and its resolutely nonurban sangfroid.

EXTEND YOUR VISIT

Since you're in the neighborhood, swing through Multnomah Village (centered on SW Capitol Highway and 35th Avenue) for food, coffee, shopping, and charm.

55 SPRING GARDEN PARK

Meadows, accessible paths, and a great play area in this recently developed park

Location: 3350 SW Dolph Ct., Southwest Portland
Acreage: 4.6
Amenities: Accessible play area, accessible restroom, paths, picnic shelters and tables, splash pad
Jurisdiction: Portland Parks and Recreation

GETTING THERE

BY CAR I-5 southbound to exit 296A (Barbur Blvd.); left onto SW Barbur Blvd.; right onto SW 30th Ave.; left onto SW Dolph Ct. **BY TRANSIT** ★★ Bus 12 (Barbur/Sandy Blvd. toward Tigard Transit Center) to 8900 Block SW Barbur (stop 194); go right on SW 30th Ave. and left on SW Dolph Ct. to the park (one-third-mile walk). **BY BIKE** ★★

For too long, Spring Garden Park was a barren hillside between two narrow residential lanes. It seemed about as anonymous as a park could get. Finally, in 2018, Portland Parks and Recreation built a proper neighborhood park. Now it's one of Portland's best, with an ideal blend of accessibility, nature, and high design.

The main entrance is on the uphill side, off SW Dolph Court. Two circular paths intersect here, Venn diagram–like, to bring nature and play into conversation. The western circle contains the play area, among the city's very best. It features accessible swings, a planetarium-themed tower, climbing nets, a ground-mounted slide, a splash pad, and an embankment of basalt pillars perfect for scrambling. The play area manages to be beautiful, widely accessible, and truly fun. Well done, Portland Parks!

The adjacent circle has picnic tables and a shelter set among a lawn and native plantings. The emphasis on native plants, though common enough in newer Portland parks, is especially noticeable here, in part because the park is almost devoid of trees. Designers turned this deficit to their advantage by re-creating a meadow full of native grasses and wildflowers. A gently graded, paved path curves through it to Spring Garden Street.

On its way down, the path passes the park's signature element, an eye-catching orb of bamboo by the sculptor Hannes Wingate. Farther downhill, through two sweeping switchbacks, it arrives at a lawn with a low, curved stone wall facing a semicircular concrete pad—designed for movies and performances.

EXTEND YOUR VISIT

Continue your voyage of Southwest discovery by visiting Multnomah Village, five blocks north along SW 35th Avenue. Cafes, restaurants, a bookstore, and more make for good rambling.

56 WOODS MEMORIAL NATURAL AREA

Secluded wooded ravine at the headwaters of Fanno Creek

Location: SW 48th Ave. and SE Wood Pkwy.
Acreage: 46
Amenities: Hiking trails (1.25 miles)
Jurisdiction: Portland Parks and Recreation

GETTING THERE

BY CAR I-5 southbound to exit 295 (Capitol Hwy.); left onto SW Taylors Ferry Rd.; right onto SW 48th Ave.; right onto SW Wood Pkwy. to trailhead. **BY TRANSIT** ★★ Bus 44 (Capitol Hwy./Mocks Crest toward PCC Sylvania) to SW Capitol and Taylors Ferry Rd. (stop 930); walk right onto Taylors Ferry Rd.; right onto SW 43rd Ave. to reach the Alice Trail. **BY BIKE** ★

This low-key natural area is pure Southwest Portland: deep forest in a ravine shoehorned among houses and steps away from the bustle of Barbur Boulevard. Come here for a short, slow walk along lovely Woods Creek.

There is nothing secret about Woods Memorial, but given its off-the-beaten-path location and lack of anything resembling a proper entrance, you might feel you discovered a lost world. Multnomah County received this forest as a gift in 1950, with the restriction that it be "used for park and playground purposes only." This was rather farsighted, given that much of the surroundings were still farmland and nearby Multnomah Village was actually a village.

Times have changed, of course, but down in Woods Memorial the trees have only grown bigger. An ageless calm has accumulated like forest duff around these Douglas-firs, cedars, and creekside willows, with their understory of Oregon grape, elderberry, thimbleberry, and the fragile, white-flowered trillium.

The walk is short: follow the Stairway Trail downhill, cross the Low Bridge, then work your way up Woods Creek to the Alice Trail (starting point for the transit directions above). Double back, or walk along SW Taylors Ferry Road a short distance to SW 46th Avenue, where a first right leads you back into the park via Wood Parkway

Exploring the woods at Woods Memorial Natural Area following a rare snowfall

(closed to cars) or the South Trail. Enjoy the cool air, maybe dip a toe (discreetly) into the creek, and soak up the negative ions. That's really all there is to do here, but it's plenty.

57 FANNO CREEK GREENWAY

Regional trail lined with parks cuts a green swath through western suburbs

Location: Along Fanno Creek from Southwest Portland to Tigard
Acreage: N/A
Amenities: See below
Jurisdiction: Tualatin Hills Park and Recreation District; Tigard

GETTING THERE

To Garden Home Recreation Center: **BY CAR** I-5 southbound to exit 296B (Multnomah Blvd.); 2.4 miles on Multnomah Blvd., then right onto SW Garden Home Rd.; first right onto SW Oleson Rd.; first left into parking area. **BY TRANSIT** ★★★

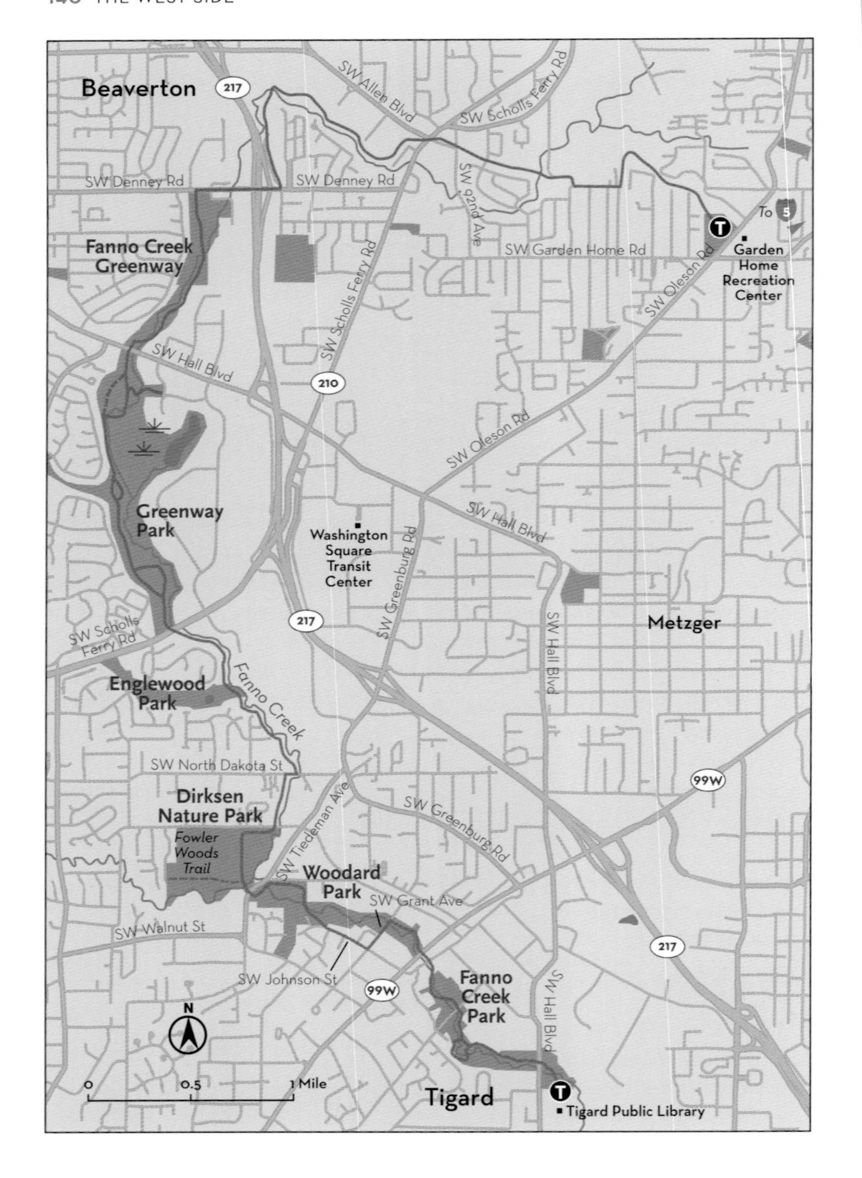

Beaverton
217
SW Allen Blvd
SW Scholls Ferry Rd
SW Denney Rd
SW Denney Rd
SW 92nd Ave
To 5
Fanno Creek Greenway
SW Garden Home Rd
Garden Home Recreation Center
SW Scholls Ferry Rd
SW Oleson Rd
SW Hall Blvd
210
SW Oleson Rd
Greenway Park
SW Hall Blvd
Washington Square Transit Center
SW Greenburg Rd
217
SW Hall Blvd
Metzger
SW Scholls Ferry Rd
Englewood Park
Fanno Creek
SW North Dakota St
99W
Dirksen Nature Park
SW Tiedeman Ave
SW Greenburg Rd
Fowler Woods Trail
Woodard Park
SW Grant Ave
SW Walnut St
217
SW Johnson St
99W
Fanno Creek Park
SW Hall Blvd
N
0
0.5
1 Mile
Tigard
Tigard Public Library

Bus 45 (Garden Home) to SW Garden Home and 71st (stop 1982); cross Oleson to the park. **BY BIKE** ★★

Rising just west of downtown Portland, Fanno Creek flows through Southwest Portland, Beaverton, and Tigard to meet the Tualatin River at Tigard's Cook Park. A greenway trail runs most of its length, connecting a series of parks beloved by west siders. The greenway and path are mostly wooded, offering a nice counterpoint to the open views along the Rock Creek Greenway, the other great West Side trail in this book.

One of the best aspects of the Fanno Creek Greenway Trail is that it alternates between restored natural areas thriving with streamside plants, birds, and even beavers, and traditional parks with lawns, picnic areas, and play structures. If you have time and energy, tour the entire greenway by bike.

The greenway trail—a paved path—starts at the Tualatin Hills Park and Recreation District's Garden Home Recreation Center. (Note this is *not* Garden Home Park, which is down the road). It snakes among subdivisions through a narrow but pleasant corridor for 2.5 miles to cross Highway 217 at SW Denney Road, then continues south along Fanno Creek. Here begins a true greenway, with meadows and forests.

Across Hall Boulevard, the path enters eighty-seven-acre Greenway Park. If you are only going to visit one park along the greenway, this should be it. The park has several play structures, basketball courts, a disc golf course, and plenty of room to enjoy a picnic on the lawn. It is adjacent to an extensive wetland. Look for native pond turtles (now a rare and threatened species) basking on logs; you may also spot a beaver. These resilient rodents are coming back to Fanno Creek after a century and a half away, and their handiwork (or mouthwork?) occasionally floods the trail.

A mile beyond Greenway Park, in Tigard, is Dirksen Nature Park. Consider a detour on the Fowler Woods Trail, which follows Summer Creek. This short walk leads through a forested wetland, a rare habitat type in the urbanized parts of the Portland metro region.

The greenway trail continues through Woodard Park, followed by a brief jog along SW Johnson Street, to reach the center of Tigard. Tigard, long a bedroom community, decided to turn itself into an urban village with a walkable and lively downtown. Consider a stop here for lunch or coffee.

South of downtown Tigard is thirty-acre Fanno Creek Park, where Fanno Creek rambles in loops (some recently re-established) through a diverse forest of oaks,

The Fanno Greenway Trail connects some of the West Side's best parks. (Photo courtesy of Tualatin Hills Park and Recreation District)

maples, Douglas-firs, and even a few ponderosa pines. Across Hall Boulevard is Tigard's beautiful library, where you can grab a snack in the lobby cafe and enjoy it at the gazebo overlooking Fanno Creek.

The route described here is about 7.5 miles one way. If you don't feel like retracing your route, Bus 76 will get you to the Washington Square Transit Center, where you can transfer to Bus 45 or walk/bike the remaining mile and a half back to Garden Home.

58 COOK, DURHAM, AND TUALATIN PARKS

Great paddling in a megapark along the Tualatin River

Location: Along the Tualatin River near SW Boones Ferry Rd.
Acreage: 79 (Cook), 45 (Durham), 27 (Tualatin)
Amenities: Many (see below)
Jurisdiction: Tigard; Durham; Tualatin

GETTING THERE

To Cook Park: **BY CAR** I-5 to exit 291 (Carman Dr.); west on Carman Dr.; left onto SW Upper Boones Ferry Rd.; right onto SW Durham Rd.; after 1 mile, left onto SW 92nd Ave. to park entrance. **BY TRANSIT** ★ Bus 12 (Barbur) to Tigard Transit Center, then Bus 76 (Hall/Greenburg) to SW Hall and Avon (stop 10631); walk a half mile south on SW 85th Ave. to enter park. (Bus 76 also serves Durham and Tualatin Parks.) **BY BIKE** ★★★ Via Fanno Creek Greenway Trail.

Here are three great connected parks at the confluence of Fanno Creek and the Tualatin River. You can see all three in a few miles' walk or bike ride, which I recommend.

Tigard's Cook Park is the largest. The northern half is mostly for sports, with well-tended soccer and baseball fields, basketball courts, and sand volleyball courts. The park's southern half is forested with paths leading down to and along the Tualatin River.

The park's boat launch, located on a big river bend, is a great place to start a canoe, kayak, or stand-up paddleboard outing; the Tualatin is slow enough in summer that you can easily paddle upstream and down. Near the dock are a small beach and a picnic shelter. As you're decently far from roads, houses, and other urban things at this point, stillness largely prevails. It's a good place to hang out and take a dip in the calm water.

East of the boat launch, a web of trails lead to the park's butterfly garden. (Some of these trails close seasonally; you can access the garden year-round on a paved path from the main parking lot, next to the restrooms.) The small, densely planted garden has different species flowering throughout the growing season, attracting a steady lepidopteran swarm. It can be magical on a summer afternoon as the lowering sun illuminates glowing, gossamer butterfly wings.

The paved path continues half a mile downstream from the butterfly garden, tracing the edge where woods and wetland meadows meet. It passes under a railroad to arrive at the Fanno Creek Greenway Trail.

At this junction, turn left to visit Durham City Park, much quieter than Cook and the best suited for a forest ramble. This path, part of the Fanno Creek Greenway Trail, parallels train tracks and then loops through a stately stand of maples, cedars, Douglas-firs, and alders. On your way back toward the junction, a side path branches left across a bridge over Fanno Creek to a picnic shelter set in a meadow. Return to the junction by the railroad underpass to complete this roughly 1-mile loop.

Continuing south along the Fanno Creek Greenway Trail, cross the Ki-a-Kuts Pedestrian Bridge, which affords a long, lovely view down the Tualatin. You'd never know that I-5 roars just around the bend!

Across the bridge is Tualatin Community Park, the smallest, but liveliest, of the trio. From the bridge, the path passes a fenced dog park—somewhat barren but with a convenient shelter for humans—and a manicured lawn often filled with sunbathers, Frisbee tossers, and office workers on lunch hour. Right before the path reaches the dog park, a soft-surface trail branches off to the left, entering woods to continue a third of a mile along the Tualatin River. This short stretch of forest trail is great, full of big trees and intermittent river views.

The paths converge at a parking area and continue underneath an old train trestle. Here you'll find another boat launch, a play area with a sand-and-water feature, tennis and basketball courts, and a good skatepark.

59 TUALATIN RIVER NATIONAL WILDLIFE REFUGE

Birds and valley views at a unique urban wildlife refuge

Location: 19255 SW Pacific Hwy., Sherwood
Acreage: 1856
Amenities: Restrooms, trails, nature center, tours and education programs
Jurisdiction: US Fish and Wildlife Service

GETTING THERE

BY CAR I-5 southbound to exit 294 (OR 99 W) westbound; continue 6.5 miles to refuge at right. **BY TRANSIT** ★★ Bus 12 (Barbur) to Tigard Transit Center; then Bus 93 (Tigard/Sherwood) to Pacific Hwy. and Tualatin River Refuge (stop 12743). **BY BIKE** ★

The story of the Tualatin River National Wildlife Refuge has been told plenty of times, but it bears repeating. The flood-prone banks of the Tualatin River have been farmed since the mid-1800s, producing hogs, corn, milk, onions, and more for the growing cities nearby.

By the 1990s, with suburbs encroaching, residents floated the idea of an urban wildlife refuge to keep some open space between Sherwood and Tigard. It was an ambitious, even audacious, idea: turn back the clock on tired-out farmland that had been tiled, ditched, drained, and altered beyond anything remotely resembling "natural." Federal wildlife officials were intrigued, though. Following a spirited

Winter is a great time for birding at Tualatin River National Wildlife Refuge.

grassroots campaign, the government designated a refuge. A local family promptly stepped up to donate the first twelve acres.

In the thirty years since, the refuge has grown enormously and struck a balance between protecting wildlife and welcoming people. Case in point is the wildlife center, located off Highway 99W. From this beautiful building, full of wood and light, you can watch the wetlands flood and contract with the changing seasons. (This occurs courtesy of the refuge managers, who have installed dikes and other water-conveyance structures to re-create natural fluctuations.) If the weather is good, spend some time on the outdoor observation deck admiring the subtle but constant changes at play in this watery panorama.

Inside the wildlife center are dioramas and exhibits telling the refuge's story. At a nature store operated by the Friends of Tualatin River National Wildlife Refuge (see Resources), volunteers set up spotting scopes and help visitors identify what they are seeing. The center and store are open 10 AM to 4 PM every day except Monday. (Note: dogs and bikes are not allowed in the refuge.)

A 1.1-mile (one way) trail, open year-round, leads from the wildlife center through a restored and maturing oak savanna to an overlook along the Tualatin River. I love this spot, which somehow makes the homely Tualatin seem idyllic, with its muddy banks draped in willows.

The trail ends at another observation deck over the wetlands. From May 1 through September 30, you can continue on a 3-mile gravel road looping this section of the refuge. (This 450-acre parcel is part of a much larger complex. The other parcels—covering over 10 miles of river frontage—are mostly closed to the public.)

It's worth reiterating that this land, once so intensively altered, now provides a home for nearly two hundred bird species. Many of them are travelers on the Pacific Flyway, a sort of migratory superhighway in the air running from Alaska to Mexico. Seen in this context, the refuge is much more than "just" a nature park. It's a critical component of a continent-spanning network. Yes! Right here, between Sherwood and Tigard, next door to a pick-and-pull junkyard! There really is room for nature in the city . . . if we make it.

60 BEAVERTON CITY PARK

Civic plaza with fountains and a farmers market in Beaverton's walkable core

Location: SW Watson Ave. and SW 5th St., Beaverton
Acreage: 2.5
Amenities: Spray feature, restroom, play area, picnic tables, farmers market
Jurisdiction: Beaverton

GETTING THERE

BY CAR OR 217 to exit 2A (SW Canyon Rd./Beaverton-Hillsboro Hwy.); west on SW Canyon Rd.; left onto SW Watson Ave. to the park at SW 5th St. **BY TRANSIT** ★★ MAX (Blue Line) to Beaverton Central; walk south past Beaverton City Hall; left at SW Millikan Way; right onto SW Watson Ave. to the park at SW 5th St. (half-mile walk). **BY BIKE** ★

Much of Beaverton is Peak Suburbia, circa 1970: cul-de-sacs, lawns, plenty of parks, and some excellent greenway trails. At the center of it all, though, is a little nineteenth-century town, walkable and charming. At *its* center is Beaverton City Park, a great public space.

In 1847, a settler named Lawrence Hall claimed land near the site of an Atfalati village called *Chakeipi*, meaning "Place of the Beaver." Hall and his fellow settlers called it "Beaverdam." Hall's gristmill, the Tualatin Valley's first, established Beaverdam as the valley's commercial hub.

The valley's fertile soils were useless without access to markets, so local farmers teamed up with Portland investors to build a plank road from Hall's mill to Portland's waterfront. This primitive highway, mostly cedar planks and mud, spanned the West Hills and played the decisive role in elevating Portland to regional dominance.

Beaverton City Park spans three blocks. The westernmost is a great grove of Douglas-firs, pines, and maples shading picnic tables and play structures. (Restrooms are at the far west end.) The central block is a lawn, at the center of which a broad plaza with benches surrounds a fountain—the type that shoots unpredictably from ground-level nozzles, to the delight of soaked kids. The easternmost block, across Hall Boulevard, is a lawn fronting Beaverton's attractive library, with skylights and exposed wooden beams enlivening its reading room.

The best time to visit the park—preferably by transit, because parking gets tight—is on Saturday mornings during spring, summer, and fall. That's when the Beaverton Farmers Market is in full swing, spilling into the park from its site next door. It bills itself as "the single largest all-agricultural market in the state" and sees upward of twenty thousand visitors on a peak day. With live music, food, and a stellar park in which to enjoy your picnic, it should be on your summer to-do list.

61 TUALATIN HILLS NATURE PARK

Wetlands, creeks, and woods at a refuge deep in the burbs

Location: 15655 SW Millikan Way, Beaverton
Acreage: 222
Amenities: Paved path (1.5 miles), trails (3.5 miles), nature center with educational programs
Jurisdiction: Tualatin Hills Park and Recreation District

GETTING THERE

BY CAR US 26 to exit 67 (NW Murray Blvd.); south on Murray Blvd. 2 miles; right onto SW Millikan Way; three-quarters of a mile to the park entrance at right. **BY TRANSIT** ★★★ MAX (Blue Line) to Merlo Rd./SW 158th; immediately south of the tracks, follow the Westside Regional Trail east a tenth of a mile, then right on the Oak Trail to enter the park. **BY BIKE** ★★★ Via Westside Regional Trail.

Occupying a low, wet woodland where Cedar Mill and Beaverton Creeks meet, the Tualatin Hills Nature Park is lush, often wet, and full of life. You can get right to its back door via the MAX light rail.

A network of paved and soft trails lace through the woods, spanning the many wet areas via bridges and boardwalks. It is great for walking year-round: shady in summer, radiant with foliage in autumn, rain-soaked and dreamy in winter, and humming with birds and native blossoms like Nootka rose and red-flowering currant in spring.

The park has a fine nature center with restrooms, a small library and store, classrooms, and a permanent exhibit. It offers environmental education programs, volunteer stewardship opportunities, and drop-in activities like yoga and tai chi. I have

Tualatin Hills Nature Park is the green heart of the West Side. (Photo courtesy of Tualatin Hills Park and Recreation District)

not sampled the classes, but this seems like an ideal setting for such contemplative practices.

Pick up a map and follow the paved Vine Maple Trail west from the nature center into dense woods. (Note: dogs are not allowed here.) Perspective and a sense of distance immediately shift as the horizons close in. At the first junction, the paved Oak Trail strikes north through a mixed oak woodland to a wetland overlook.

Across Cedar Mill Creek, the path leads out to the MAX station (your entrance point if coming by light rail). Just before leaving the park, the path meets the unpaved Old Wagon Trail to follow Cedar Mill Creek downstream. At the Mink Path, you can cut south to rejoin the Vine Maple Trail and explore a number of loops on the park's south side. The viewing spot overlooking Big Pond is a popular destination; the stretch of Big Fir Trail and Chickadee Loop beyond it are particularly nice.

This is one of those parks where I, normally an obsessive map reader, prefer to just wander. If you walked every inch of trail, you'd go almost 5 miles, but with so many loops it would be difficult to do so by accident. In other words, no matter where you end up, you won't be far from your starting point. The woods lack views (the park's name notwithstanding, there is not a hill anywhere around), but this is a blessing. Instead of topography, there is a stillness punctuated only by birdsong and the distant, faint rumble of the MAX. With a little imagination, it can sound like thunder—sublime and ominous, but also somehow comforting.

62 COOPER MOUNTAIN NATURE PARK

Sweeping views and diverse habitats on a hillside park at the edge of town

Location: 18895 SW Kemmer Rd., Beaverton
Acreage: 230
Amenities: Native plant demonstration garden, restrooms, nature play area, trails (3.5 miles), accessible path (0.75 mile), Nature House with classes
Jurisdiction: Metro; Tualatin Hills Park and Recreation District

GETTING THERE

BY CAR OR 217 to exit 2A (SW Canyon Rd./Beaverton-Hillsboro Hwy.); second right onto Beaverton-Hillsboro Hwy., which becomes SW Farmington Rd./OR 10; left onto SW 170th Ave.; right onto SW Rigert Rd.; curve left onto SW 175th Ave.; right at traffic circle onto SW Kemmer Rd. to the park at left, just before SW 190th Ave. **BY TRANSIT** None. **BY BIKE** ★

Cooper Mountain Nature Park drapes across the southern slopes of a hill where Beaverton ends and the Tualatin Valley's farms, orchards, and vineyards begin.

As big as this park is, my one complaint is that it's not big enough. The burgeoning West Side of our region, where new development strains against the urban growth boundary, needs a continuous greenbelt running thick and wild from the Tualatin River to the Tualatin Mountains—not just a few regional parks isolated by development. Still, given the speed at which bulldozers are tearing into Cooper Mountain's eastern and southern flanks, I am nevertheless grateful for what we *do* have.

What we have at Cooper Mountain Nature Park is a diverse and well-tended assemblage of habitats, easily reached by a trail network that takes maximum advantage of the land's varied topography and microclimates. If you want to tour the major native Willamette Valley habitat types without walking too far, this is a perfect place to do so. It is an excellent outdoor classroom.

The first thing you'll notice when you arrive is the view, a panorama of the Tualatin Valley with the Chehalem Mountains arcing across the horizon. The parking area is at the park's highest point, but views actually get better at a few spots lower down the trails.

At the parking area is the cheery red Nature House, used for environmental education and community programs. Take a moment to visit the adjacent native plant demonstration garden, where you can learn which native plants will thrive in your own yard.

On the other side of the Nature House is a play area with both traditional and nature-based elements. Beyond, a kiosk marks the beginning of the wheelchair-accessible, three-quarter-mile Little Prairie Loop. This path takes in much of what makes Cooper Mountain great, passing through young stands of Willamette Valley ponderosa pine to deeper, older mixed forests and a rest area at the edge of an oak-lined meadow, where native grasses have managed to hold on.

Metro manages this meadow like its other native grasslands and oak savannas, using a mix of mowing and controlled burns. These oak and grass landscapes, which so captivated early settlers as icons of an unspoiled Eden, were in fact a human creation. Kalapuyan people burned them each fall to promote desirable resources like young shoots for basket-weaving, camas bulbs for food, and improved forage for deer. Over millennia, oaks thrived as the human-set, low-intensity fires suppressed faster-growing conifers. When Euro-American settlers evicted the Kalapuyans, seasonal fire largely disappeared. This prompted a gradual decline in these beautiful, tremendously biodiverse habits. Metro is now working to reverse that trend.

From the Little Prairie Loop you can continue to additional trails across meadows, over creeks, past seasonal ponds, and through glorious oak stands. Keep in mind, there is plenty of poison oak around—stay on trails to minimize your impact and your chances of a painful rash. Also, remember you need to hike back *up* to return. On warm days, these trails can get hot once you have left the breezy summit. Plan accordingly.

Finally, don't miss the park's signature element, the listening trumpets. (Picture those old-fashioned hearing aids, called ear trumpets, but supersized and mounted on poles like viewing scopes.) They actually work! I've heard the distant call of a raptor through one, and am told that if I were to arrive at dawn I could hear great horned owls.

63 JENKINS ESTATE

Historic estate with big trees, manicured grounds, and West Side views

Location: 8005 SW Grabhorn Rd., Beaverton
Acreage: 68
Amenities: Historic residence and buildings, rhododendron garden, restrooms, paved path, trails (2 miles), accessible play area
Jurisdiction: Tualatin Hills Park and Recreation District

GETTING THERE

BY CAR OR 217 to exit 2A (SW Canyon Rd./Beaverton-Hillsboro Hwy.); second right onto Beaverton-Hillsboro Hwy., which becomes SW Farmington Rd./OR 10, for 5 miles; left onto SW Grabhorn Rd. to the park entrance at right. **BY TRANSIT** ★ MAX (Blue or Red Line) to Beaverton Transit Center; then Bus 88 (Hart/198th) to SW 198th and Farmington (stop 7071); walk three-quarters of a mile west on SW Farmington Rd. to the park's lower trailhead, just past Grabhorn Rd. **BY BIKE** ★

The Jenkins Estate is a century-old mansion perched on a hillside at the outskirts of Beaverton. It is an idyllic setting to hike forest trails and wander among landscaped gardens.

Belle Ainsworth Jenkins and her husband, Ralph, built the estate in 1912. Belle was the youngest daughter of John C. Ainsworth, the Willamette's original steamboat captain. He later founded the Oregon Steam Navigation Company, which for a time was the most powerful and lucrative transportation monopoly in the Pacific Northwest. Suffice to say, Belle was loaded.

A Saturday stroll at the elegant Jenkins Estate

Her estate shows it. In addition to the main house, there is a greenhouse, an open-air teahouse, and several outbuildings—notably the stables, complete with a dairy and an open loft where the Jenkinses held dance parties. They employed as many as twenty people to run the place.

When Belle died, childless, in 1963, the estate passed to her caretaker. Soon a real estate developer acquired it. Delivering utilities proved challenging, however, and the development delays allowed the Tualatin Hills Park and Recreation District (THPRD) to buy it in 1976. Having largely sat empty since 1963, the estate was in disrepair. Over decades, the THPRD has thoroughly restored it. Now the place practically shines.

From the main parking area, head uphill to tour the grounds. The highlights here are the primrose path and the rhododendron garden, the latter set in a grove of giant redwoods. East of the main house, a road lined with hundred-year-old elms leads up to a nineteenth-century farmhouse. Next to the house is an orchard and picnic tables with a view north toward the Tualatin Mountains.

Just uphill from the farmhouse is the Learning Garden, where the Washington County Master Gardener Association offers free classes on edible landscaping, native plants, pollinator-friendly practices, and more. Check THPRD's website (see Resources) for a schedule.

At the park's southern end, beyond a small rise, is Camp Rivendale, a summer day camp for developmentally challenged kids. The cheery playground here was the first accessible playground in the region and is justifiably popular with children of all abilities.

64 PIRATE PARK

Whimsical playground and Tualatin Valley views on a popular greenway trail

Location: Along the Rock Creek Greenway near NW Graf St., Bethany
Acreage: 16
Amenities: Accessible play area, picnic tables, paved path
Jurisdiction: Tualatin Hills Park and Recreation District

GETTING THERE

BY CAR US 26 to exit 65 (NW Bethany Blvd.) northbound; after 2.3 miles, left onto NW Graf St.; continue a quarter mile to greenway entrance at left, just before NW Sickle Terrace; park on street. **BY TRANSIT** ★★ MAX (Blue Line) to Merlo Rd./SW 158th; then Bus 67 (Bethany/158th) to NW Springville and Sickle Terrace (stop 10080); backtrack 100 yards and go right onto the Ben Graf Greenway Trail; cross NW Graf St. to enter the park. **BY BIKE** ★★★ Via Westside Regional Trail.

The Tualatin Hills Park and Recreation District (THPRD) specializes in high-quality playgrounds, and here I highlight one of their best: Pirate Park on the Rock Creek Greenway. Centered on a vaguely pirate-themed play structure, it's hugely popular. So popular, in fact, that THPRD renamed the park (formerly known as Bethany Meadows) after it.

From NW Graf Street, a paved path leads five hundred feet to the play structure, crossing Bethany Creek on a footbridge. A small stand of alder and maple separates the play area from the creek, providing a scenic backdrop, a patch of habitat, and a great place to hide booty.

Corsairs swarm the play structure underneath colorful sunshades, which, if you squint a little, slightly resemble sails. Ship's masts top a second play structure nearby. In between, several desert island palms endure Oregon's climate to round out the incongruous Blackbeard scene. The structure is accessible and generally toddler-friendly, though often covered in kids of all sizes. Freebooting knows no age limit.

THE ROCK CREEK GREENWAY TRAIL

The West Side—the urbanized part of the Tualatin Valley—has some excellent greenway trails. One of my favorites is Rock Creek, which runs from Rock Creek Powerline Park near Cornelius Pass Road to Kaiser Woods Natural Area. Along its 3.5-mile length, you can enjoy views of the Tualatin Mountains, visit Bethany Lake at the confluence of Rock and Bethany Creeks, indulge in some buccaneering at Pirate Park, and explore a patch of nature at Kaiser Woods—all via an excellent paved path. I recommend it as a first longer outing for beginning bicyclists.

The Rock Creek Greenway Trail is also a great spot from which to appreciate the invisible but mighty urban growth boundary. Pause at the little pocket park just north of Kaiser Woods, where to the west and south you'll see McMansions sitting cheek by jowl; to the east and south, bucolic fields stretch toward timbered hills. You're right on the boundary.

The urban growth boundary is meant to ensure orderly urban expansion and limit sprawl. In a fast-growing, desirable area like this, it creates a paradox. Looking to foster more walkable and sustainable communities, urban planners have mandated more density. Yet since many older, closer-in suburbs are already built out with quarter-acre (or even larger) lots, much of the desired density ends up in newer developments, typically on the margins rather than in the middle—far from freeways, transit, and jobs.

So it is here. To judge by the home prices, however, plenty of people like it. *I* certainly wouldn't mind if my daily commute involved the Rock Creek Greenway Trail.

For a break from the action, head a hundred yards west to a modest hilltop with views across the Tualatin Valley. Here, the Rock Creek and Waterhouse Trails intersect. These paved regional paths connect neighborhoods across northern Washington County. From here, one can bike or ramble in any number of directions.

EXTEND YOUR VISIT

There are more kid-friendly attractions in the neighborhood. Walk a mile east on the Rock Creek Greenway Trail to reach Kaiser Woods Natural Area, a twenty-eight-acre forested wetland with a soft-surface loop trail. This pocket natural area is just big enough to surround you with trees, birds, and a touch of wildness. Return as you came or loop north via the Bethany Creek Trail and brand-new Bethany

Young buccaneers keep busy at Pirate Park.

Creek Falls Park, where an accessible play area and picnic shelter invite further fun, pirate-related or otherwise.

65 ORENCO WOODS NATURE PARK

Historic nursery turned natural area with creek, trails, bridges, and artwork

Location: 7100 NE Birch St., Hillsboro
Acreage: 42
Amenities: Paved paths (0.5 mile), soft-surface paths (1.2 miles), accessible restrooms and playground, picnic tables and shelter
Jurisdiction: Hillsboro

GETTING THERE

BY CAR US 26 to exit 62A (Cornelius Pass Rd. S.); left onto Cornelius Pass Rd.; after three-quarters of a mile, right onto NE Cornell Rd.; left onto NE Century Blvd.; cross MAX tracks, then left onto NE Birch St.; five blocks to the park entrance. **BY TRANSIT** ★★★ MAX (Blue Line) to Orenco; backtrack to go right onto NE Century Blvd.; left onto NE Birch St. to reach the park (hlaf-mile walk). **BY BIKE** ★★★ Via Rock Creek Greenway Trail.

Don't miss the explorable artworks at Orenco Woods Nature Park.

Orenco Woods is a favorite with residents of Hillsboro, the former farm town that, with the arrival of Intel Corporation in the 1970s, became the heart of Oregon's "Silicon Forest." This park is worth seeing even if you're not from the area. It's easy to reach on MAX and is fun on foot or by bike.

The park has a split personality. The upper area, near the entrance, is a lawn with restrooms, a huge picnic shelter, and an accessible nature play area that will mostly appeal to younger kids. (The water-and-sand feature is a perennial favorite and welcome on hot days, as there's little shade in the park.) The rest of the park is a natural area sloping down to Rock Creek, which carves a mini-canyon just deep enough to provide some seclusion and some habitat for the winter steelhead, cutthroat trout, and Pacific lamprey somewhat improbably making their home in the midst of suburbia.

A short, paved loop circles the lawn, leading past Orenco's signature: a bright green and red steel apple, with seating inside, that commemorates the property's heritage. In 1906, the Oregon Nursery Company established a company town here with the portmanteau name of Orenco. It grew to become the largest nursery on the West Coast, spreading the famed Orenco apple across the nation.

The nursery closed in 1927, and the company town dissolved shortly afterward. From the 1950s until 2006, the property was a golf course. When a planned residential development stalled in the Great Recession of 2008, the nonprofit Trust for Public Land joined forces with Metro and the City of Hillsboro to conserve the area. Metro, Hillsboro, and volunteer groups have since spent time and money painstakingly restoring the golf greens and creek canyon with native species. Orenco now thrives with wildlife, despite busy Cornelius Pass Road and the MAX tracks close by.

Follow the paved Rock Creek Greenway Trail across a mighty trestle bridge for views over the canyon, or follow two soft-surface trail loops down into it. Along the way, check out the woven willow and dogwood sculptures, vaguely reminiscent of Easter Island statues, set in a Douglas-fir grove. The artist Patrick Dougherty created them in 2017.

EXTEND YOUR VISIT

The town center around the Orenco MAX station is worth a look, for good restaurants and a suburban take on New Urbanism.

66 ROOD BRIDGE PARK

Big park with the West Side's best mix of nature and recreation

Location: 4000 SE Rood Bridge Rd., Hillsboro
Acreage: 60
Amenities: Accessible restrooms, paved paths (2.25 miles), trails (1 mile), meeting facility, pavilion, picnic shelters, play area, tennis courts, paddle craft launch, rhododendron garden
Jurisdiction: Hillsboro

GETTING THERE

BY CAR OR 217 to exit 2A (SW Canyon Rd./Beaverton-Hillsboro Hwy.); west on Canyon Rd. (which becomes OR 8/Tualatin Valley Hwy.) for 6.8 miles; left onto SE Brookwood Ave.; first right onto SE Witch Hazel Rd.; right onto SE River Rd.; left onto SE Rood Bridge Rd.; left into park. **BY TRANSIT** ★ MAX (Red and Blue Line) to Beaverton Transit Center; then Bus 57 (Tualatin Valley Hwy./Forest Grove) to SE Tualatin Valley Hwy. and 24th (stop 5612); walk south on 24th; left onto SE River Rd.; right onto the Rock Creek Trail into park (three-quarter-mile walk). **BY BIKE** ★

Rood Bridge Park has enough variety and quality to warrant a visit from any corner of the region. It has active recreation covered, charm to spare, forests and meadows, and a great boat launch for river exploration—quite a feat for a park that's not really so big.

The main entrance is on Rood Bridge Road, though you can also enter along SE River Road, where a quarter-mile path (sometimes wet or even flooded in winter)

Early spring above the lake at Rood Bridge Park

follows Rock Creek. From the main entrance, head left to reach tennis courts, a play area, and three large picnic shelters. Facilities here are in excellent repair. It's clear that Hillsboro residents value and fund their parks.

Just south of the picnic shelters is a small but fine rhododendron garden with over five hundred varieties of what should be, in my opinion, the region's official flower (forget about boring roses!). The Woodland Pond loop, part paved and part gravel, circles the garden along a rocky streambed to reach a pavilion overlooking a small waterfall and pond. It's artificial but enchanting nevertheless.

South of the Woodland Pond is a meadow dotted with picnic tables. The park's designers have taken full advantage of the undulating topography here. It's a lovely spot that overlooks woods. Beyond is a small lake, mostly full of lily pads in summer, with scenic rest spots at the north and south ends.

These different park "rooms" are each very appealing. Best of all, though, is the park's "backyard," the natural area along the Tualatin River. Paths lead downhill from the meadow and lake into a forest of cottonwood, maple, and ash to converge at a footbridge over Rock Creek. Across the bridge, breaks in the trees afford views of the languid, elusive Tualatin. A soft-surface trail climbs a ridge to loop a forest, half-hidden and a touch wild, of Douglas-firs and cedars. On my last visit, it glowed with bright white trillium flowers.

Back across the bridge, the path continues upstream to the River House, a community meeting space with a view from the back patio over the park's wetlands and woods.

Along the way, it passes a small boat launch and dock. This marks the upstream end of the Tualatin River Trail, which runs almost 40 river miles to the Tualatin's mouth at Willamette Park in West Linn. Though gaining in poularity, this novice-friendly water trail is still underrated and deserves your attention. The current in summer is sluggish enough that out-and-back trips are very doable, and the paddle to Metro's Farmington Road ramp is a great half-day outing, especially with kids. See www.tualatinriverkeepers.org for more.

67 CHEHALEM RIDGE NATURE PARK

Brand-new regional park with huge views and a lot of hiking options

Location: 39551 SW Dixon Mill Rd., Gaston
Acreage: 1230
Amenities: Restroom, multiuse shelter, picnic tables, trails (3 miles; half accessible); additional trails, trailhead, and nature play area planned
Jurisdiction: Metro

GETTING THERE

BY CAR OR 217 to exit 2A (SW Canyon Rd./Beaverton-Hillsboro Hwy.); second right onto Beaverton-Hillsboro Hwy., which becomes SW Farmington Rd./OR 10; after 10.5 miles, right onto SW Hillsboro Hwy./OR 219 for three-quarters of a mile; left onto SW Unger Rd.; after 3 miles, left onto SW Dixon Mill Rd.; 2.4 miles to the park entrance at right. Parking fee. **BY TRANSIT** None. **BY BIKE** ★ Rural route via SW Unger Rd. and SW Dixon Mill Rd. is incredibly scenic for competent riders.

Chehalem Ridge is the broad, curving mountain range separating the Tualatin Valley from the Chehalem and Yamhill Valleys farther west. Formed by the same geologic forces that created the Coast Range and Cascades, it's a sort of sky island surrounded by valley lowlands. Though vineyards and estates cover its southern end, the northern end of the ridge was, until recently, a tree farm. Now it's a brand-new park with miles of trails, big views, and a decade's worth of forest restoration already under way.

A timber company owned this land for a century, feeding the local mill near Henry Hagg Lake. Given the surrounding development, though, it was only a matter of time before high-end homes replaced forestry. Fortunately, the company was open to a different idea. With assistance from the Trust for Public Land, the Metro Regional Government acquired the area in 2010.

What Metro bought was an industrially managed forest. Some areas were clear-cut, others overgrown with densely planted single-species stands where no light reached the forest floor. Metro invested years setting the forest on a more natural trajectory, thinning stands and controlling invasive plants. Along with the restoration, Metro worked overtime to engage area residents, in partnership with the Latinx communities of nearby Forest Grove, Cornelius, and Hillsboro, to plan the park. While it's too early to tell, Metro seems to have succeeded in creating a park that truly welcomes everyone.

For now, the main thing to do here is walk the forest trails. Some are also open to bikes. The main trail leads uphill from the parking area through timber stands slowly transitioning to natural forest and crosses a small creek to reach viewpoints looking east toward the city. After about 1.5 miles, the trail tops out at Iowa Hill, the property's highest point at 1135 feet. Your reward is a panorama of the Coast Range and the Wapato Lakebed nearly a thousand feet below.

The lakebed merits a little elaboration. A century ago, it was a seasonal wetland. In winter, the Tualatin River would flood, creating a lake of fifteen hundred acres or more. The Atfalati people lived in permanent villages around the lake, subsisting on its vast fields of wapato. In 1855, following a decade of encroachment by settlers, the dwindling Atfalati "agreed" under duress to relocate to the newly created Grand Ronde reservation in the Coast Range foothills.

In the 1930s, farmers diked and drained the lake to grow potatoes and onions. Over the last few decades government agencies started buying up the lakebed in hopes of one day restoring the wetlands, which help clean the Tualatin's water and provide habitat for migratory birds. In 2007, the US Fish and Wildlife Service designated part of the lakebed a national wildlife refuge. Metro, meanwhile, has acquired land in and around the lakebed to stitch together a corridor of habitat running from the lake to the ridgetop.

It's all a work in progress. But the key word here is *progress*. It's never too late to find—or make—room for nature!

68 SCOGGINS VALLEY PARK AT HENRY HAGG LAKE

Giant reservoir with swimming beaches, biking, hiking, and picnicking

Location: 50250 SW Scoggins Valley Rd., Gaston
Acreage: 1500
Amenities: Restrooms, disc golf, boat launches, picnic areas, trails; note: entrance fee
Jurisdiction: Washington County

You can almost always find solitude along Hagg Lake's extensive shoreline.

GETTING THERE

BY CAR US 26 to exit 57 (1st St./NW Glencoe Rd.) southbound; follow signs for Forest Grove: right onto NW Zion Church Rd., right onto NW Verboort Rd., left onto NW Martin Rd., left onto OR 47 south/Quince St.; after 6 miles, right onto SW Scoggins Valley Rd. to the park entrance. **BY TRANSIT** None. **BY BIKE** ★★ Via Forest Grove and SW Old Hwy. 47.

Henry Hagg Lake is a reservoir on the Upper Tualatin River that provides drinking water to Hillsboro and neighboring communities. Set in the quiet Scoggins Valley among the Coast Range foothills, it's a scenic destination. In summer, swimmers, boaters, cyclists, and campers flock here. Anglers and hikers enjoy the place year-round.

From the entrance booth, proceed to a junction where the park's office is located. From here, you can loop the lake in either direction. Just across the dam from the park entrance, Elk Recreation Area has restrooms and a nonmotorized boat launch. The main action is farther west and north at C Ramp, with a large parking lot, picnic areas, fishing pier, and a popular swimming beach. (Note: there is no lifeguard, and the lake bottom drops off steeply in places.)

If you are here for a more natural setting, continue to the Scoggins Creek Recreation Area at the back of the lake. Here you can picnic among creekside willows, alder, and cedar. As this half of the lake is a no-wake zone and water-skiers stay closer to the dam, quiet prevails. (Amen.) More excellent spots to picnic and access the water can be found between Scoggins Creek and Eagle Point Recreation Area. A highlight is the Fenders Blue area, where a short trail leads past a habitat restoration site for the endangered Fender's blue butterfly to a promontory above the lake.

A 13.5-mile trail loops the entire lakeshore, joining the road briefly in a few places. Portions of the trail can be muddy and there are plenty of short hills, but on the whole it's an easy and mostly scenic loop, good for trail runners and intermediate-level mountain bikers. The road is also a great place to ride a bike. There are a few hills and a minimal shoulder, but the traffic is light and drivers are generally courteous, making it suitable for (and popular with) riders of most abilities.

THE BANKS–VERNONIA STATE TRAIL

Running from the edge of Washington County's farmland deep into timber country, the Banks–Vernonia State Trail offers a scenic and beginner-friendly bike tour within easy reach of Portland. It's popular, but not nearly as popular as it should be. This is simply one of the best rail trails in the United States, hands down.

Beginning in Banks, the paved path climbs gently through tranquil valleys and deepening forest, passing through Stub Stewart State Park and over the divide between the Tualatin and Nehalem Valleys, to arrive 21 miles later at the village of Vernonia. Reasonably fit riders will have no trouble completing the entire route in both directions. An easier 7-mile (one way) stretch runs from the state park entrance south to the Manning trailhead. The highlight here is the century-old, seven-hundred-foot-long Buxton Trestle, which soars a dizzying eighty feet above Mendenhall Creek.

At trail's end is little Vernonia, seemingly lost in the woods. Established in the 1880s, it was a remote, hardscrabble farm town until 1924, when the Oregon-American Lumber Company opened what it claimed to be the largest sawmill in the world. The company built a rail line (you just rode it) to the Tualatin Valley to haul logs to market. Vernonia boomed. A mere thirty years later, the timber was mostly all cut, the mill obsolete, and the lumber company absorbed by ever-larger timber conglomerates. The mill closed for good in 1957, a few days before Christmas.

Though Vernonia never fully recovered, it adapted gracefully. Today, the old millpond is Vernonia Lake, a popular fishing hole, and the old mill site is a wooded park, complete with romantic mill ruins. I love this town and highly recommend a visit, whether by two wheels or four. After exploring the mill site, grab a coffee or lunch along Vernonia's rustic main street. If it's a hot day and you have the energy, head up the road a few more miles to Eddy County Park and dip in the lovely, calm (in summer!) Nehalem River.

69 STUB STEWART STATE PARK

Expansive state park in a young forest with great biking

Location: OR 47 north of Buxton
Acreage: 1673
Amenities: Restrooms, camping, cabins, nature center, 20 miles of paved and soft-surface trails, equestrian trails, disc golf, naturalist programs
Jurisdiction: Oregon State Parks

GETTING THERE

BY CAR US 26 westbound for 28 miles; bear right onto OR 47 north; 4 miles to the park entrance at right. **BY TRANSIT** None. **BY BIKE** ★★★ Via Banks-Vernonia State Trail.

L. L. "Stub" Stewart was a lumberman, legislator, and long-standing member of the State Parks Commission. His namesake, which opened in 2007, is one of Oregon's newest state parks. As this was commercial timberland for a century, some areas of the park are young, dense regrowth—not, to my taste at least, as inviting as older forests. Still, this is prime country for growing trees. The forest will return. In the meantime, the clear-cuts offer open vistas and a sense of space.

I think this park is best enjoyed on two wheels. The professionally designed mountain bike trails—including some dedicated bike-only routes—are among the region's best. Most are cross-country trails, but downhill-oriented freeriders will find options too. Additionally, one of region's best paved rail trails runs right through the park; see the sidebar on page 162.

If you are here to wander on foot, check out the small but impressive visitor center, then try the 1.5-mile loop on the Brooke Creek Trail and Widowmaker Way. For a longer trek, try the Hares Canyon Trail south to the Banks-Vernonia State Trail and then up South Caddywhomper Way to a ridgetop vista overlooking the Williams Creek valley. If you just want to have a picnic, drive straight up to the Hilltop day-use area, where shelters, restrooms, and expansive views await. This is but a small selection of the park's extensive network.

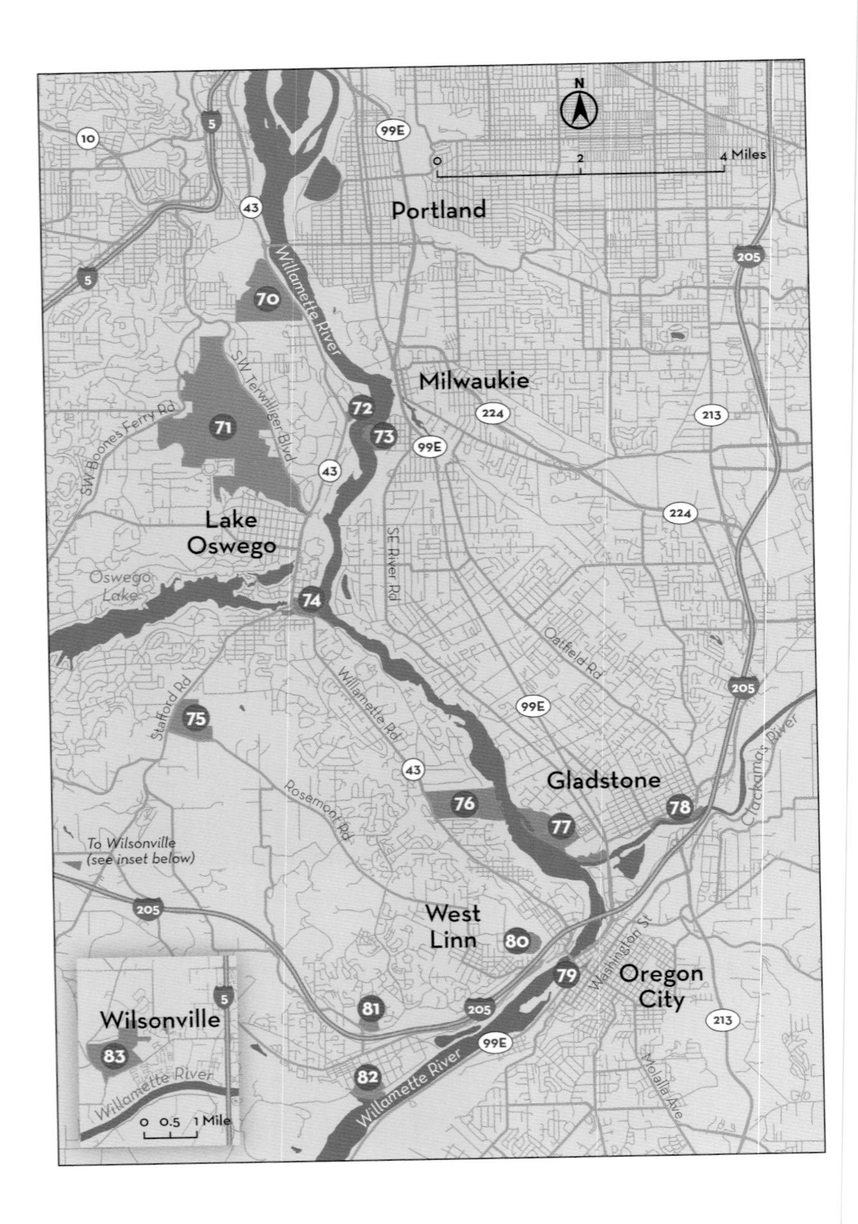

N
0
2
4 Miles
Portland
Milwaukie
Lake Oswego
Oswego Lake
Gladstone
West Linn
Oregon City
Wilsonville
Willamette River
Clackamas River
SW Terwilliger Blvd
SW Boones Ferry Rd
SE River Rd
Oatfield Rd
Willamette Rd
Stafford Rd
Rosemont Rd
Washington St
Molalla Ave
To Wilsonville (see inset below)
0 0.5 1 Mile
5
10
43
99E
205
224
213
70
71
72
73
74
75
76
77
78
79
80
81
82
83

UP THE WILLAMETTE: MILWAUKIE, OREGON CITY, WEST LINN, AND WILSONVILLE

70 RIVER VIEW NATURAL AREA

Recent addition to the West Hills' forested parks offers rugged hiking

Location: Along OR 43 south of the Sellwood Bridge
Acreage: 146
Amenities: Trails, restroom (portable)
Jurisdiction: Portland Parks and Recreation

GETTING THERE

BY CAR Upper access: I-5 to exit 297 (Terwilliger Blvd.) southbound; 1.6 miles on Terwilliger Blvd. to a traffic circle at Lewis and Clark College; left onto SW Palater Rd.; left onto SW Palatine Hill Rd. to park trailheads. Lower access: SW Macadam Ave./OR 43 southbound; 0.6 mile beyond the Sellwood Bridge, look for a small parking area at right. **BY TRANSIT** ★ Upper access: weekdays only, Bus 54 (Beaverton-Hillsdale) to SW Capitol and Terwilliger (stop 957); transfer to Bus 39

(Lewis and Clark) to SW Palater and Palatine Hill (stop 13022); walk north along Palatine Hill Rd. to trailheads. Lower access: Bus 35 (Macadam/Greeley toward Oregon City Transit Center) to SW Riverside and Radcliffe (stop 4905); backtrack a quarter mile to the trailhead. **BY BIKE** ★

Why include River View? It has a lot in common with nearby Tryon Creek State Natural Area and other wooded parks like Marquam Nature Park and Forest Park. Though smaller than those places, River View is, in my opinion, a notch wilder. It's steep, cut by precipitous ravines that expose slippery, easily eroded clay slopes. Prior to construction of the new loop trail, dozens of informal paths—don't use them!—made for dangerously steep walking. This may be urban nature, but it's not tame.

I am also biased about River View because the organization I long worked for—the Trust for Public Land—helped the city acquire this property in a somewhat improbable feat of modern-day conservation. It was the largest natural area acquisition by the city in decades.

River View Natural Area reaches from Palatine Hill down to the Willamette River, between the River View Cemetery and Lewis and Clark College. You can access it from two trailheads on top and one below, along Highway 43. A new trail loops the property in about 3.5 miles, offering solitude and a hill-climbing workout while leaving the natural area's core undisturbed. If you're not up for the full circle, try the three-quarter-mile loop from the upper trailhead, which heads down gentle slopes to a rest area deep in the forest. Given the transit connections, you can also try a one-way hike up or down.

This is a special forest for several reasons. First, it runs from nearly the top to the very bottom of its watershed, meaning that its streams, though short, are relatively clean. They deliver cold water to the Willamette River, offering a lifeline to the spawning salmon that have just navigated a hot and shadeless river through downtown. Furthermore, the forest's core has been virtually undisturbed for decades. It offers refuge for an array of wildlife, birds in particular, with over seventy species identified.

The forest is also unique in that it's a true wilderness. Not wilderness in the legal sense of "untrammeled by man"—it was cleared in the late 1800s and has been home to the homeless ever since—but in the sense that it has been sitting unmanaged and (officially) off limits for a century. The land was owned during this time by the adjacent River View Cemetery, where Portland's highest and mightiest find eternal repose. The cemetery held the forest for future expansion. But it turns out people aren't dying like they used to, or at least aren't opting for burial in ornate, landscaped settings. So the cemetery's owners concluded they would likely never need the land and in 2006 entered talks with a real estate developer.

This was prime land for high-end residences—and development would have spelled disaster for the forest and its streams. Yet public acquisition of a property worth many millions was out of the question. Then came the Great Recession of 2008, putting the kibosh for a time on almost all development. With lucky timing and by turning over every couch cushion and piggy bank, the city was able to acquire the land at about half its peak value.

Portlanders are now paying for it, through sky-high water and sewer bills. That has spawned some ire and a few lawsuits. When the dust settles, though, we will still have the forest and will be richer for it.

EXTEND YOUR VISIT

Powers Marine Park, the narrow strip of Willamette frontage opposite Highway 43 from River View Natural Area, has a quiet, wooded shoreline and beach where even in the heat of summer you will find solitude and some shade. Access it from a paved path beneath the Sellwood Bridge.

71 TRYON CREEK STATE NATURAL AREA

Lush, forested park fills a ravine in a close-in suburb

Location: 11321 SW Terwilliger Blvd.
Acreage: 660
Amenities: Nature center, restrooms, picnic areas, hiking trails (8 miles), paved trail (3 miles), naturalist programs
Jurisdiction: Oregon State Parks

GETTING THERE

BY CAR I-5 to exit 297 (Terwilliger Blvd.) southbound; follow Terwilliger Blvd. 2.7 miles to the park entrance at right. Parking fee. **BY TRANSIT** ★★ Bus 35 (Macadam/Greeley toward Oregon City Transit Center) to N. State and D Ave. (stop 5507); follow path north to the park. **BY BIKE** ★★ Via SW Terwilliger Blvd.

A quick glance at an aerial image of Portland gives it away: just south of downtown and surrounded by city is a blob of green. It's as though a chunk of Forest Park broke off and drifted south. This is Tryon Creek State Natural Area, which by dint of filling most of a canyon feels even bigger than it is. And it's pretty big.

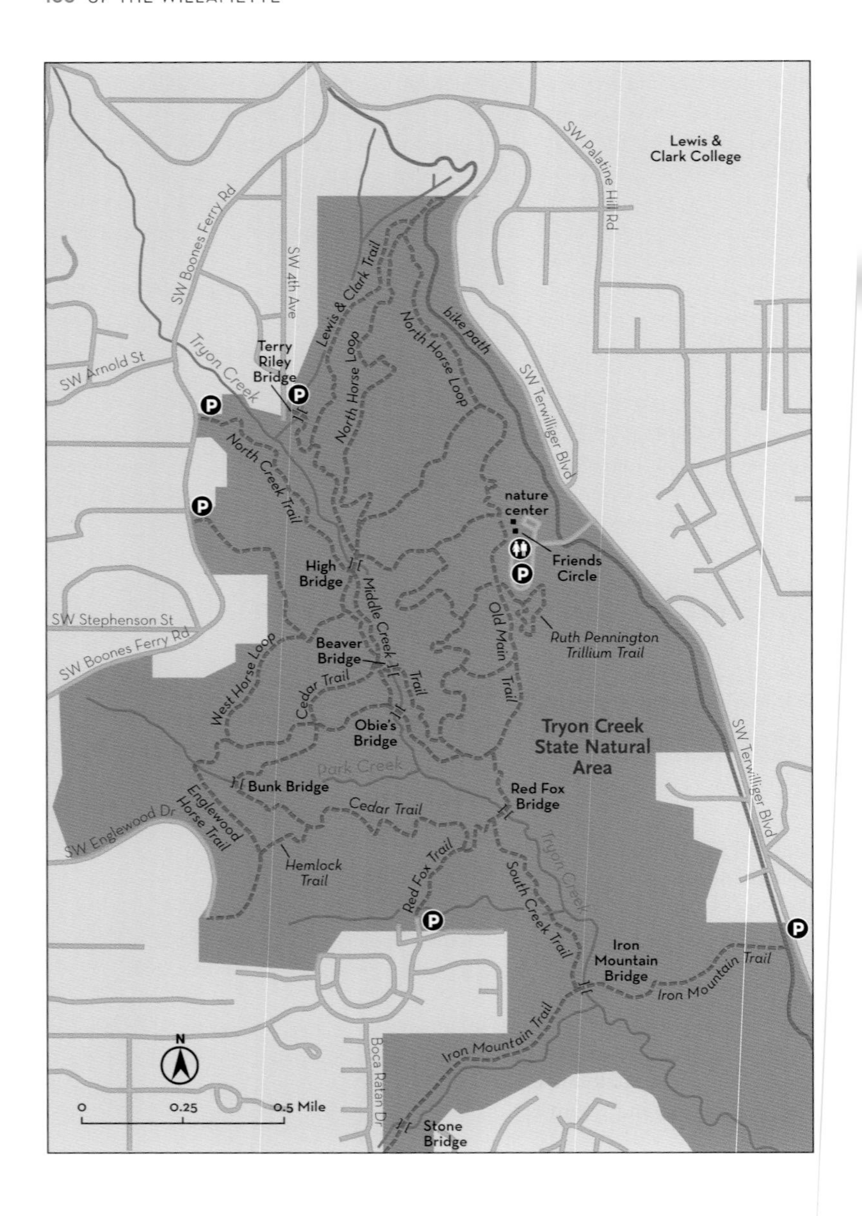

Lewis & Clark College
SW Palatine Hill Rd
SW Boones Ferry Rd
SW 4th Ave
Lewis & Clark Trail
North Horse Loop
North Horse Loop
bike path
SW Terwilliger Blvd
SW Arnold St
Tryon Creek
Terry Riley Bridge
North Creek Trail
nature center
Friends Circle
High Bridge
Middle Creek Trail
Old Main Trail
Ruth Pennington Trillium Trail
SW Stephenson St
SW Boones Ferry Rd
West Horse Loop
Beaver Bridge
Cedar Trail
Obie's Bridge
Tryon Creek State Natural Area
Park Creek
Bunk Bridge
Englewood Horse Trail
SW Englewood Dr
Cedar Trail
Red Fox Bridge
SW Terwilliger Blvd
Hemlock Trail
Red Fox Trail
South Creek Trail
Tryon Creek
Iron Mountain Bridge
Iron Mountain Trail
Iron Mountain Trail
Boca Ratan Dr
N
0
0.25
0.5 Mile
Stone Bridge

Nature play options abound at Tryon Creek State Natural Area. (Photo by Monica Vogel)

Park at the main entrance off SW Terwilliger Boulevard and head to the nature center, operated as a partnership between Oregon State Parks and the nonprofit Friends of Tryon Creek (see Resources). This band of heroic volunteers pulls ivy, tends trails, runs day camps, and welcomes thousands to the park each year.

From the nature center, trails lead in every direction. Walk south a few hundred feet to the Friends Circle, where the barrier-free, half-mile Ruth Pennington Trillium Trail offers an executive summary of the park's many virtues. The Old Main Trail also starts here. For a 2-mile loop taking in much of the park, head down the Old Main Trail. Go left onto the Red Fox Trail, cross the Red Fox Bridge, go right onto the Cedar Trail, and return via the Middle Creek Trail. The Iron Mountain Trail, through the park's lower reaches, is also excellent and often less busy.

Part of what makes this place so great, aside from its size, is its all-season accessibility. Even on blistering summer days, the shade and a perennial stream keep it comfortable. On the nastiest days of winter, you can still find dry(ish) trails and shelter from wind. The forest is deep, but not gloomy.

You may wonder how a state park of this size happened to land between Portland and Lake Oswego. This entire watershed, like much of the surrounding country, was long ago denuded to power an iron foundry at Oswego—now the site of George Rogers Park. The forest slowly grew back, just in time for a post–World War II population boom. By the 1960s, homes cloaked the surrounding hills.

In 1969, two local women caught wind of a rumor that a developer was quietly assembling properties in the canyon to build a master-planned community. Lucille Beck and Jean Siddall wanted the canyon to be a park. They realized that for this to happen, *they* needed to do it. So on the first Earth Day in 1970, they launched a grassroots campaign to buy it. By fall, they had acquired several parcels and convinced Governor Tom McCall to declare the canyon a state park. Yet development plans chugged on, caught between the governor's declaration and the county's desire for tax revenue from a development. Undaunted, Lu and Jean mobilized an epic letter-writing campaign. The developer eventually stood down, and the state acquired the land.

In the years since, the Friends of Tryon Creek have stayed busy helping Lu and Jean's vision reach fulfillment.

72 ELK ROCK GARDEN AT BISHOP CLOSE

Lofty views and serenity at one of Portland's best formal gardens

Location: 11800 S Military Ln.
Acreage: 13
Amenities: Landscaped garden with path
Jurisdiction: Private

GETTING THERE

BY CAR SW Macadam Ave./OR 43 southbound; past Sellwood Bridge, continue 1.6 miles; left onto S Military Rd.; right onto S. Military Ln. **BY TRANSIT** ★★★ Bus 35 (Macadam/Greeley toward Oregon City Transit Center) to SW Riverside and Military (stop 4900); walk down Military Rd. to Military Ln. (quarter-mile walk). **BY BIKE** ★★ Hilly but scenic route via SW Terwilliger Blvd., S. Palatine Hill Rd., and S. Military Rd.

A quiet moment at Elk Rock Garden

Elk Rock Garden is one of the prettiest places in Portland. Come here for a contemplative stroll among exquisite gardens to a dizzying view over the Willamette River.

The property and grounds were home to Peter Kerr, a Scotsman who made his fortune exporting Eastern Oregon and Washington's wheat. He lived here for sixty years, developing the garden with help from landscape architect John Olmsted and Emanuel Mische, Olmsted protégé and Portland's early parks superintendent. Over Kerr's many decades of hosting social gatherings, the garden's fame spread. Eager to see its legacy endure, Kerr donated the garden to the Episcopal Diocese of Oregon at his death in 1957, on condition that it remain a garden and open to the public.

The Episcopal diocese maintains its offices here in Kerr's former home and keeps the garden up with help from the nonprofit Friends of Elk Rock Garden. As this is a working church office at the end of a quiet residential street in a very exclusive neighborhood, don't come here to picnic, run your dog, or ride a bike. This is a quiet, sanctified place.

Sign in at the visitor center and pick up a map. Paths circle the main lawn to meet near an outdoor altar. The view takes in much of East Portland, with Mount Hood perfectly framed by trees. Magnolias, witch hazel, rhododendrons, and chrysanthemums line the way.

Beyond the lawn, the path crosses a water feature to enter woods. It soon reaches the property's far end, where you emerge atop a cliff above the river. Dark waters swirl a hundred fifty feet directly below, with Elk Rock Island just beyond. According to my research, the Elk Rock is actually the cliff on which you are standing, not the island below. The area's indigenous residents apparently hunted elk by driving them off this precipice. Though I can't verify the story, I can attest to the drama and spiritual resonance of this spot.

The path continues in a loop up and across the hillside, with more views, to return to the visitor center. That's it. Take your time.

73 SPRING PARK AND ELK ROCK ISLAND

Seasonal island with beaches, coves, and views

Location: 2001 SE Sparrow St., Milwaukie
Acreage: 20
Amenities: Trails, picnic area, play structure
Jurisdiction: Milwaukie

GETTING THERE

BY CAR SE McLoughlin Blvd./OR 99E south to Milwaukie; a half mile past the stoplight at SE Harrison St. and SE 17th Ave., bear right onto SE 22nd Ave.; right onto SE Sparrow St. to Spring Park. **BY TRANSIT** ★★ MAX (Orange Line) to SE Park Ave.; walk right onto Park Ave.; right onto SE 23rd Ave., then straight onto SE River Rd.; left onto SE Sparrow to reach the park (three-quarter-mile walk). **BY BIKE** ★★

If I had to pick one, and only one, Willamette River destination for you, it would be Elk Rock Island. This place feels like a world unto itself: a rugged, craggy rock that defies the river to go around it. In high water during late winter and early spring, it is a true island, though easily reached by a short paddle upstream from Milwaukie Bay Park. For much of the year, you can walk right to it from Spring Park across a rocky isthmus.

I love Elk Rock Island because it compresses the spirit of wildness into a tiny space. That is not to say it's wild: you will likely see other explorers if you go in summer. Nevertheless, in the short lap around the island you will find places of seclusion and mystery. The city seems to fade. The forest, the unforgiving basalt, and the relentless river come to the fore. If you have ever floated a wild river or paddled a sea kayak to a remote cove, you know the feeling. In this case, the feeling is available via the MAX train and a short walk.

Start at Spring Park Natural Area, where a basic play structure and a few picnic tables mark the start of an accessible quarter-mile path to the water. Assuming the river is low enough, pick your way across the rocks to find a well-worn trail at the island's upstream end.

Follow it along a rocky bench overlooking the water. A patch of madrones, oaks, and a few Douglas-firs eke out a living on thin soil in the island's center. Continue to a small cove with a muddy beach. It faces a towering cliff on the opposite bank—a degree of topographical drama rare along the Willamette. Atop the cliff is Elk Rock Garden.

There is a connection here. Elk Rock Garden's owner, Peter Kerr, twice owned this island. The history is muddled, but it would seem Kerr built a social club on the island around 1903, then watched, presumably with dismay, as the club changed hands and developed a reputation for licentiousness. It burned down in 1916. Two years later, Kerr sold the island to the Portland Rowing Club with, one imagines, hopes for reform. His intention seems clear enough: the deed of sale includes a restriction that the property "not . . . be used for immoral purposes, no factory, mill, construction work, or any mercantile or business use for 12 years."

Only six years later, Kerr bought the island *again*. He ultimately donated it to the city in 1941, preserved "as a pretty place for all to enjoy." I can't say for certain, but I have a hunch Kerr was simply doing what he could to preserve the peace and dignity of his clifftop estate from the vulgar rabble below.

The trail continues around the cove to surmount a rocky peninsula. From here, backtrack or loop through the forest to reach a cove facing Milwaukie. In summer, when the island connects to shore, this is a calm spot for little ones to splash along a sandy beach. From here, you soon regain the trail from the parking lot.

Elk Rock Island enjoys the distinction of being among the oldest rocks in the area. It is the hard core of an ancient volcano, thought to have erupted over forty million years ago, long predating the Columbia River flood basalts that made places like Rocky Butte and Multnomah Falls. To me, that's just one more reason to see wildness in this little patch of woods, rock, and water.

74 GEORGE ROGERS PARK

Great beach and paths at a historic ironworks

Location: 611 S. State St., Lake Oswego
Acreage: 26
Amenities: Restrooms, picnic areas, beach, sports fields, tennis courts, play structure, gardens
Jurisdiction: Lake Oswego

The old blast furnace at George Rogers Park, an icon of the area's industrial heritage

GETTING THERE

BY CAR I-5 to exit 297 (Terwilliger Blvd.) southbound; continue on Terwilliger Blvd. 4 miles to N. State St./OR 43; go right and travel through downtown Lake Oswego; left onto Ladd St.; right onto Furnace St. to the park. **BY TRANSIT** ★★★ Bus 35 (Macadam/Greeley toward Oregon City Transit Center) to State and Middlecrest (stop 5511); walk two blocks along State St. to the park entrance at Green St. **BY BIKE** ★

The best reason to visit George Rogers Park is its beach. Though small, it is perfectly situated and well cared for by Lake Oswego's parks department.

On my first visit many years ago, I was surprised to find a giant blast furnace next to the beach. It turns out that tony Lake Oswego, prior to the lakeside mansions, upscale boutiques, and Portland Trailblazers in residence, was a pioneer industrial town.

In the early days of statehood, Portland business leaders saw an opportunity to build Oregon's industrial base—and their fortunes—by producing iron locally. At the time, all iron used on the West Coast had to be shipped 17,000 miles around Cape Horn from the East Coast. That, to put it mildly, entailed a markup.

When prospectors discovered iron deposits nearby, it was as though nature had destined this spot for industry. The outlet of Sucker Lake (its name later upgraded to Oswego) provided water for power. The surrounding forests, including what is now Tryon Creek State Natural Area, had timber for charcoal. When the Oswego iron furnace roared to life in 1867, it was the West Coast's first. Local leaders saw a bright future for the fledgling town, which they confidently expected to become the "Pittsburgh of the West."

The business never fully succeeded, struggling from one financial challenge to the next. The Panic of 1893 shut off the furnace for good. The nearby pipe foundry (now Foothills Park) limped along until 1929, when another financial crash ushered in the Great Depression and ended business altogether. Now nearly all traces of this hot, dirty industry have disappeared. The furnace, however, refused to yield to the wrecking ball. It is now on the National Register of Historic Places as Oregon's oldest industrial site and the only charcoal blast furnace west of the Rockies.

Aside from the beach and furnace, the park has standard amenities: a play structure, sports fields and courts along Ladd Street, and a landscaped garden around the furnace. A paved path leads from the garden to the beach, a narrow finger of sand where Oswego's outlet creek enters the Willamette River.

Tucked in a slight river bend, the beach has great views to the east and a measure of shade from afternoon sun. The sand is soft and the water inviting. The cars are far enough away that quiet prevails. It can get crowded here, but the crowd is friendly and family-oriented. I don't hesitate to trek all the way from Southeast Portland when the weather is right for a swim.

EXTEND YOUR VISIT

If you are up for more walking, follow the Oswego Iron Heritage Trail north through downtown to visit Millennium Plaza Park on Oswego Lake and Roehr City Park on the Willamette. The interpretive signage is excellent.

75 LUSCHER FARM PARK

A preserved farm at the edge of town offers views, history, and veggies

Location: 125 Rosemont Rd., Lake Oswego
Acreage: 152
Amenities: Restrooms, picnic areas, paved interpretive trail, sports fields, fenced dog park, community gardens, tours
Jurisdiction: Lake Oswego

GETTING THERE

BY CAR I-5 to exit 297 (Terwilliger Blvd.) southbound; continue on Terwilliger Blvd. 4 miles to N. State St./OR 43; go right and travel through downtown Lake Oswego; right onto McVey Ave. (becomes Stafford Rd.); continue 2 miles; left at the traffic circle onto Rosemont Rd.; left into the park. **BY TRANSIT** Doable, not recommended. **BY BIKE** ★

Luscher Farm is a unique hybrid: working farm, museum, garden, and community park. Rudie and Ester Luscher operated a dairy here from 1944 to 1969, the last in a century of farmers. Lake Oswego acquired the farm from Rudie's estate in 1990, honoring his wish that it be preserved "to show how dairy farm people lived" in the first half of the twentieth century.

The historic farmhouse and grounds are now an outdoor museum. A city-employed farm coordinator leads an army of volunteers maintaining the grounds, tending a "children's garden" (where kids are invited to look, touch, and taste), and teaching classes on gardening, art, cooking, and more. Lucky participants might also nab one of the coveted community garden plots (organic, of course). On top of all that, volunteers maintain a two-acre garden showcasing clematis vines from around the world.

In addition to the museum and classroom, this is also actually a farm, operated as a CSA (community-supported agriculture). Find more information about farm shares and a schedule of classes and farm events on the City of Lake Oswego's website (see Resources).

The 1.5-mile Hazelia Agri-Cultural Heritage Trail begins near the farmhouse, leading past interpretive panels reflecting the breadth of history and community here. The panels are uncommonly well done. If you have the energy, walk the whole thing.

The trail first leads east, paralleling Rosemont Road on a winding path to a grove of oaks and a trailhead for the Rosemont Trail. You could follow this all the way down to the city of West Linn if so inclined. For now, return to the farmhouse and follow the Heritage Trail west, past more historic farmsteads, to end at the Cooks Butte trailhead.

EXTEND YOUR VISIT

Cooks Butte, the big hill west of Luscher Farm, has an easy, scenic trail to the top—a 1-mile round-trip from the west end of the Hazelia Agri-Cultural Heritage Trail.

76 MARY S. YOUNG STATE PARK

Trails and superb river access are among this big park's many draws

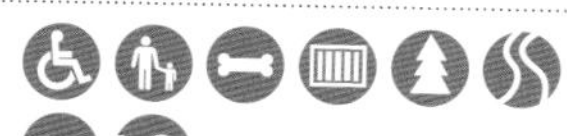

Location: 19900 Willamette Dr., West Linn
Acreage: 128
Amenities: Restrooms, sports fields, picnic shelters, dog off-leash area, dog-friendly beach, trails, paved paths, climbing rock
Jurisdiction: West Linn; Oregon State Parks

GETTING THERE

BY CAR I-5 to exit 297 (Terwilliger Blvd.) southbound; continue on Terwilliger Blvd. 4 miles to N. State St./OR 43; go right and travel through downtown Lake Oswego; past the stoplight at McVey Ave., continue 2.7 miles to the park entrance at left. **BY TRANSIT** ★★★ Bus 35 (Macadam/Greeley toward Oregon City Transit Center) to Willamette Dr. and Mapleton Dr. (stop 6300); look for the marked trail entering the park opposite, 100 feet down the road. **BY BIKE** ★

Of the parks fronting the Willamette River, this is one of my favorites. Though hemmed in on three sides by residential subdivisions, it is just big enough that you can imagine you are somewhere more remote. And a TriMet bus brings you right to the entrance.

From the parking area, the paved Riverside Loop Trail leads down to the beach. It is smooth, wide, and generally accessible, but steep in places. Several steeper soft-surface trails also lead to the river. Topography in this part of the park is surprisingly rugged, with ravines formed by Turkey and Mary S. Young Creeks cutting dramatically down to the river.

The beach is outstanding. Where Mary S. Young Creek flows into the Willamette, a river bar forms a lagoon of sorts, which is a perfect spot for kids to play in the sand and for dogs (allowed off leash in this area) to romp. A rocky outcrop studded with oaks divides this area from the beaches downstream and offers a

Miles of forest paths beckon at Mary S. Young State Park.

great vantage over the river, almost midstream. A river path continues downstream to a great swimming beach. From here, a footbridge connects to crescent-shaped Cedar Island. I love to picnic here. There's little shade, but a hint of wildness.

While the beach is the main draw, the park's trails (around 6 miles in total) are impressive. The 1.6-mile Heron Creek Loop provides a good overview. Mostly flat and well marked, it's perfect for amateur trail runners like me.

Near the parking area and the spacious dog off-leash area, look for a monument commemorating the Willamette Falls Railway. The line, built in the 1890s, carried Portland General Electric employees to the power station in West Linn. In 1904, it extended north to a riverfront amusement park called Magone's. With rental cottages; a floating dance floor; and rowboats for nighttime, waterborne assignations, one assumes it was a romantic destination.

River frontage in this neighborhood isn't cheap, so we're fortunate to have this park. It comes to us from Mary Hoadly Scarborough Young, a Lake Oswego resident who purchased this tract in the 1930s with ambitions of cattle ranching or building an estate. She had a change of heart, perhaps informed by her experience helping turn Lake Oswego's ruined iron smelter into what is now George Rogers Park. Shortly after that park opened, she and her husband donated this place to the state of Oregon. (A story, which I can't verify, claims she withheld the donation from the City of Lake Oswego out of spite over a disputed speeding ticket.) The state park, managed by West Linn, opened in the 1970s.

77 MELDRUM BAR PARK AND DAHL BEACH

Swimming, paddling, biking, and more where the Clackamas and Willamette Rivers meet

Location: 19 Meldrum Bar Park Rd., Gladstone
Acreage: 100
Amenities: Paved path, boat ramp, sports fields, restrooms, picnic tables, community garden, bike jumps, radio-controlled car course at Meldrum Bar Park; portable toilet at Dahl Beach
Jurisdiction: Gladstone

GETTING THERE

BY CAR SE McLoughlin Blvd./OR 99E south to Milwaukie; 4.6 miles south of the stoplight at SE Harrison St. and SE 17th Ave., go right onto SE Glen Echo Ave. (becomes River Rd.); right onto Meldrum Bar Park Rd. **BY TRANSIT** ★ MAX (Orange Line) to SE Park Ave.; then Bus 33 (McLoughlin/King toward Clackamas Community College) to McLoughlin and Gloucester (stop 10324); backtrack to go

Getting a jump start on summer at Dahl Beach

left at W. Gloucester St.; right onto River Rd.; immediate left onto Meldrum Bar Park Rd. to the park entrance (half-mile walk). **BY BIKE** ★★ Via Trolley Trail.

Meldrum Bar is a great place to wander along a beach, start a paddle trip, or swim. It takes its name from a gravel bar formed in the Willamette River by sediment spilling from the Clackamas River. During fishing season, the bar bustles with anglers.

Near the busy gravel bar and boat ramp, Meldrum Bar Park has a few unusual features. First is the BMX course, a maze of rolling berms and jumps. Conditions vary depending on weather and the attention paid by volunteers. When in shape it offers opportunities to catch epic air on a bike. There are a few beginner jumps, but it's mostly for experts and/or thrill-seeking types. Next to it is a miniature version of the BMX park, where intense-looking folks pilot small radio-controlled cars over jumps and obstacles. It looks ridiculous, but fun.

Back from the river, Meldrum has sports fields and a ho-hum playground. A paved path leads along the riverfront, parallel to Dahl Park Road and past a massive community garden, to some quieter access points on the Willamette.

The road ends at Dahl Beach, where the Clackamas River's clear, green water backs up against the Willamette to create a good swimming spot. The beach is wide, sandy in places and gravelly in others. In summer, the water is calm, with the main current running against the opposite bank. Thanks to the southern exposure, this spot is pleasant just about any time of year when the sun's out and the river is low enough to expose some beach.

Dahl Beach also makes a great launch point for paddling the lower Clackamas and the Willamette. One suggestion: launch a canoe or stand-up paddleboard and scoot across the Willamette's main channel to Goat Island, then work your way around to its quiet back channel. The island's downstream tip is a great place to stop for a picnic. Immediately opposite, in West Linn's Burnside Park, is a lovely meadow just up from the beach, another great spot to explore. The interior of Goat Island is also intriguing—but take care not to disturb the herons that often roost here.

78 HIGH ROCKS AND CROSS PARK

Swimming, picnicking, and questionable judgment along the lower Clackamas River

Location: 2 82nd Dr., Gladstone
Acreage: 1.5 (High Rocks), 5.6 (Cross Park)
Amenities: Restroom, paved paths (Cross Park)
Jurisdiction: Gladstone

GETTING THERE

BY CAR I-205 to exit 11 (Gladstone); west on 82nd Dr. a half mile to its end. **BY TRANSIT** ★★ MAX (Orange Line) to Milwaukie Main St.; then Bus 32 (Oatfield toward Milwaukie) to E. Arlington and Cornell (stop 132); walk two blocks south to the park. **BY BIKE** ★★

Just above its confluence with the Willamette, the Clackamas River squeezes through a narrow basalt gorge. This is High Rocks, a beloved swimming and fishing hole, where the river runs clear and deep between beautiful rock formations. I-205 zooms overhead a mere hundred yards away, adding a dull roar that diminishes, but doesn't ruin, the place's beauty.

I love the low cliffs, boulders, and ledges along this riverbank. They are dramatic in a low-key way, fit for a summer's day of exploration. That said, part of what makes High Rocks, well, *High Rocks*, is that on those summer days, hordes of people come here, many to jump off the cliffs. Often egged on by reckless friends (and sometimes alcohol, though in recent years the cops have stepped up enforcement), they routinely accomplish truly stupid feats.

(I will admit: I've jumped off some of these cliffs. It's fun. It's also dangerous. Submerged rocks and spooky currents routinely claim jumpers' lives. So come for the lovely water and, if inclined, the occasionally nail-biting spectacle—but please don't become a statistic.)

Just downstream from High Rocks is Cross Park, a more peaceful if less colorful spot, where you can enjoy a picnic at a proper picnic table and access the river from a gentler slope. There are shallow areas conducive to wading when the river level drops in summer. The park's eastern entrance is at the end of 82nd Drive, adjacent to a pedestrian bridge that leads over to the Clackamas River Greenway Trail, Clackamette Cove, and beyond to Oregon City.

Cross Park's western entrance is along East Clackamas Boulevard, where you'll find a restroom and more parking. From both ends, paths go down to a low, grassy bench along the river. If you are lucky enough to grab one of the picnic tables, enjoy. This is a prime spot to linger and swim.

EXTEND YOUR VISIT

The path in Cross Park continues west to Charles Ames Memorial Park and Gladstone's tidy main street, Portland Avenue. With its flashing stoplight, hardware store, tavern, and little post office, it could be a quiet Willamette Valley farm town. Only the gourmet coffee shop gives it away: this is—almost—Portland after all.

79 WILLAMETTE FALLS RIVERWALK

A cultural and scenic site of international significance . . . someday, hopefully

Location: SE McLoughlin Blvd./OR 99E and Main St., Oregon City
Acreage: 10
Amenities: Planned riverfront promenade through historic mill site, interpretive exhibits, restrooms, overlook on Willamette Falls
Jurisdiction: Metro; Oregon City; Confederated Tribes of Grand Ronde

GETTING THERE

BY CAR I-205 to exit 9 (Oregon City); left onto SE McLoughlin Blvd./OR 99E southbound; where McLoughlin curves east after the Arch Bridge, go right onto Main St. to reach the Riverwalk access point (subject to change as the design is finalized). **BY TRANSIT** ★★★ Bus 35 (Macadam/Greeley) to Oregon City Transit Center (stop 8762); walk six blocks southwest on Main St. to cross McLoughlin. **BY BIKE** ★

This is an admittedly unusual entry. It describes and promotes a park that does not yet exist. So why include it here? Simply put, Willamette Falls is the most important place in Oregon, maybe the entire Pacific Northwest, and it deserves a world-class park. My goal is to make you, dear reader, aware of this and urge you to learn about, advocate for, and visit the place.

Willamette Falls is the second-largest waterfall in the United States by volume, after Niagara. It used to be the third, until we drowned the Columbia River's great Celilo Falls behind a dam. Like Celilo, Willamette Falls has been a gathering place for millennia, where groups from across the Pacific Northwest and even beyond met to fish, trade, gamble, and share stories. It has been a busy, cosmopolitan site for longer than we have been a civilization. If Celilo Falls was London, Willamette Falls was Paris.

It was here that Oregon's "pioneer" history rightfully began as well; Oregon City was the first real town in Oregon and the endpoint of the Oregon Trail. The merchants who eventually built Portland got their start here. So did Oregon's first mills, powered by the falls. Mills of some sort or another—flour, lumber, paper—have operated here ever since.

Until 2011. That year, the Blue Heron Paper Mill declared bankruptcy and shut down. For the first time in 150 years, the east bank of the Willamette River at the falls went silent. No one knew what would come next, but everyone knew it would not be another mill. Some people envisioned condos and high-end stores, while others proposed bringing in a big-box store, figuring it would goose local tax revenues. Some even called for a national historical park. The problem was that none of these people owned the place—a bankruptcy court did. Given the pollution potentially buried under this century and a half of dirty activities, no one wanted to buy it.

Then, suddenly, a speculator snapped up the property for a song. He laid out grand plans and acted magnanimously toward the government agencies eager to secure public access, at long last, to the falls. Prestigious architects signed on and a public outreach campaign began. The resulting designs are fantastic. They depict a broad walkway atop basalt ledges leading past tastefully preserved industrial relics to a public gathering space and killer, close-up views of the falls. If the actual park ends up looking anything like this, it will instantly become the best public space in Oregon.

Unfortunately, the speculator proved to be, well, a speculator. He toyed with officials for years, wasting precious time and the public's money while falling behind on property taxes. Then something equally unexpected happened: he abruptly sold the property to the Confederated Tribes of Grand Ronde. Now, the land belongs to the people to whom it should always have belonged.

McLOUGHLIN PROMENADE

Relative to the millennia over which Native peoples have gathered at Willamette Falls, Oregon City is a newcomer. Still, it *was* the first incorporated city west of the Rocky Mountains—older than Portland, San Francisco, Seattle, and Los Angeles—and justly famous as the end of the Oregon Trail. Yet too few appreciate just how much history is here. A great place to experience this history is the McLoughlin Promenade, an elegant path perched atop basalt cliffs overlooking the sublime falls. Head to Main Street, filled with galleries, restaurants, and shops, and look for the Municipal Elevator.

Yes, a municipal elevator. Oregon City started on a narrow ledge immediately below Willamette Falls but quickly outgrew its perch. The city expanded onto the bluff above, necessitating an arduous walk up 722 steps. By 1912, citizens were tired of hoofing it and voted to build an elevator.

It was powered by water, despite the fact that Oregon City had already made history as the first locale in the United States to generate and transmit electricity over a long distance. Notoriously unreliable, the hydraulic elevator often stopped midway, forcing riders to evacuate via a small hatch in the bottom. The current elevator, with its wonderful midcentury modern aesthetic, replaced that rickety structure in 1955. According to the city, this is the only "vertical street" in North America.

After a short ride up, go right to reach the promenade. Lined with handbuilt stone walls, the path is a legacy of the Works Progress Administration, the Great Depression–era federal agency that put unemployed artisans to work building trails and public facilities across the country. To these workers we owe iconic places like Timberline Lodge on Mount Hood and Silver Falls State Park.

The promenade commemorates John McLoughlin. As superintendent of the British Hudson's Bay Company's Columbia Department, he was the de facto ruler of the Oregon Territory prior to American settlement. He built Fort Vancouver, oversaw the Pacific Northwest fur trade, and diligently steered Oregon Trail settlers to the Willamette Valley (and away from Puget Sound, which Britain hoped to retain). Later, sensing the inexorable tide of American settlement, he left the Hudson's Bay Company and helped establish Oregon City, becoming a leading citizen. McLoughlin's home, right across 7th Street from the promenade and elevator, is now a unit of the Fort Vancouver National Historic Site and open to the public.

The promenade leads approximately half a mile along the bluff, past Victorian homes and basalt outcrops, to end at a parking lot just north of Tumwater Drive. From here, you can cross over busy McLoughlin Boulevard on a pedestrian bridge to reach a viewpoint directly above the falls. Someday this will likely connect to the Willamette Falls Riverwalk.

If time and energy permit, explore the historic Singer Hill neighborhood east of the promenade. Its centerpiece is the Oregon City Library at 7th and John Adams Streets. One of the original Carnegie libraries, it has been carefully restored and expanded. Outside the library's new entrance is a compact park with a splash pad and play structure.

This is good news, but it adds uncertainty to the project. It is no longer clear, as of this writing at least, how the design might change and when it might get built. Patience is in order. Patience and polite pressure!

Oregon City, the region, the state, and the nation all deserve a high-caliber park here. Let's hope we get it.

80 CAMASSIA NATURAL AREA

A wonderland of oaks and camas on a flood-scoured ledge above Willamette Falls

Location: Walnut St., West Linn
Acreage: 27
Amenities: 1-mile trail network
Jurisdiction: Private

GETTING THERE

BY CAR I-5 to exit 297 (Terwilliger Blvd.) southbound; continue on Terwilliger Blvd. 4 miles to N. State St./OR 43; go right and continue through Lake Oswego to West Linn; cross underneath I-205 and bear right onto Willamette Falls Dr. (at the sign for "High School"); bear right onto Sunset Ave.; right onto Walnut St. to the parking area. **BY TRANSIT** ★★ Bus 35 (Macadam/Greeley toward Oregon City Transit Center) to Willamette Dr. and McKillican (stop 6339); walk up McKillican St. to West Linn High School; entrance to Camassia is at the south end of the school's football field. **BY BIKE** ★

Camassia Natural Area is owned by the Nature Conservancy. This little patch of woods and meadow, tucked behind the high school in suburban West Linn, has the distinction of being the global nature-conservation giant's first Oregon property,

Camas flowers paint the land purple at their namesake natural area.

which it purchased in 1962. Generations of conservancy volunteers have pulled ivy, cut blackberries, and generally loved this place.

It's easy to see why. Camassia feels like a revelation. The main entrance hides at the end of a residential street, where a small sign urges you to respect the neighbors' quiet. A nondescript opening in the trees admits you to a woodland and meadow dotted with camas flowers, mosses, exposed chunks of basalt, and stunted oak trees. I can't help but use the phrase "fairy landscape" to describe this, well, fairy landscape.

The main trail loops through the meadow and around seasonal wetlands to a viewpoint of Mount Hood. Almost directly below you, thousands of cars scream past on I-205. You can hear, but not see, them, as if the ocean were right there, out of sight. The trail continues across areas of exposed bedrock and meadows to an unusual (for this region) grove of quaking aspen. At a junction, stay left to complete the loop or go right to visit Wilderness Park (see below).

This strangely rockbound landscape, full of little trees, wet meadows, and (in April) a riot of purple camas flowers, owes its existence to the Missoula Floods. About fifteen thousand years ago, glaciers covering most of Canada extended icy fingers southward to Puget Sound and the Rockies. One such finger blocked off an entire valley near present-day Missoula, Montana. A body of water the size of Lake Erie formed behind this ice dam. Then the dam abruptly burst, unleashing a watery torrent equivalent to ten times the combined flow of all the world's rivers today.

Over three or four days, the flood swept westward, obliterating everything in its path. (The moonscape of Eastern Washington's Channeled Scablands is one result.) Rushing toward the ocean, the floods pushed through the Columbia River Gorge, backed up into the Willamette Valley, and submerged present-day Portland under as much as four hundred feet of water. The whole process repeated itself dozens of times over millennia.

The floods pushed repeatedly through the Willamette Narrows, where the river cuts a narrow cleft through the Tualatin Mountains just upstream from here. The surging waters scraped and scoured the rock, removing nearly all of the topsoil and leaving precious little on which plants could grow. The result is a beautiful, miniaturized landscape rich in rare plants.

EXTEND YOUR VISIT

Head north on the Terrace Trail to West Linn's Wilderness Park, where you can follow several miles of forested loop trails.

81 WHITE OAK SAVANNA

Find nature in the city on an oak-studded hillside above the Willamette River

Location: 2425 Tannler Dr., West Linn
Acreage: 20
Amenities: 1-mile trail, benches, nature play area (planned)
Jurisdiction: West Linn

GETTING THERE

BY CAR I-205 to exit 6 (10th St.); north on 10th St.; left at light onto Blankenship Rd.; immediate right onto Tannler Dr.; the park entrance trail is 200 yards up on the right. **BY TRANSIT** ★ Bus 35 (Macadam/Greeley) to Oregon City Transit Center; then (weekdays only) Bus 154 (Willamette/Clackamas Heights toward Willamette) to Blankenship and Tannler Dr. (stop 9297); walk up Tannler Dr. to the park entrance. **BY BIKE** ★

The White Oak Savanna is a small place, tucked on a suburban hill among homes, the freeway, and a shopping center. In my highly biased opinion, however, it's of more than purely local interest.

Just a few decades ago, this was countryside. When the I-205 freeway came through and the riverside hamlet of Willamette started growing uphill, the cows moved on and blackberries grew up. The forlorn ground seemed destined for development, likely of the soulless commercial kind. Most of the remnant oaks, struggling to survive the onslaught of invasive species, would come down. As local resident Roberta Schwarz liked to say (quoting Joni Mitchell), someone was bound to "pave paradise and put up a parking lot."

Roberta was determined to stop this. She lived up the street and admired the oaks. She couldn't stand the thought of them being cut down, or of more traffic on her already busy street. She called the mayor, local environmental groups, and even the landowner himself. Everyone expressed sympathy, but explained this place just wasn't worth saving.

For most people, that would be it. Roberta is not like most people. The polite but firm "no" set her teeth on edge and launched what would become a decade-long struggle to stem the tide of progress. Thanks to incredible persistence, a well-timed real estate crash, the help of loyal friends, and many, many bake sales, Roberta succeeded.

Oaks, camas, and river views at the White Oak Savanna

What might have been an office complex is, instead, a refuge for one of the city's last native oak stands. As ecologists start to understand just how important urban forests are for air quality and the resilience of native species to climate change, Roberta's efforts look less like NIMBYism and a lot more like wisdom. I encourage you to visit.

With help from the West Linn parks department and many youth crews, Roberta has waged an epic battle against Himalayan blackberries, removing the invaders to discover tiny oak saplings struggling hopefully through the weeds. They have since thrived and with luck, in a few centuries, will resemble the great grove of wolf trees at the property's center.

A 1-mile gravel trail, painstakingly constructed by Roberta and her volunteers, leads among these ancient oaks and up the hillside. At the top are big views across the Willamette Narrows, where the river squeezes through a canyon before plunging over Willamette Falls. Hand-crafted wooden benches line the trail, each honoring a donor to Roberta's fundraising campaign.

The city intends to install a nature play area here, which if built to its design will be among the region's best. It will be a fitting tribute to Roberta, who has introduced this place to hundreds of kids through a mind-boggling number of work parties. And it will honor the spirit that keeps people like Roberta going: the knowledge that we will only really love what we know, and will only protect what we really love.

82 WILLAMETTE PARK

Riverfront park accesses one of the region's best easy paddles

Location: 1100 12th St., West Linn
Acreage: 23
Amenities: Picnic shelters, restrooms, gazebo, stage, sports fields, volleyball courts, playground, splash pad, boat ramp and dock
Jurisdiction: West Linn

GETTING THERE

BY CAR I-205 to exit 6 (10th St.); south on 10th St.; right onto Willamette Falls Dr.; left onto 12th St. to the park. **BY TRANSIT** ★ Bus 35 (Macadam/Greeley) to Oregon City Transit Center; then (weekdays only) Bus 154 (Willamette/Clackamas Heights toward Willamette) to 10th St. and 8th Ct. (stop 9296); walk west on Willamette Falls Dr.; left onto 13th; cross Tualatin Ave. to enter park (half-mile walk). **BY BIKE** ★

I love West Linn's Willamette Park for several reasons. First is the setting: the Tualatin River, having lazed its way down the valley at a snail's pace, suddenly discovers a little gradient and rushes through riffles to join the Willamette River here. River confluences are magical places as far as I'm concerned, and this is no exception.

Second, the park itself is appealing. Its hub of activity is at 12th and Volpp Streets, tucked among a grove of cedars and Douglas-firs. Here you'll find rustic picnic shelters, a small stage where the parks department puts on concerts and movies in summer, an accessible play area, and a splash pad ringed by a low stone wall. It is an altogether pleasant spot and, unsurprisingly, gets busy at times.

Third, the park sits just downhill from the Willamette neighborhood's cozy, casually affluent main street along Willamette Falls Drive. You can take an easy walk from park to town and back along charming residential streets.

Best of all, though, is what awaits you a 1-mile paddle up the Willamette. Here, at the Willamette Narrows, the river has carved a small gorge through layers of hard basalt, squeezing among steep, forested walls and oak-dotted islands. It is arguably the best easy paddling destination around Portland.

From the park's boat ramp, officially known as Bernert Landing, paddle upstream along the near shore. The current in summer is noticeable but easy to overcome with a modicum of effort. You will pass several hideous mansions—thank goodness Willamette Park didn't fall prey to one of these!—before the woods close in. The Willamette narrows noticeably as the banks grow steeper. Soon, the forested slopes rise precipitously up four hundred feet. Aside from some powerlines and the distant hum of Highway 99, civilization mostly disappears.

Soon the islands come into view. First is Little Rock. Stay right to follow a narrow channel to a rocky inlet near the island's upstream end. This is one my favorite river spots, secluded and a bit exotic. It is a perfect picnic spot, but also very fragile. It will take only a few careless users to trash the place.

Farther upstream is Rock Island, with more basalt outcrops clad in sedum and flowers. I like to paddle to the upstream end and thread through narrow channels on river right to return downstream. It takes a little bit of paddling skill to pass through these constrictions, presuming the current isn't too strong. If it is, stick to the main river channel. If river levels are low, expect to get stuck (not unenjoyably) in a few places.

You could explore all day in these rocky, watery byways—taking care to keep a light touch. Return as you came.

83 GRAHAM OAKS NATURE PARK

Watch native habitat restoration in action at this regional park in the making

Location: 11825 SW Wilsonville Rd., Wilsonville
Acreage: 250
Amenities: Accessible restrooms, picnic shelter, trails (3 miles)
Jurisdiction: Metro

GETTING THERE

BY CAR I-5 to exit 283 (Wilsonville Rd.) westbound; 1.5 miles to the park at right. **BY TRANSIT** Doable, not recommended. **BY BIKE** ★

At Graham Oaks, a new natural area is taking shape. Metro acquired this 250-acre site decades ago to build a landfill, but changed course in the face of community opposition. Instead, they launched an ambitious effort to restore long-abandoned farm fields to a grassland dotted with oaks, of the sort that once blanketed the Willamette Valley.

When it officially opened in 2010, Graham Oaks Nature Park still looked pretty much like an old cornfield awaiting the bulldozers and homebuilders. One journalist quipped it should be called "Graham Oak" since there was, indeed, only one oak tree, surrounded by a newly planted crop of saplings and shrubs.

Fast-forward a decade and these plants—Oregon white oaks, Willamette Valley ponderosa pines, spirea, wild roses, and others—are starting to grow up. The one hundred million native grass and wildflower seeds Metro sowed are likewise making their presence known.

A great way to explore the park is via Metro's audio tour, recorded by local guidebook author Laura Foster. It starts at the parking area along Wilsonville Road, where there are restrooms and a picnic shelter. A short path leads to the Gateway Plaza, with interpretive signs and an overview of the park. Metro created these signs in coordination with the Confederated Tribes of Grand Ronde, whose members include descendants of the Kalapuyan people who lived here before Euro-American settlers expropriated their land.

The park's main route is the paved Tonquin Trail, which will eventually connect Graham Oaks to points north, including the Fanno Creek Greenway Trail. It leads past the stately Elder Oak, estimated at one hundred fifty to two hundred years old. Spur trails lead east to wetlands along Arrowhead Creek and west to a patch of old forest along Mill Creek, where a few of the Douglas-firs are as much as seven hundred years old. At both spots, as at the Elder Oak, benches and interpretive signs highlight the ecological edges and transition areas that make this park an inviting home for wildlife.

Squint and you can imagine this place in 2100, with the field covered in Elder Oaks, their spreading branches and massive trunks etching intricate patterns across the sky. If that's hard to imagine, consider the Lone Fir Cemetery—a cathedral of giant trees that, a century and half ago, had only one.

The future forest at Graham Oaks Nature Park

EXTEND YOUR VISIT

Next door to Graham Oaks is Villebois, Oregon's largest master-planned residential community. Its many paths and New Urbanist details make for an interesting walk. Prior to Villebois, the Dammasch State Hospital stood here. It was an old-school "insane" asylum, like its counterpart in Salem, the setting for the film of Ken Kesey's *One Flew Over the Cuckoo's Nest.* Doctors at Dammasch carried out electroshock therapy and forced sterilization on "defectives," e.g., epileptics, the developmentally disabled, psychotic patients, and convicted rapists. Amazingly, this modern-day eugenics program lingered into the 1980s. The state razed Dammasch in 2005, not long after a state employee "accidentally" shredded most of the hospital's records.

A mile-long tunnel connected Dammasch to the Callahan Center, a rehabilitation facility for injured state workers built in the 1970s. Callahan's hulking, bunker-like concrete building later housed the Living Enrichment Center, a New Age megachurch that went spectacularly bankrupt and shuttered in 2004. The building has since been demolished to make way for an expansion of Villebois.

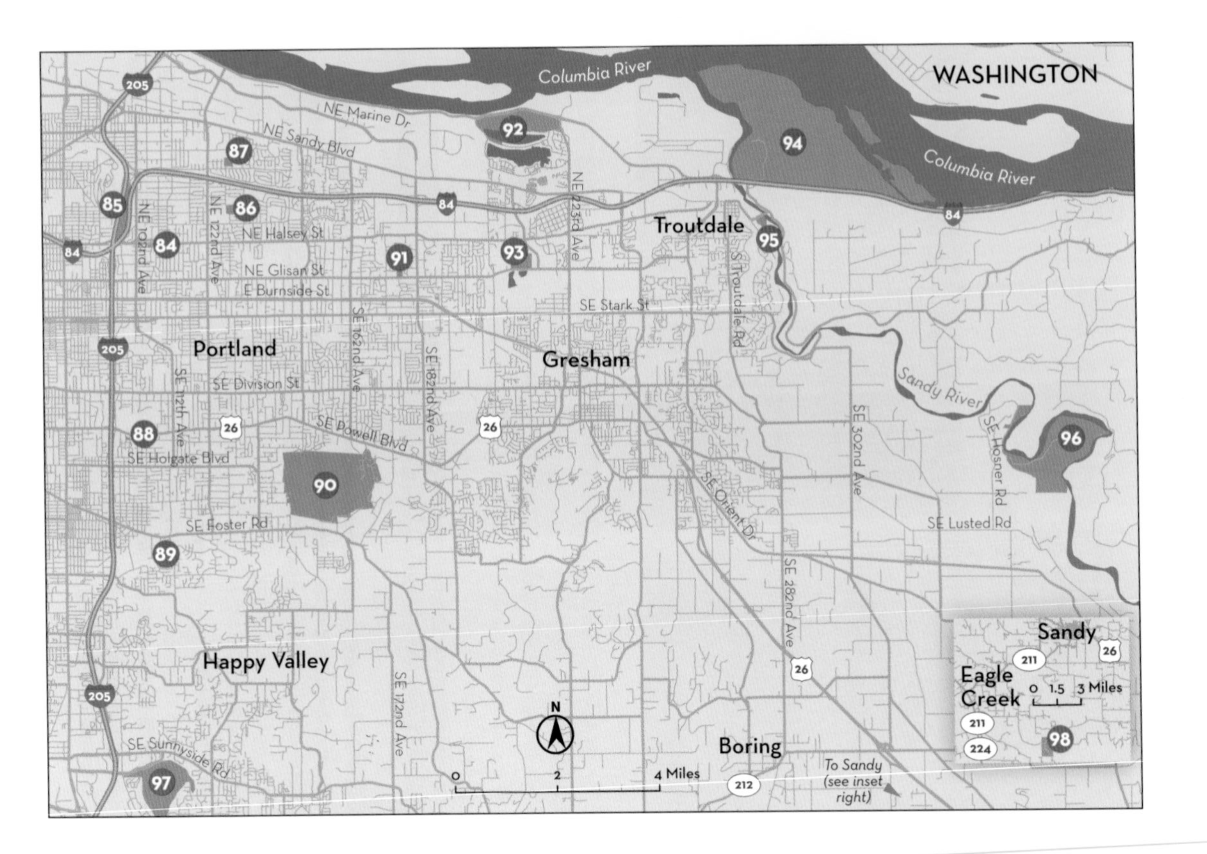
WASHINGTON
Columbia River
Columbia River
NE Marine Dr
NE Sandy Blvd
NE Halsey St
NE Glisan St
E Burnside St
SE Stark St
SE Division St
SE Powell Blvd
SE Holgate Blvd
SE Foster Rd
SE Sunnyside Rd
NE 102nd Ave
NE 122nd Ave
SE 112th Ave
SE 162nd Ave
SE 182nd Ave
NE 223rd Ave
S Troutdale Rd
SE Orient Dr
SE 172nd Ave
SE 282nd Ave
SE 302nd Ave
SE Hosner Rd
SE Lusted Rd
Sandy River
Portland
Gresham
Troutdale
Happy Valley
Boring
To Sandy (see inset right)
Sandy
Eagle Creek
0 1.5 3 Miles
0 2 4 Miles
N
84
205
26
211
212
224
84
85
86
87
88
89
90
91
92
93
94
95
96
97
98

EAST PORTLAND, GRESHAM, AND BEYOND

84 GATEWAY DISCOVERY PARK

Long-awaited urban park for a neighborhood in transition

Location: NE Halsey St. and NE 106th Ave.
Acreage: 3.2
Amenities: Plaza and lawn, restrooms, inclusive playground, skatepark, spray feature
Jurisdiction: Portland Parks and Recreation

GETTING THERE

BY CAR I-84 eastbound to exit 7 (Halsey/NE 99th Ave.); straight on NE Halsey St. to NE 106th Ave.; the park is on the right. **BY TRANSIT** ★★ MAX (Blue, Green, or Red Line) to Gateway Transit Center; walk east to NE 102nd Ave.; go left one block, then right onto NE Wasco St.; two blocks to the park (half-mile walk). **BY BIKE** ★★ Via I-205 Path.

Astride converging transit lines and freeways, with easy access to downtown and a quick escape to Mount Hood and the Columbia River Gorge, the Gateway neighborhood brims with potential. Portland's army of urban planners envision a more dense and pedestrian-oriented neighborhood than today's worn and charmless commercial strip. Brand-new Gateway Discovery Park heralds this change. It is beautiful and, for the time being, a bit out of place—an urban plaza without much "city" around it.

The park is a hybrid. The western half is a neighborhood park with native plantings ringing a brightly colored, turf-covered play area. This is the city's second barrier-free, inclusive play space. Harper's Playground, a nonprofit that created the inclusive play space at Arbor Lodge Park, advised on the design and helped raise funds to build it. The turf mound is an instant classic, mobbed by kids sledding down on cardboard scraps—an innovation probably not envisioned by the landscape architects. The elaborate splash pad helps compensate for a lack of shade here.

The park's eastern half is part lawn and part hardscape plaza reminiscent of downtown's Director Park. Portland Parks and Recreation programs this area in summer with kids' games, all-age dance classes, free concerts, tennis lessons, and more. Visit on a weekend and you will stumble onto something fun.

Cafe tables along 106th Avenue make a great place for snacking, chatting, and people watching. A food-cart pod planned for the lot next door will likely be ready by the time you read this.

This is a vibrant and appealing place. With luck, both current and future residents will get a chance to appreciate it as the city grows inexorably up around.

85 GATEWAY GREEN

Mountain biking and nature play in a former no-man's-land among freeways

Location: Along I-205 Multi-Use Path, Gateway neighborhood
Acreage: 25
Amenities: Mountain bike trails (3 miles), pump track, jump lines, portable toilet
Jurisdiction: Portland Parks and Recreation

GETTING THERE

BY CAR I-84 eastbound to exit 7 (Halsey/NE 99th Ave.); right onto NE 99th Ave.; park along 99th or surrounding streets; walk/bike along NE Multnomah St. to Gateway Transit Center; enter the I-205 Multi-Use Path and proceed north a quarter mile to the park entrance. **BY TRANSIT** ★★★ MAX (Red, Blue, or Green Line) to Gateway Transit Center, then follow directions above. **BY BIKE** ★★★ Via I-205 Path.

Gateway Green is still taking shape but the pump track is already a classic.

If you're looking for one of Portland's shockingly few places to mountain bike, come to Gateway Green. If not, visit anyway to enjoy the woods and watch this exciting new park take shape.

Gateway Green is unique in many ways. First, you can't drive there. The only access is via the I-205 bicycle and pedestrian path, about a quarter mile from the Gateway Transit Center. This is because the park fills a long, narrow strip of land completely encircled by freeways and rail lines.

In the 1940s, the county jail stood here, a hulking mass of basalt blocks blasted from the cliffs of Rocky Butte. It was demolished in the 1980s to make way for I-205, which crosses over, parallels, and merges with I-84 in a tangle of ramps and overpasses. These effectively cut off the former jail site from the surrounding city. It became a true no-man's-land, visited only by transients and trespassers. Drivers sped past, barely registering the overgrown forest and meadows.

Locals noticed, though. To them—residents of the Madison South, Hazelwood, and Parkrose Heights neighborhoods—it was the local woods. Affluent and established neighborhoods farther west had Mount Tabor Park, Forest Park, and the like. Why shouldn't they have something like that? After all, the marooned land was a nature park just waiting to happen.

There were plenty of reasons why a park wasn't viable: access constraints, tepid interest from the landowner (the state department of transportation), lack of money, a perception it was a no-go area, and more. Gateway Green's champions methodically checked each reason off the list. "Patient persistence"—that's how Linda Robinson, who alongside fellow resident Ted Gilbert has worked tirelessly since 2005 to create the park, describes it.

Linda and Ted imagined a natural area, not necessarily a mountain bike park. But in the long-running and often heated debate between mountain bikers and nature advocates over biking in Forest Park, Gateway Green emerged as a rare spot of agreement. In a city sorely lacking for trails, and in a neighborhood with plenty of kids lacking adequate access to parks, Gateway Green found its purpose.

With a lot of volunteer help and government support, the Friends of Gateway Green (see Resources) built a mountain biking trail network and a bike skills park called the Dirt Lab. Riders will find a pump track, jump lines, downhill-oriented "gravity" lines, and some traditional single track. There is also an innovative adaptive cycling feature for all riders, including those with disabilities.

Beyond biking, Gateway Green offers a nature play area, a lawn for picnics, and a restroom, all clustered around the new entrance plaza adjacent to the I-205 path. With hundreds of newly planted trees and ongoing construction, it retains a provisional feel. Still, it's already a great biking destination and is on its way to being a great park as well.

86 JOHN LUBY PARK

An urban refuge among giant trees

Location: NE 128th Ave. and NE Brazee St.
Acreage: 11
Amenities: Paths, picnic tables, play structure, restrooms
Jurisdiction: Portland Parks and Recreation

GETTING THERE

BY CAR I-84 eastbound to exit 10 (NE 122nd Ave.); left onto NE 122nd Ave.; left onto NE Russell St.; right onto NE 127th Ave. to park. **BY TRANSIT** ★★ MAX (Blue Line) to E. 122nd Ave.; then Bus 73 (122nd toward Parkrose/Sumner Transit Center) to NE 122nd and Brazee (stop 6620); walk north on NE 122nd Ave.; right onto NE

Russell St.; right onto NE 127th Ave. to the park. **BY BIKE** ★★ Via I-84 Pedestrian Path and NE 132nd Ave.

There's not a lot at John Luby Park: a patch of trees threaded with paths and bookended by a field in one corner and a modest playground in the other. But these trees are magnificent, and a rarity in this overdeveloped and underserved neighborhood. For views and flashy new play structures, visit nearby Luuwit View Park. At John Luby, expect a welcome quiet.

On clear winter afternoons, the light rakes at a low angle across the forest floor, setting the trees aglow. When the bitter east winds, scourge of East County, turn neighboring parks to wastelands, John Luby stays still and inviting. Giant Douglas-firs deflect winter rain, which trickles to earth in a fine mist. In summer, the park offers a cool refuge from the noise and heat of NE 122nd Avenue.

It's just big enough that if you lay out a picnic right in the center, you can forget you're in the midst of a sprawling city. Sit still, try some *shinrin-yoku* (that's "forest bathing" in Japanese—but keep your clothes on), and feel some gratitude that these woods escaped the bulldozer. Hard as it may be to imagine, most of East Portland once looked this way.

EXTEND YOUR VISIT

Jog the wooded, 2-mile soft-surface path at Metro's nearby Glendoveer Golf Course. You can also enjoy a round of footgolf (argyle socks recommended but not required). See www.playglendoveer.com for more details.

87 LUUWIT VIEW PARK

Mountain views, eye-popping colors, and more at this new community park

Location: NE 127th Ave. and NE Fremont St.
Acreage: 16
Amenities: Dog park, basketball courts, climbing structure, pavilion, picnic tables, Ping-Pong tables, play structure, public art, restrooms, running path, skatepark, spray feature
Jurisdiction: Portland Parks and Recreation

GETTING THERE

BY CAR I-84 eastbound to exit 10 (NE 122nd Ave.); right onto NE 122nd Ave.; right onto NE Fremont St.; left onto NE 127th Ave. to the park. **BY TRANSIT** ★★ MAX (Blue Line) to E. 122nd Ave.; then Bus 73 (122nd toward Parkrose/Sumner

Poised for flight, Mauricio Robalino's sculpture takes center stage at Luuwit View Park.

Transit Center) to NE 122nd and Fremont (stop 8907); walk four blocks east to the entrance at NE 127th Ave. **BY BIKE** ★★

The Argay Terrace neighborhood waited a long time for a park at this site, which for decades was an empty field sandwiched between an elementary school and Portland's last real urban farm. The park that finally opened in 2017 is called Luuwit (pronounced "loo-WIT") View, after the Chinook *Wawa* name for the volcano we know as Mount St. Helens.

The modern name comes courtesy of Captain George Vancouver, who sailed up the river in 1792. He took the liberty of renaming Luuwit after his friend, Alleyne Fitzherbert, the Baron St. Helens. Like his contemporaries Peter Rainier and

Samuel Hood, Fitzherbert never set foot anywhere near the Pacific Northwest. Unfortunately, Vancouver's name stuck nevertheless.

Luuwit View really feels like a destination, worth visiting from anywhere in the region. The park's centerpiece is a striking galvanized steel picnic shelter, a gleaming jumble of triangles designed to accommodate concerts, performances, and family gatherings. The sloping topography creates a natural amphitheater here, bookended by a play area and a stark mound capped by a soaring, abstract bird. It was created by Tacoma-based Ecuadorian artist Mauricio Robalino.

This assemblage, which practically screams "design," is out of context among the cul-de-sacs and midcentury ranch homes of quiet Argay Terrace. This is an urban space in a staunchly suburban setting.

But change is coming. After five generations of farming, the neighboring Rossi Farm is poised to sow a new crop of townhomes and commercial buildings on its thirty acres. If current plans come to fruition, it should be a dense, vibrant, and pedestrian-focused neighborhood strongly tied to the park.

The park is already plenty busy, especially the extensive play area. Along with a misting spray feature, it has elaborate woven-rope climbing structures, ground-level slides, foam-covered sculpted obstacles, and a variety of swings. It is both accessible and challenging to kids of many ages and abilities.

In the southwest corner is a capacious, fenced dog park with killer views of both Luuwit (Mount St. Helens) and Wy'East (more recently known as Mount Hood). On the opposite end, downhill, is a place denoted in park plans as the "teen area." It has a climbing wall, basketball courts, a skatepark, and one of my favorite elements: a trio of bubblegum-pink Ping-Pong tables. I wonder how well this color will age, but for the time being, the tables exuberantly frame winter views of snowy Luuwit. If there's a more grandiose setting for a Ping-Pong table, I'd like to see it.

88 ED BENEDICT PARK AND PORTLAND MEMORY GARDEN

Popular neighborhood park with a "green" skatepark and unique healing garden

Location: SE 104th Ave. and SE Powell Blvd.
Acreage: 13
Amenities: Garden, accessible play area and restroom, picnic tables, skatepark, basketball court, sports fields
Jurisdiction: Portland Parks and Recreation

Gathering to reflect and reminisce at the Portland Memory Garden

GETTING THERE

BY CAR I-205 to exit 19 (Powell Blvd.) eastbound; right onto SE 104th Ave. and immediate right into the park. **BY TRANSIT** ★★★ Bus 9 (Powell Blvd. toward Gresham Transit Center) to SE Powell and 102nd (stop 4562) and the park. **BY BIKE** ★★★ Via I-205 Path.

Ed Benedict Park spans three blocks along SE Powell Boulevard, just east of I-205 at the base of Kelly Butte. The state bought these parcels to build the Mount Hood Freeway, which would have plowed a gash through Southeast Portland had citizens not mobilized to stop it. Thanks largely to the efforts of Ed Benedict, a local resident and state legislator, the land was repurposed as a park.

The park's most interesting feature, and the reason I include it here, is the Portland Memory Garden. This half-acre garden is specifically for people living with Alzheimer's and other memory disorders, and their caregivers. As a sign near the entrance explains, the garden "provides four seasons of plants and flowers in raised beds that have been chosen to stimulate the senses and to spark past memories." At the time of its opening in 2002, it was one of only eight such parks in the nation. Portland is fortunate to have this place, which I suspect is not widely known among park-goers.

Enter at the corner of 104th Avenue and SE Bush Street. An elegant black fence surrounds the garden, providing a safe space for visitors to wander the oval path looping a central courtyard. Restrooms and a water fountain are nearby. The plants' scents, textures, and colors invite meditation and reverie; the experience, as Marcel Proust put it, is of "utmost profundity, evanescence, and mystery—with a quiet suggestion of infinity." As it was intended, the garden feels like a place outside of time.

By contrast, the rest of Ed Benedict Park typically thrums with action. The soccer fields, basketball courts, and tree-ringed play area all see a lot of use in this kid-heavy neighborhood.

At the park's northwestern end is its other unique feature: a "green" skatepark that captures its own storm water via a swale planted with vine maple, cedars, and other wet-tolerant plants. The plantings run down the center of the skatepark, with additional swales collecting runoff from Powell Boulevard. I find it especially satisfying to watch skateboarders catching air over a little stream flowing among sedges and grinding on curbs within arm's reach of native trees and shrubs.

89 LEACH BOTANICAL GARDEN

Historic estate in a lush creek canyon with trails and gardens

Location: 6704 SE 122nd Ave.
Acreage: 17
Amenities: Garden (tours available), paths, restrooms, gift shop; note: park is closed Mondays
Jurisdiction: Portland Parks and Recreation

GETTING THERE

BY CAR I-205 to exit 17 (SE Foster Rd.) eastbound; right onto SE 122nd Ave.; right into parking lot just across a bridge over Johnson Creek. **BY TRANSIT** ★★ MAX (Green Line) to Lents/SE Foster; walk down stairs to cross Foster Rd. and SE Woodstock Blvd.; at Woodstock, take Bus 73 (122nd Ave. toward Parkrose/Sumner Transit Center) to SE 122nd and Foster (stop 6626); walk a quarter mile south on SE 122nd Ave. **BY BIKE** ★★

At the risk of exceeding my quota, I hereby declare Leach Botanical Garden a "must-see" among Portland parks. It's neither more beautiful nor more significant than peers like Hoyt Arboretum or Elk Rock Garden, but it is somehow more exquisite, its splendor more compressed and concentrated. This characteristic still surprises me after repeat visits.

Outside the Manor House at Leach Botanical Garden (Photo by Mary Edmeades)

Part of what makes the garden so remarkable is that it seems somehow secret. One of East Portland's thoroughfares is 122nd Avenue, lined with big-box stores, car dealerships, and largely soulless apartment buildings. Yet when the wide, windswept avenue crosses equally charisma-challenged Foster Road, it abruptly narrows and dips into a wooded ravine, as if determined to get out of town. If you blink, you miss the little bridge over Johnson Creek and the wrought-iron gate marking the entrance to "Sleepy Hollow"—the garden.

Park at the lot just over that bridge and walk through that gate. You'll soon arrive at a little white manor, understated but enchanting. This was home to John and Lilla Leach, he a pharmacist and she an eminent botanist. They built this home in 1937 and lived here until the early 1970s. The garden is a living memorial to their lives spent botanizing across the Northwest and above all in Southern Oregon's Siskiyou Mountains. The home is now a visitor center, gift shop, and event venue. You can pick up a self-guided walking tour brochure here.

Enclosed in forest, the garden's many paths reward slow walking and close looking. Paths lead uphill, past a rock garden, to the main collections. Here are over a hundred fern varieties, heathers (including species endemic to the Siskiyous, discovered by Lilla), medicinal herbs, bamboo, wildflowers from across the region, and much more, packed into a few captivating acres.

From the entrance and the terrace next to the manor house, cobbled paths lead downhill to Johnson Creek and a small footbridge. Across the creek is an almost impossibly charming stone house, John and Lilla's summer cottage. Park benches just beyond offer a vantage from which to admire the manor and garden.

Although this place has been in city ownership since 1972, only in recent years has it started to shake its reputation as the "secret garden." Recognizing it, at last, as an underappreciated treasure in a neighborhood too long neglected, the city and the nonprofit garden leaders have embarked on a major renovation and expansion. New elements include an elevated "forest canopy" walkway, a much-needed parking lot expansion, and a work by sculptor Michihiro Kosuge called *Contemplative Place*, a collection of massive basalt blocks marking points of the compass.

The secret garden is getting even better, and ever less secret.

90 POWELL BUTTE NATURE PARK

Panoramic views, trails, and open space at East Portland's best natural area

Location: SE Powell Blvd. and SE 162nd Ave.
Acreage: 611
Amenities: Restrooms, approximately 12 miles of trails, nature center
Jurisdiction: Portland Parks and Recreation

GETTING THERE

BY CAR I-205 to exit 19 (Powell Blvd.) eastbound; right onto SE 162nd Ave. and park entrance road; continue a half mile uphill to the parking area. **BY TRANSIT** ★★★ Bus 9 (Powell Blvd. toward Gresham Transit Center) to SE Powell and 162nd Ave. (stop 13957); walk up the entrance road a half mile to the visitor center. Alternative access: Bus 17 (Holgate/Broadway toward Holgate/134th Dr.) to SE Holgate and 136th (stop 2708); walk east one block to the Holgate trailhead. **BY BIKE** ★★★ Via Springwater Corridor.

Powell Butte is the best place to hike within city limits on Portland's East Side. An extinct volcanic cinder cone that rises above the surrounding city, it is an island of open space in a sea of residential development. Powell Butte's steep sides are cloaked with forest; most of its wide, gentle summit is a meadow. This diversity of topography and vegetation offers a variety of experiences, from wide-open rambling to secluded forest switchbacks. Mountain bikers, trail runners, dog walkers, birders, picnickers, and urban naturalists all find reasons to treasure the place.

Most people start at the small visitor center next to the parking area, with restrooms and exhibits telling the butte's story. A nineteenth-century farm laboriously cleared from the forest, it was acquired nearly a century ago by the city for a future reservoir. Dairy farmers leased the land from the city and grazed cows on the butte well into the 1970s, when subdivisions already climbed its flanks. The reservoir was built in 1981, with a second in 2014. The land is now officially a water facility *and* a nature park.

From the visitor center, the Mountain View Trail leads three-quarters of a mile up a paved and gently graded path to the butte's high point. A toposcope, or mountain finder, identifies the many buttes and summits visible on a clear day. The mountains are impressive enough, but what's really special about this view is how expansive it feels, balanced between the buttes east of Portland and the Willamette River's broad basin. It feels higher and more exposed than the six hundred feet of elevation would suggest. The summer sun can be intense, the winter east winds bitter. Dress accordingly.

From the top, trails fan out in every direction. Head east then south on Summit Lane for an easy loop around the summit to Meadowland Lane, passing abandoned orchards and oak savannas. Or head straight west to the Douglas-fir Trail, leading down switchbacks into the forest. From here you can complete an approximately 3.5-mile loop via the Cedar Grove and Elderberry Trails that will rival any hike of similar distance in the Columbia River Gorge or the West Hills.

If you get away from the crowds (and keep your dog on leash), you will be surprised at just how much wildlife lives here. I've seen pheasants, turkey vultures, more banana slugs and woolly bears than I can count, and plenty of deer. I'm told that with stealth and a little luck, you can spot a coyote or even a gray fox. I'll keep trying.

91 NADAKA NATURE PARK

Woods, nature play, and community

Location: NE Glisan St. at NE 176th Ave.
Acreage: 12
Amenities: Restrooms, nature play area, picnic areas, trails
Jurisdiction: Gresham

GETTING THERE

BY CAR I-84 to exit 13 (NE 181st Ave.) southbound; continue on NE 181st Ave. for 1 mile, then right onto NE Glisan St.; parking lot (at St. Aidan's Episcopal Church) is at right after two blocks. **BY TRANSIT** ★★ Max (Blue Line) to E. 172nd Ave.; walk

Impromptu parade at Nadaka Nature Park. (Photo courtesy of Billy Hustace and Friends of Nadaka)

north on NE 172nd Ave.; cross NE Glisan St. and go right to reach the park (two-thirds of a mile walk). **BY BIKE** ★

Nadaka Nature Park is a precious patch of woods in a neighborhood otherwise sorely lacking them. Located off a dreary stretch of NE Glisan Street in Gresham's Rockwood neighborhood, it's a modest place many people haven't heard of. They should, because in addition to its little forest, Nadaka has one of the region's best nature play areas.

The Rockwood neighborhood has more people of color and more children per capita than nearly anywhere else in the region. It also has precious few developed parks. In flusher times, Gresham acquired parkland like these woods, which were previously home to the Camp Fire organization's "Nature Day Kamp." (NaDaKa, get it?) Budgets have since tightened, Gresham's parks department has withered, and many park properties remain minimally developed or still vacant.

Such was the case with Nadaka. Tucked away on a neighborhood street, it was little known and little loved. When I first saw the place in 2008, it was frankly pathetic: ten acres of ivy-infested trees surrounded by chain-link and razor wire fencing. (The fence kept out illicit activity by keeping out *all* activity. Nature Day Kamp had come to look like prison camp.) Thousands of residents, many of them kids lacking anything green within walking distance, lived a stone's throw from this nature preserve and could hardly access it.

Then, the owner of a small, vacant parcel between Nadaka and Glisan Street passed away. A "for sale" sign went up, and with it an opportunity to connect the park to the neighborhood, make a proper entrance, and take down that fence. Neighborhood associations, the adjacent St. Aidan's Episcopal Church, the Portland Audubon Society, and others joined forces to launch the Friends of Nadaka Nature Park. In the depths of the Great Recession, with public budgets under unprecedented strain, they convinced Gresham's leaders to support their vision for a place that would welcome neighbors rather than shut them out.

The Friends of Nadaka led a community-based effort to transform that little vacant lot into a full park. Several years, thousands of volunteer hours, and a million dollars later, Nadaka boasts Gresham's largest community garden, a (mostly) restored forest, and a universally accessible play area made entirely of natural materials. Highlights include a log-climbing structure in the shape of an indigenous longhouse and a rock garden with sand and a water pump for river making.

The Friends, who manage the park with the city, want it to "nurture nature, food, and families." They program park activities around this vision. For the park's many immigrant neighbors who have come here from rural places, this often means establishing a garden they can work with multiple generations of family, to perhaps re-establish a connection to land that was lost when they settled in their adopted home. Visit their website (see Resources) to view the events calendar and support the park.

92 BLUE LAKE REGIONAL PARK

Hugely popular regional park with beach, boats, play areas, and more

Location: 21224 NE Blue Lake Rd., Fairview
Acreage: 185
Amenities: Paths, restrooms, swimming beach, fishing pier, play areas, splash pad, paved and gravel paths (2 miles), disc golf course, basketball and volleyball courts, sports fields, picnic shelters and tables, seasonal paddleboat and canoe rentals, native plant discovery garden, wetlands with boardwalk and overlook
Jurisdiction: Metro

A rare moment of calm on the lakefront path at Blue Lake Regional Park

GETTING THERE

BY CAR I-84 to exit 14 (Fairview Pkwy.) northbound; right onto Sandy Blvd.; left onto NE 223rd Ave.; left onto NE Blue Lake Rd.; left into the park. Parking fee. **BY TRANSIT** Doable, not recommended. **BY BIKE** ★★★ Via Marine Drive Path/40-Mile Loop to the park's north entrance.

Blue Lake Regional Park is a blockbuster, welcoming as many as fifteen thousand visitors on a peak day. The crowds can get thick, but it's precisely these languid days when Blue Lake is at its best. This is a true urban getaway, a park for the people. Come ready to celebrate Portland's all-too-brief summer with a beautiful cross section of our community.

The park has what is probably the best lake-swimming beach in the city. There's no lifeguard, but conditions are safe for all but the youngest swimmers. Next door is a fishing pier (the lake has resident bluegill, bass, and crappie, with trout stocked seasonally). On warm days between Memorial Day and Labor Day, you can rent a paddleboat, rowboat, or canoe here for a reasonable fee. This is a great way for beginners to get started with zero hassle.

Like the Columbia Slough, Blue Lake receives water underground from the Columbia River. The Great River of the West exerts incredible force against its bed, pushing water through gravel and cobblestones to rise as springs along its banks. In addition to these springs, Blue Lake used to receive water aboveground from the Columbia's seasonal floods. In 1939, a levee was built and stopped this. Cut off from the river's annual flushing, Blue Lake grew more stagnant and has struggled with water quality ever since. Fortunately, Metro closely monitors the lake to ensure safe swimming.

The park has a *lot* going on beyond the lake. The eighteen-hole disc golf course is "gold" rated and popular with novices and experts alike. Picnic tables are seemingly everywhere. A cluster along the lakefront are first come, first served but many of the picnic shelters require reservations. There are four(!) different play areas, including a nature play area near the boat rental. It's not elaborate, but the inverted root wad is attractive, and the pile of wood keeps kids occupied building forts. The splash pad, near the beach and restrooms, and complete with water cannons, is beloved.

At the west end, farther from the crowds, a trail leads through wetlands to a viewing platform. That this area is quiet on even the busiest days adds a great dimension to the park.

From the wetlands, a second loop extends south to the park's far corner. Here, along the lake's western shore, stand a pair of carved cedar columns framing a view of Mount Hood. Nearby are benches in the shape of cedar canoes and a basalt sculpture of a sinker weight, of the sort used to hold fishing nets. These are a memorial to the Chinookan village of Nichaqwli. It stood near here until the 1830s, when its inhabitants, like many of the forty thousand or so people who lived along the lower Columbia, perished in an epidemic of malaria.

As I write these words, under a stay-at-home order due to the COVID-19 pandemic, I struggle to imagine what it must have been like to endure such a catastrophe. I pay my respects and hope for better days, free from care, spent at Blue Lake's beguiling beach.

93 SALISH PONDS WETLAND PARK

Wander among wetlands, ponds, and a creek through a recovering landscape

Location: NE Fairview Pkwy. and NE Glisan St., Gresham
Acreage: 70
Amenities: Trails, benches, viewing dock
Jurisdiction: Fairview

Nature is thriving at this former gravel quarry.

GETTING THERE

BY CAR I-84 to exit 14 (Fairview Pkwy.) southbound; continue 1 mile; right onto NE Glisan St., then immediately right into the "Lodges at Lake Salish" apartment complex; park parking is at left. **BY TRANSIT** ★★ Bus 77 (Broadway/Halsey toward Troutdale) to NE Halsey and Fairview Pkwy. (stop 2415); backtrack and cross Fairview Pkwy.; follow it south 100 yards to an access road leading down to the Salish Ponds Trail. **BY BIKE** ★★★ Via Gresham-Fairview Trail or I-84 Pedestrian Path.

At Salish Ponds Wetland Park, nature is taking root after years of neglect. The land was extensively quarried in the 1950s to build I-84 nearby. When construction was complete, mining dwindled, ending altogether in the early 1980s. Ignored for a decade, the pits finally ended up with the City of Fairview, which combined them with adjacent wetlands as a park.

For years, the ponds were mostly known for ludicrously easy fishing, thanks to annual stocking by the Oregon Department of Fish and Wildlife. Erosion along the shores eventually led the state to cease pond stocking. In 2008, Fairview secured a grant from Metro, the regional government, to restore the denuded banks and upgrade the trails. In the years since, nature has continued to tip the balance from "no-man's-land" to "urban wilderness."

The 0.65-mile East Pond Trail loops (you guessed it) the east pond, often bustling with waterfowl and still popular with anglers. This is a great path for jogging. At a junction north of the pond, the Salish Ponds Trail continues north along Fairview Creek through a wetland of ash, willow, and cattails. Don't be surprised to spot a coyote prowling around. Follow the trail underneath Fairview Parkway, past the parking lot for Target, and into a patch of woods with cedars, Douglas-firs, and oaks. This is a lovely spot, tucked away from the surrounding subdivisions. It's the kind of woods every kid needs near home.

EXTEND YOUR VISIT

Across a covered bridge, continue if you like to Fairview Community Park, a petite park next to Fairview's slightly surreal New Urbanist town center. You'll find restrooms, a small lawn with a gazebo and picnic tables, and a decent play structure. (From the ponds to here is about three-quarters of a mile.) Then backtrack to the ponds.

94 SANDY RIVER DELTA

A paradise for walkers, birders, and dogs, laced with paths exploring the river's floodplain

Location: Historic Columbia River Hwy., Troutdale
Acreage: 1400
Amenities: Restrooms, trails, public art, river access
Jurisdiction: US Forest Service

GETTING THERE

BY CAR I-84 to exit 18 (Lewis and Clark State Recreation Site); right at the stop sign to loop underneath the freeway; continue straight on frontage road into the park. **BY TRANSIT** ★ Bus 77 (Broadway/Halsey toward Troutdale) to NW Graham/257th and 257th Way (stop 9470); walk north past the Columbia Gorge Outlets and go right onto the pedestrian path paralleling the freeway; cross over the Sandy River and go left at a junction to cross under the freeway; continue east along the frontage road into the park (three-quarter-mile walk). **BY BIKE** ★★★ Via Marine Drive Path/40-Mile Loop to I-84 pedestrian bridge over the Sandy River.

At the edge of the Columbia River Gorge National Scenic Area, the Sandy River Delta offers wide-open spaces for rambling and running your dog.

The Sandy River spills from a glacier high on Mount Hood, carrying enormous quantities of silt. At its confluence with the Columbia, it drops this silt to form a vast delta. During the twentieth century, the delta was diked, drained, grazed, nearly developed as an industrial park, and then left to be overrun with invasive plants.

A new chapter started in 1990 when the US Forest Service bought the land as a gateway to the national scenic area. With help from the Friends of the Sandy River Delta (see Resources), they have been gradually restoring it. Now it's a great place to wander, welcoming people and their four-legged friends. The Forest Service likes to remind visitors this isn't a dog park. While that's technically true, this place is as close to dog Valhalla as you'll find anywhere. Expect to encounter *lots* of dogs running joyously off leash. This opportunity is what attracts the majority of visitors.

Several trails lead from the parking area. The Confluence Trail, wide and the most accessible, goes one and a quarter miles to the Columbia River, ending at an elegant bird blind raised above the forest floor. Designed by landscape architect Maya Lin, it's one of six public artworks along the lower Columbia River that make up the Confluence Project (see Resources). Each work references a passage from Lewis and Clark's journal of their 1805–1806 journey through the Pacific Northwest. Inscribed in the bird blind's locust wood slats are names of wildlife species Lewis and Clark spotted. It's a poignant reflection on what has been lost and what has endured in this landscape.

Note that dogs must stay on leash on the Confluence Trail. (They are allowed off leash everywhere else except the parking lot.) Two other trails also lead to the bird blind. The Boundary Trail (1.5 miles one way) mostly parallels the Confluence Trail, offering a dog-friendly approach. The Meadow Trail (2 miles one way) leads to a broad clearing, crosses the Confluence Trail, and then strikes east to leave the crowds behind. This stretch can be wet in winter and a little overgrown in spring, but is worth exploring.

The Ranch Dike Trail (1.25 miles one way) winds through woods to the 1000 Acres Road (closed to vehicles), then runs atop an old dike to join the Confluence Trail. Sheltered and raised above the floodplain, it's great on wet days or when the famous Columbia River Gorge winds blow.

The Old Channel Trail, my favorite, runs three-quarters of a mile from the Confluence Trail to the 1000 Acres Road along the Sandy's historical "upper" channel, which was blocked by a dam in 1932. The channel has recently been restored and is now actively scouring the floodplain. It's a great spot to watch a living river at work.

Beyond 1000 Acres Road, the Old Channel Trail continues west across a low area to the main or "lower" river channel. At high water this area can be inaccessible, but when reachable it's a delightful pandemonium of dogs playing, swimming, and digging in the sand. There may be no happier canines in the Portland metro area than right here.

From this beach you can continue upriver to complete a loop. Be warned, there are often homeless encampments on this stretch of river. Over many visits I've yet to encounter an unfriendly person, but the area is undeniably intimidating. Most walkers prefer to backtrack along the Old Channel Trail to the 1000 Acres Road.

EXTEND YOUR VISIT

Just upstream along the Sandy River, the Lewis and Clark State Recreation Site offers picnic facilities, rock climbing on Broughton Bluff, and developed river access for boating and swimming.

95 GLENN OTTO COMMUNITY PARK

Popular swimming hole on the Sandy River, with room to wander

Location: 1102 E. Historic Columbia River Hwy., Troutdale
Acreage: 6.4
Amenities: Seasonally guarded swimming beach, trails, picnic tables, play area, meeting hall, restrooms
Jurisdiction: Troutdale

GETTING THERE

BY CAR I-84 to exit 18 (Lewis and Clark State Recreation Site); left at stop sign onto Historic Columbia River Hwy.; after a half mile, right to cross the Sandy River; first left into park. **BY TRANSIT** ★★ MAX (Blue Line) to Gresham Transit Center; transfer to Bus 80 (Kane/Troutdale Rd.) to the park (stop 13314, end of the line). **BY BIKE** ★★ Via Marine Drive Path/40-Mile Loop, I-84 pedestrian bridge, and Historic Columbia River Hwy.

Troutdale's Glenn Otto Community Park is one of the best and most popular swimming holes in the region. You can take a city bus straight there, wander a few

Warming up before a cold swim at Glen Otto Park

hundred yards to a sandy beach, and jump into the clear and cold Sandy River. In the heat of summer, plan for a crowd.

The Sandy flows from a glacier high on Mount Hood and through rugged canyons before spreading in its delta. At the river's last big bend, where it deflects against the unyielding rock of Broughton Bluff, it creates an eddy at river left, perfect for swimming.

At low water, that is. In early summer, hot temperatures routinely tempt unwary swimmers into cold, swift glacial snowmelt. The result has too often been fatal. Later in summer, flows drop, the current slows, and the water becomes merely cool, rather than dangerously frigid. From Memorial Day to Labor Day, the park has lifeguards on duty from 10 AM to 8 PM—but don't let their presence lull you into complacency.

From the parking lot, the main trail drops down to the floodplain and soon reaches the beach. Next to it, a paved path to the right stays on high ground, passing a caretaker's house to reach a charming green with picnic shelters and a play structure. This part of the park, skipped by the hordes heading to the beach, is very appealing.

MULTNOMAH FALLS IS CALLING, AND YOU MUST GO

This is a guide to Portland-area parks. So why highlight *the most visited natural site* in the Pacific Northwest, 30 miles east of the city and mobbed by two million people each year? Especially when there are literally dozens of other world-class waterfalls nearby?

Well, three reasons. First, it's *Multnomah Falls!* Every Portlander needs to see Oregon's most iconic cateract. Period. It's your civic duty. We nearly lost this place to the Eagle Creek Fire in 2017 and should never take it for granted.

Second, it's quite easy to reach by public transit. Just catch the Columbia Gorge Express bus from the Gateway Transit Center in East Portland. Given how insanely hard it can be to find parking near the falls, you're wise to choose public transit even if you have a car.

Third, great recreation options abound within a short walk or bike ride of the falls.

So, rather than offer the falls a perfunctory glance as you whiz past on the freeway, or join in a carmageddon parking battle, why not load your bike on the bus and spend a day exploring the area at human speed? That's doing it Portland style!

When you arrive, you must immediately visit the century-old Benson Bridge, located between the falls' two sections up a short, paved trail. You may have to wait patiently in line for your selfie here, but honestly it's worth it. This is simply a spectacular place—especially in winter when the creek is in flood. The air positively vibrates with the water's roar. Elemental forces are on thunderous display, serenely uninterested in the hopes and fears of the humans crowding its base.

From the bridge, you can continue on a steep trail (#441) to the upper falls and, if you are up for it, complete a strenuous 5-mile loop through the Mark O. Hatfield Wilderness to Wahkeena Falls. You'll encounter more waterfalls and dizzying, at times downright precipitous, drop-offs. You will also see ubiquitous evidence of the Eagle Creek Fire's devastation—and signs of the forest's recovery.

If that sounds too ambitious, do the loop in reverse to reach Wahkeena Falls in a relatively flat mile on a trail (#442) paralleling the Historic Columbia River Highway. This is only the closest of many incredible hiking options nearby. Regardless of itinerary and ambition, don't forget to stop at the historic Multnomah Falls Lodge, built in 1924, for ice cream, restrooms, and a souvenir. This could be a fine end, or brilliant beginning, to a human-powered day of Gorge adventure.

Sooner or later, though, you'll want to visit the water. Head downhill on the main path to reach the beach. If the crowds are too thick, wander upstream, where more beaches await.

If solitude is what you're mostly after, consider visiting in fall. The crowds have thinned, but the river is still low enough that the gravel bars invite roaming, and the swimming is still good. Unmarked, but obvious, trails continue upstream about a quarter mile to a gravel bar and then wind back among willows for a three-quarter-mile loop.

EXTEND YOUR VISIT

If Glenn Otto's beach is just too busy, try Lewis and Clark State Recreation Site across the river and downstream. Or, walk up the road a quarter mile to visit the Troutdale Historical Society's Harlow House. From here, a trail leads up the surprisingly wild Beaver Creek Canyon for about a mile (one way).

96 OXBOW REGIONAL PARK

Superb natural area in a forested canyon on the Sandy River

Location: 3010 SE Oxbow Pkwy., Gresham
Acreage: 1000
Amenities: Restrooms (with showers), picnic areas and shelters, campground (open year-round), boat launch, trails (12 miles), play structure, naturalist programs; note: entrance fee
Jurisdiction: Metro

GETTING THERE

BY CAR I-84 to exit 17 (Troutdale); follow NW Frontage Rd. to Graham Rd. southbound; left onto Historic Columbia River Hwy. into downtown Troutdale; right onto Buxton Rd. (becomes S. Troutdale Rd.); after 3.2 miles, bear left onto SE Division Dr.; after 1.5 miles, bear right onto SE Oxbow Dr.; after 2.2 miles, left onto SE Hosner Rd. to the park entrance. **BY TRANSIT** None. **BY BIKE** ★ Scenic, challenging route via SE 302nd Ave. and SE Oxbow Dr.

Oxbow Regional Park fills a giant bend in the Sandy River, at the downstream end of its wild gorge. Barely forty-five minutes from downtown Portland, it's as good as or better than plenty of state or even national parks.

The best thing about Oxbow is the Sandy River itself, federally designated as "Wild and Scenic." Rising on Mount Hood, it flows cold and swift, collecting the

Salmon River before entering a remote canyon. Roads are few and distant, leaving the floodplain intact. The park's 4 miles of river frontage include bluffs, wooded shores, and vast gravel bars. From most of the park's beaches you can't see a single sign of civilization.

Aside from the river, Oxbow Park has excellent hiking, with a river-level trail running the length of the park and a loop through vanishingly rare low-elevation old-growth forest. The campground, picnic areas, and play area are all excellent, designed and maintained to keep the setting as natural as possible. Even when busy, the park feels serene.

Job number one is to visit the river. That could be as simple as a picnic at one of the many roadside access points. If you are up for a short walk, visit the Floodplain Trail near the visitor center. It leads a quarter mile across a sandy, willow-studded bar to a wide gravel beach.

If you want to get in the river, the gravel bar upstream of the campground is a great choice. From the boat launch parking area, a trail leads along the top of a steep bluff, then down through switchbacks to the beach. Pause at the bluff to ponder the river's power.

In 2009, floodwaters took a bite out of this bank, sending a chunk of road and several campsites into the river. The flood exposed stumps in the bank that were likely buried in 1780, when an eruption on Mount Hood sent a lahar—essentially a huge surge of mud—down the Sandy River. The lahar buried this area fifty feet deep in sediment and created the vast, sandy delta at the river's mouth. Twelve years after the eruption, Lieutenant William Broughton, in service to Captain George Vancouver's expedition, encountered the delta on an exploratory foray up the Columbia River. The delta's sandbars extended nearly across the Columbia, prompting Broughton to call it the "Quicksand River." He bestowed some imperialist names on the distant volcanoes and then sailed back downriver in defeat.

Swimming at Oxbow is awesome, but keep in mind that in winter and spring the river is much higher, and many of the gravel bars are submerged. This is a good time to keep a safe distance and explore the trail network instead. Respect this river's power!

Finally, plan a visit around a naturalist program. They cover the usual topics—wildlife and natural history—but also include music and storytelling nights celebrating the region's diverse cultural traditions. The highlight is in October at the Salmon Homecoming, a two-day event marking the seasonal return of spawning salmon. Programmed in cooperation with local tribes, it brings an indigenous perspective to this profound natural phenomenon through ceremonies and stories.

Best of all, it provides an opportunity to watch the salmon close-up. The sight of these creatures surging upriver en masse, at the edge of death, is truly moving. This event is popular, so book in advance.

97 MOUNT TALBERT NATURE PARK

Quiet trails wind around a wooded, wild volcanic butte

Location: 10945 SE Mather Rd., Clackamas
Acreage: 224
Amenities: Restrooms, trails (4 miles), picnic shelter
Jurisdiction: Metro; North Clackamas Parks and Recreation District

GETTING THERE

BY CAR I-205 to exit 14 (Sunnybrook Blvd.) eastbound; right onto SE 97th Ave.; after three-quarters of a mile, left onto SE Mather Rd.; go one-quarter mile and turn left into the park. **BY TRANSIT** ★★ MAX (Green Line) to Clackamas Transit Center; then Bus 155 (Sunnyside) to SE Sunnyside and 117th (stop 10580) for the north trailhead. **BY BIKE** ★★ Via I-205 Path, SE Lawnfield Rd., SE 97th Ave., and SE Mather Rd.

A keen reader will have noticed that many of Portland's nature parks west of the Willamette River are in the Tualatin Mountains, aka the West Hills, and those east are on buttes. Mount Talbert is one of these buttes and, like its colleagues Rocky, Powell, and Hogan, is an extinct volcano. All belong to the Boring Volcanic Field, so named for their proximity to the town of Boring. These wooded hills are, geologically speaking, part of the Cascade Mountain Range.

The volcanic field was more, well, *interesting* two and a half million years ago, when tectonic forces ripped tears in the earth's crust. Over the space of a million years, these fissures periodically oozed lava and shot cinders across the Portland region. The biggest remnant of this activity is Larch Mountain, a prominent shield volcano. (Check out the mountain finder at Powell Butte for help spotting it.)

Mount Talbert is actually an old lava dome, like the plug in the crater of Mount St. Helens that periodically—and ominously—bulges. Talbert, its eruptive days long over, is significantly more "boring."

Though not the biggest of buttes, Mount Talbert is among the least sullied by development—remarkably so, given its proximity to the freeway and a major

Forest friends at Mount Talbert Nature Park (Photo by Jon Vogel)

shopping mall. The region's voters have repeatedly chosen to fund natural area protection through Metro, the regional government, and Metro was astute enough to buy this mountain while it was still for sale.

The park's main trailhead and parking area are on the south side, off Mather Road. Here you'll find restrooms, a picnic shelter, and a short circle of accessible (packed gravel) trail. A dirt trail heads steadily uphill to the Park Loop Trail, by which you can climb over Talbert's top (views are limited) via the Summit and West Ridge Trails.

If time allows, follow the Park Loop north and downhill to Mount Scott Creek. The creek isn't readily accessible, but the riparian area is secluded and delightfully cool on a hot summer's day. From here, the trail crosses a footbridge and ends at the northern trailhead on Sunnyside Road (see transit directions above).

To me, the park feels wilder than you might guess given its surroundings. Odds are good you'll spook a deer somewhere, hear pileated woodpeckers working for their lunch, and perhaps even spot a coyote. You will also see signs of restoration in the form of girdled trees and logged areas. Metro's goal here is to promote more Oregon white oak, which once covered the southern slopes of Talbert and neighboring hills.

EXTEND YOUR VISIT

Just across I-205 are the North Clackamas Aquatic Park, one of the region's best places for indoor watery kid fun, and the adjacent 3-Creeks Natural Area, a semi-wild woods at the confluence of Mount Scott, Phillips, and Deer Creeks. In the dry season, this is a great place to see what "old-growth" oaks look like. Note: there are sometimes homeless camps here. Exercise appropriate caution—and compassion.

98 EAGLE FERN COUNTY PARK

Precious old growth—with more in the making—along pristine streams

Location: 27505 SE Eagle Fern Rd., Eagle Creek
Acreage: 171
Amenities: Restrooms, picnic shelters, play structure, trails (3 miles), swimming hole
Jurisdiction: Clackamas County

GETTING THERE

BY CAR I-205 to exit 13 (OR 224) toward Estacada; after 2 miles, left at the stoplight onto OR 212-224; after 1.5 miles, bear right at stoplight to stay on OR 224; continue 10.7 miles, then go left onto SE Wildcat Mountain Dr. (becomes SE Eagle Fern Rd.); park entrance is at right after 4.2 miles. Parking fee. **BY TRANSIT** None. **BY BIKE** ★

Eagle Fern County Park has some of the most spectacular, and rare, low-elevation old-growth forest in the region. These ancient trees, some as big around as houses, fill a patch of woods miraculously spared from the logger's axe a century ago. They line the banks of Eagle Creek, a crystal stream rising in the Salmon-Huckleberry Wilderness on Mount Hood to flow down rugged and remote canyons. I can't say enough about what a special place this is.

Paradise in the Pacific Northwest: a summer's day at Eagle Fern Park

The park itself is modest. Near the parking area are a restroom, a new play structure, and good interpretive kiosks. Down the entrance road, past the caretaker buildings, a slightly incongruous baseball diamond fills a forest clearing like some pagan ceremonial glade. Beyond, a great wooden A-frame shelters a dozen or more picnic tables.

A suspension bridge crosses the creek to access several short hiking loops among the forest giants. Half-mile Loop C has numbered signposts corresponding to a trail guide usually available at a kiosk by the bridge. (Since the kiosk is sometimes empty and cell reception is limited in the park, you might want to download the guide in advance at the Clackamas County Parks website— see Resources.)

In winter, this place is spectacularly gloomy, the sun seemingly unable to even crest the surrounding hills. In summer, it's a duff-scented paradise of shade cleaved by the creek, its sun-speckled rocks shimmering under the lazy current. Kids splash in the cool water as grown-ups relax on the bank. You probably won't find solitude, but in these few acres you can find all the beauty and solace you might seek in a week's wilderness trip.

I say "these few acres" because the part of the park with hiking trails, creek access, and amenities covers only about twenty acres. Most of the park is trackless forest, some ancient.

Next door to the park is a very different forest, a patchwork of clear-cuts, weeds, and single-species plantings. Until recently, a big timber corporation owned this land and managed it for maximal production. In 2019, a local government agency—the Clackamas Soil and Water Conservation District—bought it specifically to manage the forest for local benefits, guided by local priorities. Here, that means clean water, wildlife habitat, recreation opportunities, and limited timber harvests. It's now called the Eagle Creek Community Forest.

What is currently a tree farm will transition over time to a mixed-age and structurally diverse forest, closer to what you see at Eagle Fern County Park. Even if you have little interest in ecology, you can't help but be struck by the difference between a natural forest and a humanmade one. With time and appropriate management, that difference will fade.

The conservation district and partners also intend to build a trail network in the community forest for hiking and mountain biking.

This is part of an ambitious effort to coordinate forest restoration and recreation access across nearly fifteen hundred contiguous acres, at the heart of which is Eagle Fern County Park. This kind of conservation story too often goes untold. It shouldn't. This is a major accomplishment. In the coming years, Eagle Creek will receive its due as one of the region's most significant natural areas.

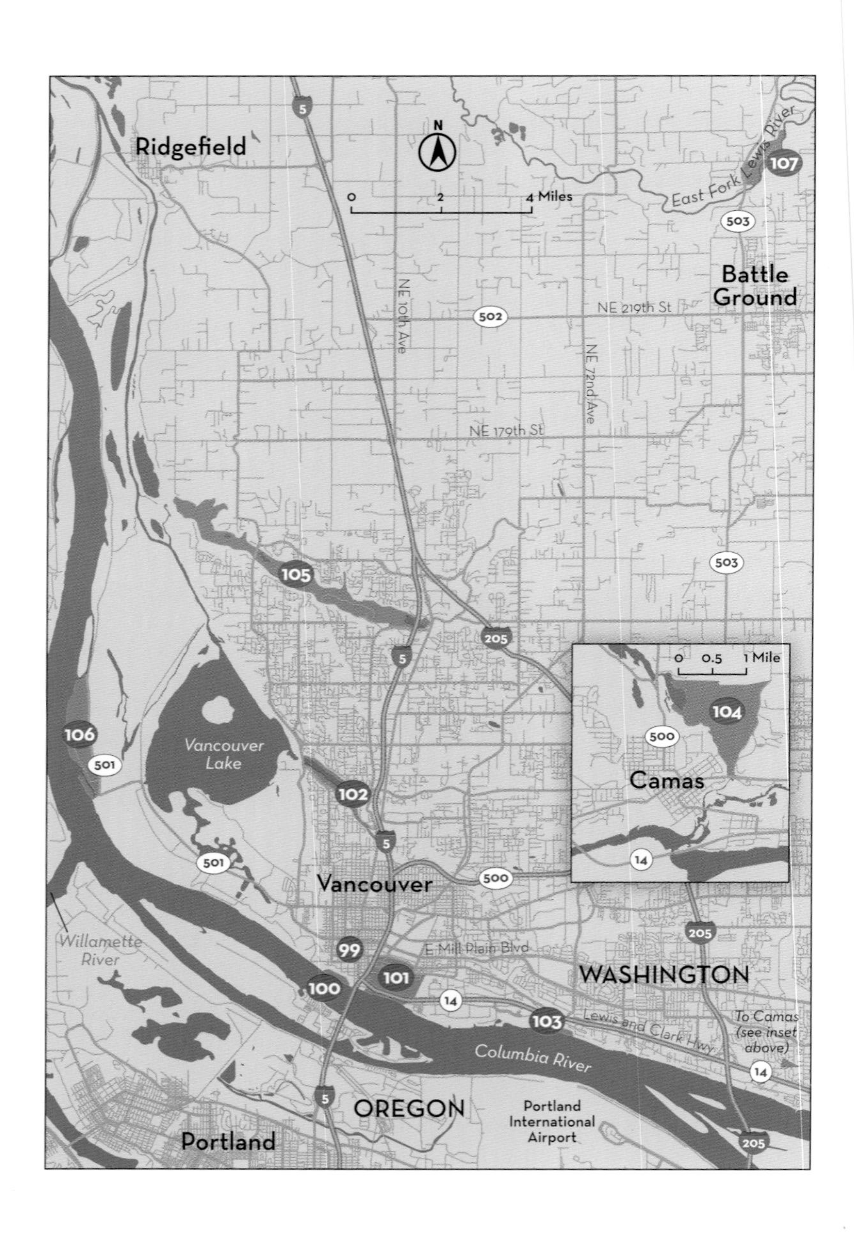

Ridgefield
N
0 2 4 Miles
East Fork Lewis River
107
503
Battle Ground
NE 219th St
502
NE 10th Ave
NE 72nd Ave
NE 179th St
105
503
205
5
0 0.5 1 Mile
104
500
Camas
14
106
501
Vancouver Lake
102
5
501
Vancouver
500
Willamette River
99
E Mill Plain Blvd
205
WASHINGTON
101
100
14
103
Lewis and Clark Hwy
To Camas (see inset above)
Columbia River
14
5
OREGON
Portland International Airport
Portland
205

ACROSS THE COLUMBIA: VANCOUVER AND CLARK COUNTY

99 ESTHER SHORT PARK

Urban park and plaza anchoring Vancouver's downtown revival

Location: W. 8th St. and Columbia St., Vancouver
Acreage: 5
Amenities: Food vendors, picnic shelter/stage, playground, plaza, rose garden, accessible restrooms, spray feature and fountain
Jurisdiction: Vancouver, Washington

GETTING THERE

BY CAR I-5 to exit 1B (City Center) in Washington; continue on 6th St. four blocks to the park. **BY TRANSIT** ★★ MAX (Yellow Line) to Expo Center; then C-TRAN Bus 60 (Delta Park Regional) to Broadway and 7th St. (stop 631); walk three blocks west to the park. **BY BIKE** ★★ Via I-5 bike path and Columbia River Renaissance Trail.

Esther Short is not a big park, but there are several reasons to visit. First, according to the City of Vancouver, it is the oldest public square in Washington. Mrs. Short gave it to the fledgling city in 1855. The story of how she came to own the land in the first place is a classic tale of settlement in the West.

One Henry Williamson first claimed the land (i.e., expropriated it from local Chinookan people), but like many early Northwest settlers, he hurried straight off to California where *real* money could be made. While he was gone, Esther Short's husband, Amos, murdered the caretaker of Williamson's claim, and then somehow managed to secure the claim for himself. Amos then promptly drowned in a shipwreck, leaving his widow, Esther, an unwitting local land baron. Perhaps with a conscience to clear, she bequeathed this parcel and much of the current Port of Vancouver lands for public use.

More recently, the park has become an emblem of Vancouver's urban transformation. By the late twentieth century, Vancouver had a moribund downtown hollowed out by sprawling suburbs. Empty storefronts lined Main and Broadway Streets even as the freeway bridges to Portland jammed with commuters. Esther Short Park and environs were a dingy no-go zone.

Vancouver's 1990s-era mayor, Royce Pollard, was determined to turn downtown around. Part of his plan entailed making Esther Short Park appealing again. When the mayor himself was menaced in the park—at an event designed to showcase its family-friendliness, no less!—he doubled down, pouring millions into a thorough park renovation and new development on the surrounding blocks. By the turn of the millennium, new condo towers were rising, parking was actually getting a little tough to find, and Esther Short Park was thriving.

If you can, visit the park during the farmers market (weekends, mid-March to late October), which purports to be the second largest in Washington. The crowds can be thick, but it's a great atmosphere.

The park's center of activity is the large plaza at 6th and Columbia Streets. One of the best features here is a fountain, like a Keller Fountain (see Portland Open Space Sequence) in miniature, where water flows over an artful jumble of basalt columns. Closer to 8th Street is a central pavilion ringed by an oval path and fronted by a statue honoring Mrs. Short. Concerts and festivals are frequent here during summer. Just beyond is a tidy playground.

EXTEND YOUR VISIT

When you're finished, head over to Main Street and take in the new shops. You can even find Portland-quality coffee now. While I understand Vancouverites are split on whether this is a step forward or backward, to me the answer is clear enough.

100 VANCOUVER WATERFRONT PARK

Long-awaited new park and urban development on a formerly industrial riverfront

Location: 695 Waterfront Way, Vancouver
Acreage: 7.3
Amenities: Paths, pier, playground, restaurants, regional trail
Jurisdiction: Vancouver, Washington

GETTING THERE

BY CAR I-5 to exit 1B (City Center) in Washington; continue on 6th St. past Esther Short Park to a traffic circle; left onto Esther St. to the park. **BY TRANSIT** ★★ MAX (Yellow Line) to Expo Center; then C-TRAN Bus 60 (Delta Park Regional) to Broadway and 7th St. (stop 631); walk to 6th St. and follow the driving directions above. **BY BIKE** ★★ Via I-5 bike path and Columbia River Renaissance Trail.

This place has been decades in the making. When early Vancouver resident Esther Short donated this land to the city in 1855, she meant to promote economic development and public access. The latter part never quite happened. As Vancouver transformed from fur trading outpost to river port, the riverfront filled with lumber and paper mills, grain elevators, concrete plants, tank farms, and shipping terminals. No parks, though.

Until now. Vancouver Waterfront Park is part of a thirty-two-acre site that for nearly a century was a paper mill. When it closed in 2006, the time was right for a new use. Well, almost right. Buoyed by downtown Vancouver's revival, real estate developers acquired the mill site and proposed a new city of gleaming high-rises and a park. It seemed improbable enough at the time, then downright fantastical when the Great Recession of 2008 set in.

The development persevered, though, and inched slowly forward. The developers wisely started with the park, donating 7.3 acres of land to the city and helping fund construction. It opened in 2018. The planned city of high-rises is now, at last, filling in behind the park. Marquee restaurants and leading civic organizations have already moved in.

The park's centerpiece is Grant Street Pier, a cantilevered promontory jutting ninety airy feet over the Columbia River like a ship's prow. It's exciting to step out over the water, especially in winter, when you can almost feel the power of the river below.

A new neighborhood is taking shape around Vancouver Waterfront Park.

Next to the pier is a fountain celebrating Vancouver's re-embrace of the Columbia River. It echoes the famous fountains of Portland's Open Space Sequence, evoking the elemental power of water to shape land. Water spills from atop a black stone monolith, etched with images of the great river's source lakes, to flow across pavers to a shallow pool. Along its course, this river in miniature gathers water emerging from beneath hewn stone blocks representing the Columbia's major tributaries.

West of the pier, the park is quieter. A path leads to a play area with a climbing net and a sandy "upland beach," safely distant from the mighty river. Next to it, steps lead down to the real thing. Here the bank is gentle, and the riprap provides some wading spots at low water. (Keep in mind, the Columbia is powerful year-round and should be approached with respect!) Beyond the beach, a picnic area provides a measure of seclusion.

At the park's other end, a promenade leads to an amphitheater built out over the water. Beyond is the Port of Vancouver's Terminal 1, where a monthly night market serves up food and entertainment. The port plans to redevelop this property as a full-blown public market. Between this project and the long-delayed but inevitable replacement of the I-5 Bridge, Vancouver's waterfront will remain dynamic for some time to come.

EXTEND YOUR VISIT

The park connects to the Columbia River Renaissance Trail, which passes Fort Vancouver en route to Wintler Park 5 miles upriver.

101 FORT VANCOUVER NATIONAL HISTORIC SITE

Must-see national park featuring reconstructed fur trade fort, barracks, museum, and public art

Location: 1501 E. Evergreen Blvd., Vancouver
Acreage: 207
Amenities: Visitor center with restrooms, food, and gift shop; historic buildings and artifacts; tours; extensive grounds with paths and picnic areas
Jurisdiction: National Park Service

GETTING THERE

BY CAR I-5 to exit 1C (E. Mill Plain Blvd.) eastbound in Washington; first right onto Fort Vancouver Way; left at traffic circle onto E. Evergreen Blvd.; visitor center is at right. **BY TRANSIT** ★★ MAX (Yellow Line) to Expo Center; then C-TRAN Bus 60 (Delta Park Regional) to Broadway and Evergreen Blvd. (stop 632); walk east (over freeway) three-quarters of a mile to the park. **BY BIKE** ★★ Via I-5 bike path and Columbia River Renaissance Trail.

Tucked across the Columbia River in sleepy (but secretly hip) Vancouver, half-hidden by freeways, lies the region's most important historic site after Willamette Falls: Fort Vancouver. Here, two centuries ago, the Hudson's Bay Company built its Pacific Northwest headquarters, drawing the peoples of four continents into relationships that changed them all—and set the trajectory for much of the region's subsequent development.

Chinookan people have lived and traded along the Lower Columbia since time immemorial. Accustomed to foreigners, they were unfazed when the first Europeans arrived by ship in the 1790s. Aside from their bigger boats and better metal goods, these "Bostons" (the Chinookan catchall for Euro-Americans) were just another group moving along the great watery highway. As across much of the West, the encounter was commercial and mostly peaceful.

Soon enough, though, the "Bostons"—they were actually British—decided to stick around. In 1824, the Hudson's Bay Company set up a home base from which to drain the Pacific Northwest of beavers. They were racing against upstart

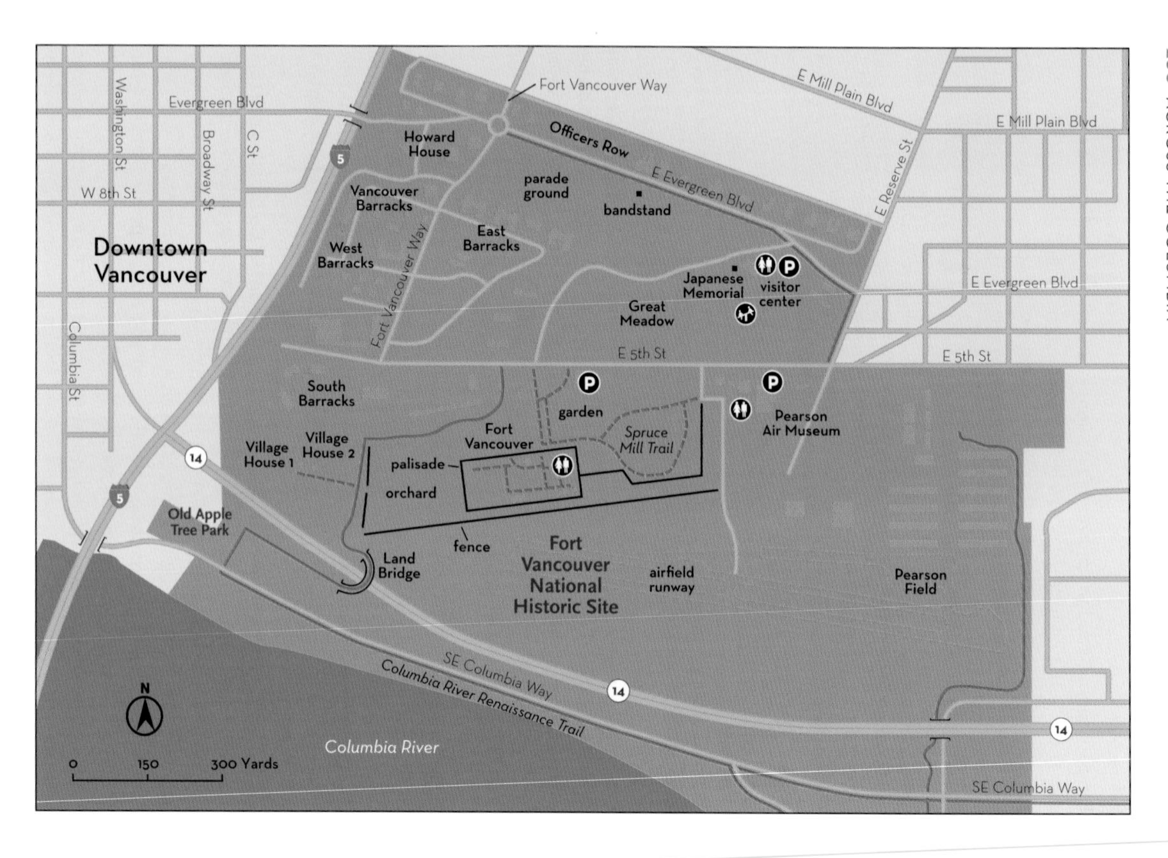
Evergreen Blvd
Washington St
Broadway St
C St
W 8th St
Downtown Vancouver
Columbia St
Fort Vancouver Way
E Mill Plain Blvd
E Mill Plain Blvd
Officers Row
Howard House
parade ground
E Evergreen Blvd
bandstand
E Reserve St
Vancouver Barracks
East Barracks
West Barracks
Fort Vancouver Way
Japanese Memorial
visitor center
E Evergreen Blvd
Great Meadow
E 5th St
E 5th St
South Barracks
garden
Pearson Air Museum
Fort Vancouver
Spruce Mill Trail
Village House 1
Village House 2
palisade
orchard
Old Apple Tree Park
fence
Land Bridge
Fort Vancouver National Historic Site
airfield runway
Pearson Field
SE Columbia Way
Columbia River Renaissance Trail
Columbia River
SE Columbia Way
N
0
150
300 Yards
5
14

American fur traders, themselves busy killing every beaver east of the Rockies. Unlike the rough-and-ready American trappers, mostly lone operators, the Hudson's Bay Company was organized. It carefully planned and built a network of trading forts from Astoria to the Upper Snake country, collecting furs from tribes across the Columbia basin and shipping them in bulk down the great river. It was an immense operation, a model of capitalist efficiency. Fort Vancouver was its nerve center, directing operations across an area the size of Europe and answering directly to bosses in Montreal and London.

Young French Canadians and Brits manned the fort in multiyear stints unimaginably far from home. Many stayed on to settle Willamette Valley farms when their terms of service ended. A thriving Native village grew up alongside the fort, inhabited by local Chinookan people and more than a few Hawaiians recruited as laborers by traders returning from China, where most furs were sold. This was a complex multicultural encounter, shaped by the imperatives of global capital and geopolitical jockeying. Presiding over it all was "the father of Oregon," Chief Factor John McLoughlin.

Then, abruptly, it ended. After only a few decades, the beavers nearly disappeared. The whims of fashion shifted, too, making beaver hats suddenly passé. Then the Oregon Trail opened, and American settlers arrived in droves, uninterested in furs but desperate for land. The Hudson's Bay Company held on a bit longer—but by the Civil War, it was American soldiers, not British fur traders, who controlled the territory.

Start at the park visitor center for an overview. Then make a beeline to the reconstructed fort, rebuilt exactly on its original footprint. Within the wooden palisades, the adjacent freeway's roar recedes. You can almost imagine living here in the 1830s, when for a typical Hudson's Bay employee this was the end of the earth. Wander the museum and check out the blacksmith shop, bakery, and trading station. On weekends you may meet reenactors eager to explain fort life two centuries ago.

When you've finished, wander toward the river and cross the freeway on a gracefully curving pedestrian bridge. This was built in 2008 as part of the Confluence Project, brainchild of architect Maya Lin. Lin, famed designer of the National Vietnam Veterans Memorial in Washington, DC, spent a decade creating public art along the Columbia River, reflecting on the region's profound social and environmental change since Lewis and Clark's journey. Across the bridge is Old Apple Tree Park, consisting of a wizened little tree ringed by a wrought-iron fence. In 1911, Washington's official fruit inspector for the Lower Columbia examined the tree and declared it the oldest in the state, likely dating to 1830. (Subsequent researchers have concluded that an entire orchard likely stood nearby, but disappeared long ago.) As a result, this tree is often called the "matriarch" of Washington's $2 billion apple industry.

Across SE Columbia Way, dip a toe in the Columbia River and then backtrack to the fort. Now you face a choice. Continue east to visit the museum at Pearson Field, adjacent to the fort, and explore this airfield's history. It originally served as polo grounds for American army officers and later one of the first modern airfields on the West Coast. Alternatively, head north to wander among the late-nineteenth-century Vancouver Barracks, following interpretive signs. In winter, you can take a lantern-lit nighttime guided tour.

If you have time and energy left, wander along Officers Row and finish with a visit to the Japanese Memorial. It commemorates three young Japanese sailors, sole survivors of a shipwreck. They washed ashore north of here in 1834, were captured and briefly enslaved by the Makah people, and then were ransomed and sent back home to Japan (via London!) by Chief Factor McLoughlin. It's just one of the many stories—of migration, cosmopolitanism, change, and resilience—that hallow the ground of this incredible place.

102 BURNT BRIDGE CREEK GREENWAY

Elegant parks and open spaces linked by a ribbon of green

Location (Stewart Glen trailhead): NW Bernie Dr. and NW Fruit Valley Rd., Vancouver **(Hazel Dell trailhead, for transit):** NE Hazel Dell Ave. and Alki Rd., Hazel Dell
Acreage: 115 (Stewart Glen area)
Amenities: Restrooms, picnic areas, paved path
Jurisdiction: Vancouver, Washington

GETTING THERE

BY CAR I-5 to exit 4 (NE 78th St.) westbound in Washington; continue on 78th St. to go left onto NW Lakeshore Ave.; first left onto NW Bernie Dr. and into the Stewart Glen trailhead parking area. **BY TRANSIT** ★ MAX (Yellow Line) to Expo Center; then C-TRAN Bus 60 (Delta Park Regional) to Broadway and Evergreen Blvd. (stop 632) in downtown Vancouver; then Bus 31 (Hazel Dell) to the 5200 block (stop 4148). Continue on the sidewalk past Alki Rd. to the Hazel Dell greenway entrance. **BY BIKE** ★

The Burnt Bridge Creek Greenway cuts an 8-mile green swath through older Vancouver neighborhoods, following Burnt Bridge Creek among wetlands, forests, and fields. It may be the region's best greenway trail. I focus here on the western end, a broad bottomland meadow below forested bluffs called Stewart Glen. This is my favorite stretch of the greenway and worth a visit for its own sake.

If you're driving, start at the Stewart Glen trailhead at the far western end of the greenway. Here, Burnt Bridge Creek backs up behind a levee. A culvert underneath NW Lakeshore Avenue admits water slowly into Vancouver Lake, just out of sight downstream. This constriction causes a good bit of Stewart Glen to flood in the winter, attracting waterfowl. I love to visit at this time, when the valley feels especially isolated and wild.

From the parking area, a paved path descends gently through the woods to the valley bottom, skirting the meadow's edge. Burnt Bridge Creek meanders through the middle of the valley, expanding and contracting with the changing seasons. In summer, tall grass hides it. Sometimes the parks department mows a strip parallel to the creek, making it easier to explore.

The main, paved path stays well clear of the creek, hugging the south side of the meadow. Forests rise steeply to the south, walling off this little valley from its urban surroundings. Hazel Dell and Northwest Vancouver neighborhoods fill the highlands above you, but down here, you barely see or hear them. Instead, there are only woods, field, and stream. It's delightful. If you stumbled upon this vale tramping through the English countryside, you'd head to the pub (there would doubtless be a pub nearby) and linger all day. It's all too easy to forget you're in the middle of a sprawling American city. Yet that makes it all the more special.

The path continues for about a mile between woods and meadow. Then it enters a clearing and soon splits in two. The right branch hugs the forest edge and the left branch runs along Burnt Bridge Creek. Just opposite the creek is a small farm, which as of this writing has been in the same family since 1883. I love this spot. It's a humble corner of countryside tucked in the shadow of I-5, a mere quarter mile distant.

The two branches of the path converge again at the far end of the clearing. A park bench here offers a vantage back over Stewart Glen. A short distance farther, the path crosses Burnt Bridge Creek to reach Alki Road, a lonely farm lane. You've come a mile and half from the Stewart Glen parking area. Linger on the shady bank of the creek, soak up the stillness, and then make your way back.

EXTEND YOUR VISIT

If you want to see more of the greenway, I recommend continuing to Leverich Park for a 5-mile total round-trip. Across Alki Road, the path continues to NE Hazel Dell Avenue and crosses I-5 via a scenic pedestrian bridge. Across the freeway, take your first right and continue downhill, past a road gate, to quiet NE Leverich Park Way. After several blocks following the sidewalk, the path reenters forest at the north end of Leverich Park.

Leverich is one of the city's oldest parks, dating back to the 1930s. It's a tasteful and simple succession of forest and glades, hemmed in by the creek's narrow valley. It has a popular disc golf course, a no-frills play structure, and some well-situated creekside picnic areas.

The greenway trail continues beyond Leverich another 4 miles to Meadowbrook Marsh. This stretch is plenty scenic, though less secluded and natural. It makes for a great bike ride.

103 WINTLER COMMUNITY PARK

A cozy, often busy beach—worth the trip to Vancouver

Location: 6400 SE Beach Dr., Vancouver
Acreage: 13
Amenities: Beach, restrooms (seasonal), regional trail
Jurisdiction: Vancouver, Washington

GETTING THERE

BY CAR I-5 to exit 1A (SR 14) eastbound in Washington; from SR 14, take exit 3 and go right onto SE Shorewood Dr., then immediately left onto SE Beach Dr.; continue to road's end at the park. Parking fee. **BY TRANSIT** Doable, not recommended. **BY BIKE** ★★ Via I-5 bike path and Columbia River Renaissance Trail.

Wintler Community Park is the only real swimming beach in Vancouver and, as such, it can be busy. The limited parking options help control crowds, but if you want seclusion on a hot summer weekend, this is not your first choice. That said, it's a lovely little beach.

Broughton Beach, immediately across the river, is easier to reach and has more room to play and roam. By contrast, Wintler offers intimacy and a southern exposure, great on those marginal weather days. Highway 14 is just far enough away that quiet mostly prevails, presuming no one is blasting music. Mount Hood looms across the river. Mature trees provide a measure of shelter from the cold-season downstream winds and screen out most of the surrounding suburbs.

A great way to visit Wintler, especially if parking looks tight (or you don't want to pay the parking fee), is to drive instead to the Water Resources Education Center next to Vancouver's wastewater treatment plant. The exhibits here are kid-oriented but edifying for everyone, and the adjacent wetlands are a great place to spot bald eagles and osprey. From here, walk or bike one very scenic mile along the Columbia River Renaissance Trail to reach Wintler's beach.

104 LACAMAS REGIONAL PARK

Waterfalls, forest, and lakes at a stellar regional park

Location: 3344 NE Everett St., Camas
Acreage: 312
Amenities: Beach, picnic shelter and tables, play structures, trails, restrooms
Jurisdiction: Clark County, Washington

GETTING THERE

BY CAR I-205 to exit 27 (SR 14) eastbound in Washington; from SR 14, take exit 12 (Camas); continue through a traffic circle onto NW 6th Ave.; before downtown Camas, turn left onto Division St.; past Crown Park, turn right onto NE 17th Ave. and then left onto NE Everett St.; continue another mile to the park entrance at right. **BY TRANSIT** ★ MAX (Yellow Line) to Expo Center; then C-TRAN Bus 60 (Delta Park Regional) to Broadway and Evergreen Blvd. (stop 632) in downtown Vancouver; then Bus 92 (Camas/Washougal) to NE 3rd Ave. and Crown Rd. (stop 2315); walk across 3rd Ave. and backtrack a short distance to the Lacamas Park Trail lower trailhead. **BY BIKE** ★

Camasonians, I'm about to share with the world what you already know. Lacamas Regional Park is amazing. I have found more variety, natural beauty, and occasionally even solitude in these three hundred acres than in many much larger sites. There is a lot to do and discover.

The park's main entrance is at Round Lake, but if you are up for hiking, I recommend starting at the lower trailhead on 3rd Avenue. From here, head up the Lacamas Park Trail to McEnry Bridge over Lacamas Creek's Lower Falls. At low water, the creek slithers down chutes carved through bedrock. A rough trail leads

Lacamas Regional Park has an extensive trail network—and space for lazy picnics too.

down to the creek at the falls' base, which is ideal for wading at low water. (Note: this creek can become a dangerous torrent in winter.)

The main trail, actually a narrow service road, heads east and up into forest. Side trails, some surprisingly rugged, branch off the main route. The short spur trail down to Woodburn Falls is especially nice. The nearby "Camas Lily" loop (a little less than a mile and moderately steep) is also worth a side trip, especially during late spring when the hillside lights up with purple blossoms.

The main trail reaches a junction on the south shore of Round Lake. This is a natural lake augmented by a dam, built in 1883 to supply water to Camas' original raison d'être, the paper mill. The lake's east path is hilly and more isolated. The west path is busier but leads past a side trail to the "Potholes," a scenic series of waterfalls and pools. This is another justifiably popular swimming spot in summer. If you have the energy, circle the lake and return to Lower Falls via the trail following Lacamas Creek though oaks, camas, and basalt outcrops. All in all, this is about 5 miles and very much worth the effort.

If you don't want to hike that far, drive straight to the (main) Round Lake parking area on Everett Street. Here on the shore of Round Lake you'll find picnic tables, restrooms, a small play structure, lofty trees, and great spots to access the lake. You can also reach the Potholes via a short trail that leads right over the dam, offering a close-up view.

Whether you roam or stick near the lake, you will likely be surprised at how picturesque this park is, and even how wild it feels in places. I highly recommend it.

EXTEND YOUR VISIT

Just across Everett Street is Fallen Leaf Lake Park, a forested pond nestled at the foot of a bluff. It's a great picnic spot. Next door is Lacamas Lake, good for paddling or running along the nearly 30-mile Lacamas Heritage Trail, a portion of which follows the lakeshore.

Alternately, from the 3rd Avenue trailhead, you can easily cross 3rd Avenue on foot and go right onto SE Crown Road to reach the Washougal Greenway Trail, which winds through a natural area along the beautiful Washougal River's lowest reach.

105 SALMON CREEK REGIONAL PARK AND KLINELINE POND

Riverside greenway and popular swimming hole

Location: 1112 NE 117th St., Vancouver
Acreage: 154
Amenities: Swimming area with seasonal lifeguard, restrooms, picnic tables, splash pad, play structure, paved creekside greenway path
Jurisdiction: Clark County, Washington

GETTING THERE

BY CAR I-5 to exit 5 (NE 99th St.) eastbound in Washington; left at first light onto NE Hwy. 99; left onto NE 117th St.; cross under freeway and turn right into the park. Parking fee. **BY TRANSIT** Doable, not recommended. **BY BIKE** ★

A century ago, gravel mines lined Salmon Creek, supplying a good deal of Clark County's aggregate. The stream is still recovering from all that mining. Amazingly enough, salmon have persisted, helped by restoration efforts begun in the 1990s. While the stream will never be what it was, Salmon Creek Regional Park and Klineline Pond make the most of this legacy. They offer two very different but equally appealing experiences.

One of the biggest former gravel pits is now Klineline Pond, named in honor of local gravel baron Harry Klineline. His company dug this and neighboring pits to supply the US Army in World War II. (Many of Salmon Creek's ancient cobbles now underlie the roads in Vancouver Barracks, the late-nineteenth-century US military fort that's part of Fort Vancouver National Historic Site.) When the pit played out in the 1970s, the state bought it and turned it into a fishing and swimming hole.

Now a county park, Klineline Pond has a fishing dock, lawns, a splash pad, and a swimming beach with seasonal lifeguards. It's a great place for little kids to get in the water. Like many local swimming holes, it gets busy on the best days of summer.

The Salmon Creek Greenway, by contrast, is rarely crowded. From Klineline Pond, a paved path heads west for 3 miles to the Felida Bridge, running along streamside wetlands and through bottomland forests of ash, red alder, and black cottonwood. Portions of the greenway path veer far from the creek, which in wet months fills its floodplain nearly half a mile across. Houses line the bluffs above the creek, but once you leave the vicinity of Klineline and I-5, you will be struck by how isolated the greenway can feel. It's worth going all the way to Felida and back if time and energy allow.

106 FRENCHMAN'S BAR REGIONAL PARK

Vast and often deserted Columbia River beach, great for watching ships

Location: 9612 NW Lower River Rd., Vancouver
Acreage: 120
Amenities: Restrooms, good paths for running, picnic tables, enormous (and reservable) picnic shelters, sand volleyball courts, play structure
Jurisdiction: Clark County, Washington

GETTING THERE

BY CAR I-5 to exit 1C (E. Mill Plain Blvd.) westbound in Washington; continue to Fourth Plain Blvd. (becomes NW Lower River Rd./SR 501); 5 miles past Mill/Fourth Plain junction, bear left to stay on SR 501 north; continue 2 miles to the park entrance at left. Parking fee. **BY TRANSIT** None. **BY BIKE** ★★ Via I-5 bike path, Columbia River Renaissance Trail, Mill Plain Blvd., SR 501.

Frenchman's Bar is a big, broad beach located where the Columbia River lumbers north after gathering the waters of the Willamette River. It feels marooned in the river's vast floodplain, in a wilderness between Sauvie Island and Vancouver Lake. It offers the same spaciousness and quiet as found on Sauvie's beloved beaches, but with a shorter drive and a mellower crowd.

The park's eight sand volleyball courts and gigantic picnic shelters draw big groups, but if you're here to run, swim, or just soak up the emptiness, you will have no trouble finding room. The beach faces west, capturing lovely sunsets and the full force of westerly winds, so come prepared for a range of temperatures.

The park's downstream end is more sheltered. Wander a mile among cottonwoods to reach a small beach opposite Caterpillar Island, where you'll find shallows great for wading. Upstream, the wide beach offers less shelter but plenty of room to run your dog. If *you're* the one who needs running, a paved path leads nearly 3 miles, atop a lonely dike part of the way, to Vancouver Lake Regional Park. It's also a great place to take kids on their first longer ride.

One of my favorite things to do at Frenchman's Bar is watch the container ships to-ing and fro-ing from the ports of Vancouver and Portland. Some of these ships are astoundingly massive, and the shipping channel runs right in front of the beach. Indeed, the river's relatively abrupt drop-off from the beach is why the county recommends against swimming here. That said, in summer you'll find plenty of swimmers. Proceed at your own risk.

EXTEND YOUR VISIT

Add a visit to nearby Vancouver Lake Regional Park for safer swimming (but still no lifeguard) and good paddling options.

107 LEWISVILLE REGIONAL PARK

Century-old forestland park along a superb river

Location: 26411 NE Lewisville Hwy., Battle Ground
Acreage: 154
Amenities: Restrooms, picnic tables, reservable picnic shelters, play structures, tennis and basketball courts, swimming hole, boat launch
Jurisdiction: Clark County, Washington

GETTING THERE

BY CAR I-5 to exit 9 (NE 179th St.) in Washington; continue straight onto NE 10th Ave.; right onto 219th St.; in Battle Ground, go left onto NW 10th Ave./SR 503; continue 3 miles to the park entrance at right. Parking fee. **BY TRANSIT** None. **BY BIKE** ★

At the far northern edge of the Portland metro area is another gift from the New Deal: woodsy Lewisville Regional Park. Clark County's first and arguably best park, it fronts a mile and a half of the East Fork Lewis River, one of the most beautiful and intact waterways in the region.

The park dates back to 1936, when workers from the Works Progress Administration built the trails, picnic shelters, bathhouses, and other rustic structures now included on the National Register of Historic Places. Like Timberline Lodge on Mount Hood and Silver Falls State Park in the Willamette Valley, Lewisville Regional Park exudes craftsmanship, charm, and reverence for nature.

The park has just about everything you'd want in a large regional park: sports fields, huge lawns lined with shade trees, picnic areas, and two excellent playgrounds. A 2.8-mile path loops the park, running under wooded bluffs west of the entrance road and along the river. Mostly wide and smooth, it's a great place to run or hike.

In my opinion, the biggest draw, even more than the rustic buildings and the towering trees, is the river itself. The East Fork rises in the Gifford Pinchot National Forest to flow west across Clark County, spilling over Sunset, Moulton, and Lucia Falls (each with excellent parks) to join the main Lewis River near Woodland. Though its upper reaches have been logged and its floodplain mined for gravel, the river is still in good shape. The water is clear, clean, and home to plenty of salmon. On a warm summer day when the water level is low, the swimming hole at Lewisville is excellent. Find it near the "Larch" picnic area.

Lewisville is also a great place for a large gathering. Many of the picnic shelters, which date back to the 1930s and have character to spare, can be reserved at a reasonable cost. They hold anywhere from twenty to two hundred people and include woodstoves or fireplaces, great for keeping a group warm on rainy days.

Interestingly, the river *doesn't* honor Meriwether Lewis of the Lewis and Clark expedition. Known for millennia as *Cahwâhnahiooks* by the Cowlitz people, it takes its "official" name from Adolphus Lewes, an early settler employed by John McLoughlin at the Hudson's Bay Company (see Fort Vancouver National Historic Site for more). Lewes established a land claim nearby and saw fit to name the river after himself. Do we fault his vanity or pity his misfortune in sharing a name with someone so much more consequential?

OPPOSITE: *Rock-skipping lessons at Lewisville Regional Park*

TRAIL

Acknowledgments

My greatest thanks go to my wife, Jen, who has been my outdoor and life companion for twenty years. To my son, Lee, I owe a debt of gratitude for inspiring me to write this book and for accompanying me on more park outings than he might have wished. (At least we'll have published proof your childhood wasn't spent indoors!)

Thanks are also due to my mother, Rachel, who visited parks with me and tolerated long, not totally consensual conversations about conservation, climate change, and politics. Likewise my brother, Neal, his wife, Abbie, their kids, David and Tess, and my in-laws: Mark Raymond, Anneliese Zemp, Charlie Zemp-Raymond, Tim Raymond, and Marj Raymond. All have supported and encouraged me—and posed for the camera more than once. I also thank Matt Scotten for his friendship, his camera, and his Portland native's perspective on this ever-changing city.

Thanks also to those who reviewed all or a portion of my manuscript: Mike Houck, Mike Abbaté, Bruce Barbarasch, and Bill Hawkins. I wish to thank my colleagues at the Land Trust Alliance, who, in addition to being committed and inspiring conservation professionals, have gamely supported my work on this "side" project. Lastly, I'd like to thank Kate Rogers and Janet Kimball at Mountaineers Books for their continued willingness to entertain my opinions about Portland!

OPPOSITE: *Following the leader to the Sandy River Delta*

Further Exploration

The hardest part of this project was deciding what to omit. So here I'm going to cheat a bit, cramming in a few more destinations just as worthy as those profiled in the main text.

MORE NATURE PLAY

- **Camille Park** (Tualatin Hills Park and Recreation District) has a nature play area with big logs set in a native oak prairie with blooming purple camas in spring.
- **Hyland Woods Natural Area** (Tualatin Hills Park and Recreation District) has a 1.5-acre "Off-Trail Play Area" where kids (and adults!) can build forts, romp, and basically go feral in the woods like we used to do.
- The **Portland Children's Museum** has a 1.3-acre "Outdoor Adventure" area offering kids of all ages, even toddlers, a range of nature play experiences. It's truly excellent, but you have to buy admission to the museum to use it.

MORE NATURAL AREAS

- **Jackson Bottom Wetlands Preserve** (Hillsboro), along the Tualatin River, offers hiking and bird-watching on par with the Tualatin River National Wildlife Refuge.
- **Marshall Park** (Portland) fills a wooded canyon along upper Tryon Creek. Admire a charming stone bridge over the creek and consider a longer hike down to Tryon Creek State Natural Area.
- **Noble Woods Park** (Hillsboro) has 1.5 miles of trails and a stretch of Rock Creek flowing through mature forest.
- **Whipple Creek Regional Park** (Clark County) is a large forested park outside of Ridgefield, Washington, with about 4 miles of trails and several historic structures. It has great hiking and is popular with equestrians.

VIEWS

- **Bald Peak State Park** (Hillsboro) has vast views west across the wine and farm country of the Chehalem Valley in Yamhill County, with Newberg in the distance. This is one of my favorite vistas in the region.

- **Crown Point** (Oregon State Parks) has the classic view of the Columbia River Gorge. For fewer crowds and better picnic and walking options, check out **Cape Horn** (US Forest Service) directly across the river, where you can hike to the Nancy Russell Overlook for an arguably even *more* stunning vista.
- **Hogan Butte Nature Park** (Gresham) has an interpretive trail and views across the Columbia River and toward Mount Hood.

PLACES TO GET IN (OR NEAR) WATER

- **The Clackamas River:** Carver and Barton Parks (Clackamas County) are hugely popular with summer floaters. Farther upstream, Milo McIver State Park has another great day-floating section and, I'm told, the best disc golf course in the state. Lesser-known Metzler Park (Clackamas County), in the woods along pristine Clear Creek, has family-friendly camping, summer movie nights in the central meadow, and a sweet little swimming hole.
- **The Columbia River:** Captain William Clark Regional Park (Clark County) in Washougal at Cottonwood Beach has an accessible, paved path along a dike with wide-open river views. The path continues to Steigerwald Lake National Wildlife Refuge, where a portion of the Columbia's once-vast floodplain is under restoration. Downriver, Ridgefield National Wildlife Refuge has easy paddling and an interpretive driving loop—a great way to see habitat and spot wildlife for the mobility-impaired. Also at the Ridgefield refuge is the Cathlapotle Plankhouse, a modern replica of a traditional Chinookan dwelling. Archaeological and oral history evidence indicates the village of Cathlapotle, noted in Lewis and Clark's journals, stood here from approximately 1450 to 1830.
- **The East Fork Lewis River:** The East Fork is a treasure. Moulton Falls Regional Park has two spectacular waterfalls: the eponymous falls and Yacolt Falls on Big Creek, across the road from the main parking area. From Moulton, you can hike or bike several miles downriver on a quiet and accessible rail trail to reach Lucia Falls Regional Park, with another fantastic falls. Downstream, Daybreak Regional Park has picnic areas, good swimming, and a boat launch. Finally, Paradise Point State Park has an *awesome* cliff-jumping spot—but you didn't hear it from me!
- **The Sandy River:** Dodge Park (Portland) has picnic areas, a playground, and prime riverfront for lounging and swimming. Dabney State Recreation Area has a great swimming beach. The easy—in summer—float from here to Oxbow or Glenn Otto is a classic.

Resources

Along with help from current and retired park professionals, I relied on these sources for many historical and logistical details. Note there are many more "Friends of" groups than those listed below. Check the relevant park agency's website; most have a directory of friends groups and other community partners.

BOOKS

Abbott, Carl. *Portland in Three Centuries: The Place and the People* (Corvallis: Oregon State University Press, 2011). A concise and engaging history from the dean of Portland historians.

Boschetto, Eli. *Urban Trails Portland: Beaverton, Lake Oswego, Troutdale* (Seattle: Mountaineers Books, 2018). Curated guide to walking and cycling the region's trails.

Foster, Laura. *Portland Hill Walks: Twenty Explorations in Parks and Neighborhoods* (Portland: Timber Press, 2005); *Portland City Walks: Twenty Explorations In and Around Town* (Portland: Timber Press, 2008); and *Portland Stair Walks: Explore Portland, Oregon's Public Stairways* (Portland: Microcosm Publishing, 2019). Excellent guides brimming with local history, geography, and culture.

Hawkins, William. *The Legacy of Olmsted Brothers in Portland, Oregon* (published by author, 2014). Well-illustrated volume tells the history of Portland's parks, focusing on John Olmsted's pivotal visit and its lasting influence.

Hockaday, Joan. *Greenscapes: Olmsted's Pacific Northwest* (Pullman, WA: Washington State University Press, 2009). A more academic but still fascinating take on the Olmsted legacy region-wide.

Houck, Michael. *Wild in the City: Exploring the Intertwine: The Portland-Vancouver Region's Network of Parks, Trails, and Natural Areas* (Corvallis: Oregon State University Press, 2011). Comprehensive guide to the region's natural heritage, packed with stories and information about the ongoing efforts to make this great place even better.

Houle, Marcy Cottrell, and Eric Goetze. *One City's Wilderness: Portland's Forest Park* (Corvallis: Oregon State University Press, 2010). Definitive guide to Forest Park's human and natural history, with trail descriptions and maps.

Nelson, Donald. *Portland's Washington Park: A Pictorial History* (published by author, 2010) and *The South Park Blocks: A Neighborhood History* (published by author, 2008). Archival photographs with historical context. Nelson has authored additional Portland pictorial histories, including ones about St. Johns and East Portland.

Portland (OR) Park Board and Olmsted Brothers. "Report on a System of Parks and Boulevards" (1904). This is the actual Olmsted report, a quick and essential read for Portland park fans. Available at pdxscholar.library.pdx.edu/oscdl_cityarchives/32.

Romano, Craig. *Day Hiking: Columbia River Gorge* (Seattle: Mountaineers Books, 2011). Among the best of many hiking guides to the Gorge, Portland's big backyard.

Wozniak, Owen. *Biking Portland: 55 Rides from the Willamette Valley to Vancouver* (Seattle: Mountaineers Books, 2012). Explore the region by bike! Rides range from 5 miles to 50, skewing toward family-friendly routes that offer plenty of reasons to stop along the way. I read it and thought it was pretty good.

WEBSITES

Bike Portland (www.bikeportland.org) has covered the bicycling scene since 2005 and is essential for news, views, and context on our public spaces.

Bike There! (gis.oregonmetro.gov/bikethere), an online map created by the Metro Regional Government, is a one-stop shop for planning your bike route to the park.

"The Columbia River—A Photographic Journey" by Lyn Topinka (www.columbiariverimages.com) documents locations Lewis and Clark camped on their 1805–1806 sojourn in the Pacific Northwest. It has an incredible level of detail and mentions many of the parks covered in this book.

Columbia Slough Watershed Council (www.columbiaslough.org) stewards and advocates for the slough. They also lead excellent multicultural programs designed to help people—especially kids—explore it.

The Confluence Project (www.confluenceproject.org) tells the story of the Columbia River through indigenous voices, with programming and events focused on the Confluence Project sites created by architect Maya Lin.

Explore Washington Park (www.explorewashingtonpark.org) provides information on the park's attractions and parking/transit options.

4T Trail Loop (www.4t-trail.org) has details, directions, and background on a route through the West Hills utilizing hiking trails, the aerial tram, the Portland Streetcar, and the MAX light rail.

Forest Park Conservancy (www.forestparkconservancy.org) leads the massive effort to care for our greatest park. They mobilize volunteers to repair trails, restore habitat, and connect the park to the community.

Friends of Crystal Springs Rhododendron Garden (www.rhodies.org) help maintain the garden. Visit them online for a tour schedule.

Friends of Gateway Green (www.gatewaygreenpdx.org) have worked long and hard to turn Gateway Green from dream to reality. They continue raising money and recruiting friends to get the park built.

Friends of Lone Fir Cemetery (www.friendsoflonefircemetery.org) help Metro preserve and restore the cemetery, and educate the public about its history through monthly walking tours and a richly informative website.

Friends of Mount Tabor Park (www.taborfriends.org) organize work parties and maintain park maps, available online and at their visitor center in the park.

Friends of Nadaka Nature Park (www.friendsofnadaka.org) led the effort to open up Nadaka and create a new park along NE Glisan Street. Now they work to ensure the park lives up to its vision of "nature, food, and families."

Friends of the Overlook House (www.historicoverlookhouse.org) have information on visiting and renting the historic home near Overlook Park.

Friends of the Sandy River Delta (www.fsrd.org) valiantly battle blackberries, remove shocking amounts of dog poop, and help the Forest Service implement an ambitious long-term restoration plan.

Friends of Tryon Creek (www.tryonfriends.org) came together in 1970 to create Tryon Creek State Natural Area. They now partner with Oregon State Parks to maintain the trails, manage habitat, and lead outdoor education programs.

Friends of Tualatin River National Wildlife Refuge (www.friendsoftualatinrefuge.org) help to steward and advocate for the refuge, offer environmental education programs, and operate a nature store at the visitor center.

Human Access Project (www.humanaccessproject.com) connects Portlanders to the Willamette River by championing access, restoration, and river fun.

Metro (www.oregonmetro.gov/parks) offers recommended itineraries, field guides, and even a few audio tours of its regional parks.

Northwest Family Daycation (www.nwfamilydaycation.com), a project of the Intertwine Alliance and the US Fish and Wildlife Service, is a crowdsourced smartphone app with "curated itineraries made by locals" centered on parks and natural areas.

Oregon Encyclopedia (www.oregonencyclopedia.org), created by the Oregon Historical Society, was my main resource for historical research. It has articles on a range of subjects, all written by relevant experts.

Pittock Mansion Society (www.pittockmansion.org) operates the museum at Pittock Mansion. Learn some history and find out what's on display at the mansion at their website.

Portland Parks and Recreation (www.portlandoregon.gov/parks) has a useful "find a park" feature and a lot of parks history. The bureau's Urban Forestry program operates a Tree Inventory Project, which has created tree guides and story maps like the one mentioned in the Alberta Park entry. Mapped parks include Cathedral, Irving, Laurelhurst, Peninsula, and Woodlawn.

"Portland's Transportation History" (www.portlandoregon.gov/transportation/36416) has a collection of annotated images perfect for geeking out on Portland's historical geography.

PARK AGENCIES

Beaverton: www.beavertonoregon.gov
Clackamas County: www.clackamas.us/parks
Clark County, Washington: www.clark.wa.gov/public-works/clark-county-parks
Durham: www.durham-oregon.us/parks
Fairview: www.fairvieworegon.gov
Gladstone: www.ci.gladstone.or.us/parksites
Gresham: www.greshamoregon.gov/parks-and-recreation
Hillsboro: www.hillsboro-oregon.gov/departments/parks-recreation
Lake Oswego: www.ci.oswego.or.us/parksrec
Metro Regional Government: www.oregonmetro.gov/parks
Milwaukie: www.milwaukieoregon.gov/parksites
National Park Service, Fort Vancouver: www.nps.gov/fova
North Clackamas Parks and Recreation District: www.ncprd.com
Oregon City: www.orcity.org/parksandrecreation
Oregon State Parks: www.oregonstateparks.org
Portland Parks and Recreation: www.portlandoregon.gov/parks
Tigard: www.tigard-or.gov/recreation
Troutdale: www.troutdaleoregon.gov
Tualatin: www.tualatinoregon.gov/recreation
Tualatin Hills Park and Recreation District: www.thprd.org
US Fish and Wildlife Service, Tualatin River National Wildlife Refuge: www.fws.gov/refuge/tualatin_river
US Forest Service, Columbia River Gorge National Scenic Area: www.fs.usda.gov/crgnsa
Vancouver, Washington: www.cityofvancouver.us/parksrec
Washington County: www.co.washington.or.us
West Linn: www.westlinnoregon.gov/parksrec

SUPPORT PARKS!

Volunteer to clean up trash, remove invasive plants, build trails, and restore native habitats. There are literally too many opportunities to list. Start with the relevant park agency; nearly all have volunteer programs. Also check out SOLVE (www.solveoregon.org) and the Nature Conservancy (www.nature.org/oregonevents); both organize park cleanups and native plantings across the region.

Donate to organizations that champion parks. Start with the Intertwine Alliance (www.theintertwine.org), which supports a coalition working to preserve and nurture a healthy regional system of parks, trails, and natural areas. Many of the alliance's one-hundred-plus partners are nonprofits doing essential work in the region; check the website for information and links to partners.

Vote to fund parks! There are few issues—pandemics, climate change, socioeconomic inequality, mental health—that *don't* relate to parks in some way. Parks are not an amenity! They are essential "green infrastructure."

Act to show your love of parks. Use parks and let decision makers know how much you care about them. Protect parks from harm by staying on trails and observing leash laws and seasonal closures. (You may be surprised to see the research on how significantly dogs disturb wildlife.) Assist parks by making your own yard a stepping-stone in a network of connected native habitats. How? Check out the Backyard Habitat Certification Program, comanaged by Portland Audubon and Columbia Land Trust (www.backyardhabitats.org).

Index

About the Author

Longtime Portland resident Owen Wozniak is a program manager at the Land Trust Alliance, where he supports nonprofit land trusts protecting climate-resilient natural places across the Pacific Northwest. Owen also serves on the board of directors of the Intertwine Alliance, a coalition of public, private, and nonprofit organizations working to integrate nature more deeply into the Portland-Vancouver metropolitan region.

Wozniak is the author of several hiking and biking guidebooks, including *Biking Portland*, and loves to ski, bike, and explore the Portland region's parks and open spaces with his nine-year-old son, Lee, and his wife, Jen.

recreation • lifestyle • conservation

MOUNTAINEERS BOOKS including its two imprints, Skipstone and Braided River, is a leading publisher of quality outdoor recreation, sustainability, and conservation titles. As a 501(c)(3) nonprofit, we are committed to supporting the environmental and educational goals of our organization by providing expert information on human-powered adventure, sustainable practices at home and on the trail, and preservation of wilderness.

Our publications are made possible through the generosity of donors, and through sales of 700 titles on outdoor recreation, sustainable lifestyle, and conservation. To donate, purchase books, or learn more, visit us online:

MOUNTAINEERS BOOKS
1001 SW Klickitat Way, Suite 201 • Seattle, WA 98134
800-553-4453 • mbooks@mountaineersbooks.org • www.mountaineersbooks.org

An independent nonprofit publisher since 1960

Mountaineers Books is proud to support the Leave No Trace Center for Outdoor Ethics, whose mission is to promote and inspire responsible outdoor recreation through education, research, and partnerships. The Leave No Trace program is focused specifically on human-powered (nonmotorized) recreation. For more information, visit www.lnt.org.